From
Fortran
to C

From Fortran to C

James F. Kerrigan

Windcrest®/McGraw-Hill

FIRST EDITION
SECOND PRINTING

© 1991 by **Windcrest Books**, an imprint of TAB Books.
TAB Books is a division of McGraw-Hill, Inc.
The name "Windcrest" is a registered trademark of TAB Books.

Library of Congress Cataloging-in-Publication Data

Kerrigan, James F.
    From Fortran to C / by James F. Kerrigan.
        p.   cm.
    Includes bibliographical references and index.
    ISBN 0-8306-8661-4   ISBN 0-8306-7661-9 (pbk.)
    1. C (Computer program language)   I. Title.
    QA76.73.C15K48   1991   91-2666
    005.26'2—dc20   CIP

TAB Books offers software for sale. For information and a catalog, please contact
TAB Software Department, Blue Ridge Summit, PA 17294-0850.

Acquisitions Editor: Stephen Moore
Book Editor: David M. McCandless
Director of Production: Katherine G. Brown
Book Design: Jaclyn J. Boone

WP1

To Julia, Elvina, and Rae.

Contents

APPENDICES

Acknowledgments

Nearly two years have passed since the original plans for this book were laid. During this period, I have enjoyed direct and indirect support from many friends and professional colleagues. At times, this support was specific to the topic of this book. More often, however, it was just an unspoken understanding that blank looks on my face meant that I had taken a brief "mental break" from the current discussion and started thinking about some aspect of Fortran or C. Now, with this project complete, there is hope that I will return to giving such friends and colleagues my undivided attention.

At TAB Books, I thank Kimberlee Burdick, Lisa Manahan, and Julie Ritter for their assistance over the duration of this project, as well as David McCandless for his editorial skill. Also, I appreciate the confidence in this project shown by Steve Fitzgerald and Robert Ostrander. I am especially indebted to Stephen Moore for his initial interest in the subject, his support during the proposal through delivery phases, and his guidance through the publishing process. It is unlikely that this text would ever have appeared were it not for Stephen's help.

Without my family's assistance, I am absolutely certain that this book would not exist. My sons—Ian, Phillip, and Evan—were very considerate of the amount of time I diverted to writing.

Finally, I am in debt to my wife, Ellen. She has shown so much patience and given so much support that I'll be hard pressed to ever be able to repay her.

Introduction

At first, experienced programmers struggle with learning a new programming language. It is frustrating to know that some task could be accomplished in seconds with the old language but will take minutes (or possibly hours) to code in the new language. I've written this book for the experienced Fortran programmers, to help them gain an understanding of the C programming language and to facilitate that process.

Learning C may be either a goal in its own right, preparation for development on a new hardware platform, or required to take advantage of an interface to external programs. C is rapidly becoming the language of choice as the first language learned by new programmers, mainly because of the deployment and availability of hardware platforms on which C is a native element. In addition, many applications software packages in the areas of database management, graphics, and screen management are delivered with a programming language interface defined for C and, often, no other language. These three areas are reason enough to learn C.

This book is structured both as an introduction and as a reference to help in the transition from Fortran to C. Chapter 1 outlines the history of the two languages and attempts to explain the circumstances behind a growing movement from Fortran to C. Chapters 2, 3, and 4 introduce C language specifications with detailed comparison to their Fortran counterparts. In each of these chapters, many C languages features are demonstrated by a complete Fortran program followed by the corresponding complete C program. These three chapters form a background understanding of what C "looks like" and how a C program is structured. These chapters can be read in order.

Chapter 5 is a reference work. In it, a separate section is dedicated to each Fortran statement with text and example programs explaining that statement's counterpart(s) in C. Each section in the chapter begins with a few lines summarizing the Fortran syntax of the statement, a list of the primary C language features directly associated with the Fortran statement, and a list of additional C statements, operators, and functions used in that section but related to the Fortran statement. Every section in Chapter 5 has at least one full Fortran program that uses the particular Fortran statement, a list of the output of that Fortran program, and a full C program that does the same thing as the Fortran program. Both programs' logic, features, and special twists are explained in the text. Chapter 5 was written in this fashion so that the experienced Fortran programmer could quickly turn to information specific to one Fortran statement and learn about C language counterparts to that statement. Because this chapter is written in a reference style, it can prove difficult to read straight through.

Chapter 6 covers how both languages handle arrays. Chapter 7 reviews several issues of interprogram communications from the perspective of the software development process. Chapter 8 presents terminal, sequential file, and direct access file input/output operations. Chapter 9 is the "miscellaneous" category and develops half a dozen features of C that are not present in the Fortran programming language. Chapter 10 summarizes the book and also discusses the new Fortran "extended" language specification.

Four appendices list C compilers, Fortran compilers, Fortran-to-C translations tools, and standard published references for both languages. Finally, an index helps the reader navigate through the book and track down references to specific Fortran and C features.

Annually, many books are published with Fortran as the primary subject and others with C as the main focus. Few, however, deal at all with both languages in any way; and fewer still, in any substantive way. This book deals squarely with how these two languages relate to each other in form, content, and style. Hopefully, this book can help reduce the time and effort it takes for the experienced Fortran programmer to acquire a knowledge of the C programming language.

1
Why C?

Traditional roles for the Fortran and C programming languages are changing. Created in the mid-1950s, Fortran has been the language of choice for the scientific and engineering programming community. Fifteen years later, C was developed as a system programming language. Despite the large body of source code written in either language that represent traditional usage, counter-examples such as an operating system in Fortran or a collection of mathematical functions coded in C do exist. Over the last 20 years, utilization of Fortran and C have merged as both serve as the foundation for an increasing number of commercial application programs. In the 1980s, C use has surpassed that of Fortran for the reasons that C is available on a wide range of homogeneous hardware platforms and is the predominant computer language learned by new programmers. As programmers gain experience on these various computer systems, one can reasonably expect that a significant fraction of new software development will be in C. Both trends lead to the increasing use of the C programming language in situations traditionally associated with Fortran.

Historically, Fortran was developed as a programming language for the IBM 700 series of scientific calculators (Perlis, 1978). The goal of the original project was to produce a compiler that could generate runfiles that executed at least as fast as runfiles created from hand-coded assembly language. The project began in late 1953, produced a language specification document in November, 1954, a programmer's reference manual in October, 1956, and was delivered to customers in April, 1957 (Backus, 1978). A year later, Fortran II was delivered with a major new feature of being able to manage separately compiled subroutines. In the winter of 1958–1959, Fortran III was delivered and included the "A" format as a new feature. Fortran IV became the basis of the American National Standards Institute's efforts to develop a standard for the Fortran programming language. The "Fortran 66" standard resulting from that four year project was finally approved in March, 1966. Work on the next ANSI standard, "Fortran 77", started in 1970 and the final report was approved in April, 1978. Significant language features introduced in "Fortran 77" were the character data type, user-specified lower and upper bounds for array dimensions, arithmetic expressions allowed in statements where the previous standard only sanctioned constants, the if-then-else control construct, list-directed input and output, and numerous file related enhancements (Brainerd, 1978).

After nine years of work, a draft for a new standard, "Fortran 8x", was finished in May, 1987. As of October, 1990, it appears that "Fortran 8x" will not replace "Fortran 77" but will be a companion specification called "Fortran Extended". Its final form is expected to include features to provide for array operators, user-defined data structures, free-form source format including 132-character statements with a new method to indicate comments, and dynamic storage allocation (Metcalf and Reid, 1989; Adams, 1990; and Adams et. al., 1990). Each "standard" Fortran represents efforts to consolidate machine-specific dialects of the language and to develop and guide the implementation of new features

Historically, C was developed at Bell Laboratories as a system programming language to implement a new operating system on a DEC PDP-11 minicomputer. The project began in 1972, and a language description was published six years later (Kernighan and Ritchie, 1978). C is a compact, terse programming language that includes data types, data operations, the ability (and need) to manipulate addresses, and an uncomplicated but complete set of flow-control constructions. In 1983, the American National Standards Institute formed a committee to produce a C programming language standard. This "ANSI C" standard was completed in May, 1988, and was expected to be approved by March, 1989. Major new features of this standard are function prototyping, a more fully defined library of support functions, program locales (i.e., support for local practices such as date and time presentation, monetary values, etc.), preprocessing compiler directives, and an ability to create and manage "characters" that are too large to store in one byte.

In parallel to the development of this standard, the original language description has been revised and reissued (Kernighan and Ritchie, 1988). Vendors of the several C compilers for microcomputers have already brought "ANSI C" compilers to market. Throughout its history, C has been closely associated with the UNIX operating system, with system programming in general, and with the challenge of writing "portable" code that can be easily transferred from whichever computer was used in the development to any one of many target computers.

Why C? In a survey of 57 out of the top 200 software companies, over 20 companies are developing in C and only 3 are developing in Fortran (Rinaldi, 1988). On UNIX-based computer systems and workstations installed in the engineering community, the ratio of existing Fortran code to C code might be as high as 100-to-1, but new packages and programs are being developed in C (Nemeth, 1987). TABLE 1-1 shows the results of an informal survey of published books on Fortran and on C. Fully three- quarters of the books are specific to the language rather than to any discipline. The remaining titles are distributed among computer graphics, personal computer implementations, science and engineering disciplines, and comparisons to other computer languages. A fifth of the Fortran titles cover science and engineering subjects, but a significant number of C books are published covering computer graphics and science and engineering topics. C is positioned to become the programming language of choice for new software in the traditional engineering and scientific role traditionally associated with Fortran.

Table 1-1   Survey of Fortran and C Book Titles. Data from *Books in Print* and *Forthcoming Books* (New York: R.R. Bowker, 1988 – 89).

Subject	Fortran	C
Graphics	1	7
Language syntax	30	35
Advanced texts	50	56
Introductory texts	70	50
Personal computer related	8	12
Science and engineering	42	5
Ada related	0	1
Algol related	2	0
Assembly language related	2	0
BASIC related	1	4
Pascal related	4	5
PL/I related	2	0
Total	*212*	*175*

Experienced Fortran programmers have served the scientific and engineering end-user community for many years. They have developed a wide range of software packages including portions of computer operating systems, programs designed to calculate the value of specialized mathematical formulae, graphic display libraries, etc. The skill gained by the programmers who designed, wrote, and maintain such source code is twofold. First, they acquired an intimate knowledge of the industry for which the programs were created. Second, when programming, they exercised a full understanding of the Fortran language. To preserve the value of such programmer's knowledge of their respective industrial applications, this book allows such Fortran programmers to continue to be productive but employ a different programming language, C.

Reference

Adams, Jeanne C. *Fortran 90: A Programmer's Guide.* New York: McGraw-Hill, 1990.

Adams, Jeanne C., et. al. *Handbook of Fortran 90: Complete ANSI Reference.* New York: McGraw-Hill, 1990.

Backus, John W. "The History of Fortran I, II, and III." *History of Programming Languages,* edited by Richard L. Wexelblat, 25-74. New York: Academic Press, Inc., 1981.

Brainerd, Walter S. "Fortran 77." *Communications of the Association for Computing Machinery,* Vol.21, No.10 (October 1978): 806-820.

Kernighan, Brian W., and Dennis M. Ritchie. *The C Programming Language.* Englewood Cliffs: Prentice-Hall, Inc., 1978.

———, *The C Programming Language.* Englewood Cliffs: Prentice-Hall, Inc., 1988.

Metcalf, Michael, and John K. Reid. *Fortran 8x Explained.* Oxford: Clarendon Press, 1989.

Nemeth, Alan. "Interview with Bill Poduska." *UNIX Review,* Vol.5, No.12 (December 1987): 64-74.

Perlis, Alan J. "The American Side of the Development of ALGOL." *History of Programming Languages,* edited by Richard L. Wexelblat, 75-91. New York: Academic Press, Inc. 1981

Rinaldi, Damian. "Ceding Territory to UNIX(s), Aiming Software at Niches." *Software Magazine,* Vol.8, No.14, (November 1988): 21-23.

2
Program structure

Fundamental to every programming language is a set of "housekeeping" rules. Certain rules govern which characters are permitted to appear in source code, others identify legal syntax for a line of source code, and a final group specifies how to delimit subprograms from a main program. These rules transcend elements of "programming style" that may be in vogue for any language. Compilers detecting violations of these rules will flag errors and might stop processing the source code file should the problem be especially severe. Fortran and C have surprisingly similar sets of housekeeping rules.

Character set

With one exception, the entire Fortran character set is available in the C character set. The character set for Fortran and C include the twenty-six capital letters of the alphabet and the ten digits. While C formally includes the twenty-six lowercase letters of the alphabet, such lowercase letters, although not recognized by the ANSI standard for Fortran, are commonly supported by modern Fortran compilers. In other words, many Fortran compilers will accept source code containing statements written with lowercase letters as if written with uppercase letters. However, no Fortran compiler in compliance with the ANSI standard would distinguish variables names, function names, subroutine names, and such on the basis of case: variable X is identical to variable x. Uppercase versus lowercase is a significant issue in C: variable X is completely different from variable x.

Both languages accept the following twelve "special" characters:

    space = + − * / ( ) , . ' :

C goes on to define the following eighteen "graphics" characters:

! " # % & ; < > ? [\ ] ^ _ { | } ~

Finally, C also represents seven formatting commands by these character pairs:

/a   alert ... usually the terminal "bell"
/b   backspace
/f   form feed
/n   new line
/r   carriage return
/t   horizontal tab
/v   vertical tab

The only character defined by Fortran but not by C as an element of the character set appropriate for source code is the dollar sign. However, the dollar sign has no special significance in the ANSI standard and is not a required element in any part of Fortran syntax. Still, it is often used in extensions to the language to signify system-specific library names, compiler directives, or unique formatting commands.

Source code syntax

Position has significance in a line of Fortran source code. The initial line of a Fortran statement has blanks or a statement number in columns one through five, a blank or a zero in column six, Fortran statements beginning in column seven, and terminates at the 72nd column. A Fortran statement can be continued from the initial line on up to 19 continuation lines. A continuation line has blanks in the first five columns, any legal character except a blank or a zero in column six, Fortran statements beginning in column seven, and terminates at the 72nd column. With a total of 20 lines—initial line plus continuations—a single Fortran statement is limited by the ANSI standard to a maximum of 1,320 characters.

Comment lines are all blank or have the letter C or the character * in the first column with additional text, if any, in columns two to the end of the line. Comment lines can appear anywhere in a program unit from the beginning of the source code file until the end statement. ANSI standard compliant Fortran compilers must accept comment lines placed before the program, block data, function, or subroutine statement but are not required to accept comment lines placed after the end statement.

In contrast, position has no significance in a line of C source code. Instead, virtually every C statement is finished with a semicolon. Where Fortran terminates scanning source code lines at column 72, C statements are scanned until this semicolon character appears. New C programmers quite often forget about the terminal semicolon.

Because a C statement's length is determined by the terminal semicolon instead of by the column number, a single C statement can span multi-

...ored on a
...e as a resul
...tem V in a cl
...improved acces

ple source lines. Simply end the initial line with the backslash character or divide the statement at the end of a token or argument, such as

```
        main( )
    {

        char *string;
        string = "This short line seems" \
                " very, very long.";
/*      Display as: This short line seems very, very long. */
        printf ( "%s \ n",
                string );
        return;
    }
```

C limits a logical line of source code to a total of 509 characters. In the previous C example, the two physical lines of source code that define the variable string comprise one logical line of source and are subject to the limit of 509 characters. Similarly, the two physical lines of source code that invoke the printf function are considered to be one logical line of source and also must be shorter than 509 characters. Comments in C start with the two-character token /* and end with the two-character token */. This definition permits several comment styles, such as

```
/*      This is a single line comment. */


        i = 123; /* This comment follows source code. */


/*
/*      This comment has multiple "open-comment"
/*      delimiters, but only one "close-comment". */

/*      This is a standard, multiple line
        comment with one open and one close
        comment delimiter.                          */


/*      Lastly, this is an alternative style for the
 *      multiple line comment with one open and one close
 *      comment delimiter.
 */
```

Comments may appear anywhere in the source code file. However, a comment may not appear within the delimiters of another comment. For example, an initial comment written as

```
/*      Beginning of initial comment.
        End of initial comment. */
```

cannot be augmented with a secondary comment, such as

```
/*      Beginning of initial comment.
/*      ILLEGAL . . . added comment . . . ILLEGAL */
        End of initial comment. */
```

because the added comment becomes embedded within the limits of the initial comment. This restriction can be troublesome because a programmer is apt to try to "comment-out" a section of code that already contains comments. In doing so, old comment lines may then be contained within the delimiters for the new comment leading to a compilation failure because C compilers do not allow embedded comments.

Program and procedures

In both Fortran and C, a program consists of a single main program and one or more procedures. Procedures in Fortran can be block data subprograms, entry points into subprograms, external functions, intrinsic functions, statement functions, or subroutines. Procedures in C can be intrinsic functions, library functions, macros, or user-written functions. In both languages, all source code for a program can be presented to the compiler in one file starting with the main program and followed by other procedures in any order. Both languages permit the source code for a program to be prepared with one procedure per file, compiled separately, and then rejoined into an executable unit with a "link/loader" provided by the host operating system.

As a device in explaining program structure, FIG. 2-1 is a trivial Fortran program that uses a subroutine, a function, and a statement function. Figure 2-2 is the C counterpart to FIG. 2-1. In both programs, variables are named according to this convention: the first letter signifies Fortran or C; the second letter indicates if the variable is used in a function, a subroutine, or a statement function; the next part indicates if the variable is input or output to the appropriate subprogram; and the last letter indicates if the variable is a variable or a constant. Both programs produce output (see FIG. 2-3) that is a running commentary of the passage of control as well as the values of constants, equations, and variables.

The main program

Any executable file has one and only one "main" program. Fortran allows the programmer to name the main program through the use of the `program` statement. C is more restrictive in that the main program starts with the main statement and that the main program cannot be given a name by the programmer. Another major difference between Fortran and C regarding the main program is that a main program in C can "take" arguments from the environment that invoked it, while a main program in Fortran can't. These arguments could be the value of constants to use in the program, the names of files to operate on, a keyword or value to control the level of debug and trace information generated by the program, etc. In the example in FIG. 2-2, the void qualifier in the main statement indicates that this particular program takes no arguments. C main program arguments are described in greater detail in the entry for the Fortran `program` statement in Chapter 5.

2-1 Fortran program demonstrating various function types.

```
        program main
        integer   ffinv
        integer   ffoutv
        integer   frinv
        integer   froutv
        integer   fsinv
        integer   fsinc
        integer   fsoutv
        integer   sfun
        external  func
        external  rout
        sfun ( fsinv, fsinc ) = fsinv + fsinc
        ffinv   = 1
        ffoutv = 0
        frinv   = 1
        froutv = 0
        fsinv   = 1
        fsinc   = 0
        fsoutv = 0
        write ( 6,100 )
100     format ( / 1H , 'MAIN: beginning of program' )
c
c       Invoke a Fortran subroutine.
        write ( 6,200 ) frinv, froutv
200     format ( / 1H , 'MAIN: ', i1, ' + 2 = ', i1  )
        call rout ( frinv, 2, froutv )
        write ( 6,300 ) frinv, froutv
300     format (   1H , 'MAIN: ', i1, ' + 2 = ', i1  )
c
c       Invoke a Fortran function.
        write ( 6,400 ) ffinv, ffoutv
400     format ( / 1H , 'MAIN: ', i1, ' + 2 = ', i1  )
        ffoutv = func ( ffinv, 2 )
        write ( 6,500 ) ffinv, ffoutv
500     format (   1H , 'MAIN: ', i1, ' + 2 = ', i1  )
c
c       Invoke a Fortran statement function.
        write ( 6,600 ) fsinv, fsoutv
600     format ( / 1H , 'MAIN: ', i1, ' + 2 = ', i1  )
        fsoutv = sfun ( fsinv, 2 )
        write ( 6,700 ) fsinv, fsoutv
700     format (   1H , 'MAIN: ', i1, ' + 2 = ', i1  )
        write ( 6,800 )
800     format ( / 1H , 'MAIN: end of program' / )
        stop
        end

        subroutine rout ( frinv, frinc, froutv )
        integer frinv
        integer frinc
        integer froutv
        write ( 6,100 )
100     format (   1H , 'ROUT: beginning of routine' )
        froutv = 0
        write ( 6,200 ) frinv, frinc, froutv
200     format (   1H , 'ROOT: ', i1, '   ', i1, '   ', i1  )
        froutv = frinv + frinc
        write ( 6,300 ) frinv, frinc, froutv
```

```
300  format (    1H , 'ROOT: ', i1, ' + ', i1, ' = ', i1  )
     write ( 6,400 )
400  format (    1H , 'ROUT: end of routine' )
     return
     end

     function func (  ffinv, ffinc  )
     integer ffinv
     integer ffinc
     integer ffoutv
     write ( 6,100 )
100  format (    1H , 'FUNC: beginning of function' )
     write ( 6,200 ) ffinv, ffinc, ffoutv
200  format (    1H , 'FUNC: ', i1, '  ', i1, '  ', i1  )
     ffoutv = ffinv + ffinc
     write ( 6,300 ) ffinv, ffinc, ffoutv
300  format (    1H , 'FUNC: ', i1, ' + ', i1, ' = ', i1  )
     write ( 6,400 )
400  format (    1H , 'FUNC: end of function' )
     func = ffoutv
     return
     end
```

2-2   C program demonstrating various function types.

```
     #define sfun( csinv, csinc) csinv + csinc

     main ( void )
{
     int    cfinv   = 1;
     int    cfoutv  = 0;
     int    crinv   = 1;
     int    croutv  = 0;
     int    csinv   = 1;
     int    csinc      ;
     int    csoutv  = 0;
     int    func ( ) ;
     void   rout ( ) ;
     printf  (     " \nMAIN:  beginning of program \n \n" );
/*
     Invoke a     "Fortran subroutine-like" function. */
     printf  (     "MAIN: %d    2    %d \n",    crinv,   croutv  );
     rout ( crinv, 2, &croutv );
     printf  (     "MAIN: %d + 2 = %d \n \n", crinv,   croutv  );
/*
     Invoke a "Fortran function-like" function. */
     printf  (     "MAIN: %d    2    %d \n",    cfinv,   cfoutv  );
     cfoutv  =   func ( cfinv, 2 );
     printf  (     "MAIN: %d + 2 = %d \n \n", cfinv,   cfoutv  );
/*
     Invoke a "Fortran statement function-like" macro. */
     printf  (     "MAIN: %d    2    %d \n",    csinv,   csoutv  );
     csoutv  =   sfun ( csinv, 2 );
```

2-2 Continued.

```
    printf  (    "MAIN:    %d  +  2  =  %d\n\n", csinv,    csoutv );
    printf  (    "MAIN:    end of program \n" );
    return;
}

    void rout ( int crinv, int crinc, int *croutv )
{
    printf  (    "ROUT:    beginning of routine \n" );
    *croutv = 0;
    printf  (    "ROUT:    %d      %d      %d\n",    crinv,crinc,*croutv);
    *croutv = crinv + crinc;
    printf  (    "ROUT:    %d  +  %d =  %d\n",    crinv,crinc,*croutv);
    printf  (    "ROUT:    end of routine \n" );
    return;
}

    int func ( int cfinv, int cfinc )
{
    int cfoutv = 0;
    printf  (    "FUNC:    beginning of function \n" );
    printf  (    "FUNC:    %d      %d      %d\n",    cfinv,cfinc,cfoutv );
    cfoutv = cfinv + cfinc;
    printf  (    "FUNC:    %d  +  %d =  %d\n",    cfinv,cfinc,cfoutv );
    printf  (    "FUNC:    end of function \n" );
    return (    cfoutv );
}
```

2-3 Output of programs in Fig. 2-1 and 2-2.

```
MAIN:  beginning of program

MAIN:  1    2    0
ROUT:  beginning of routine
ROUT:  1    2    0
ROUT:  1 + 2 = 3
ROUT:  end of routine
MAIN:  1 + 2 = 3

MAIN:  1    2    0
FUNC:  beginning of function
FUNC:  1    2    0
FUNC:  1 + 2 = 3
FUNC:  end of function
MAIN:  1 + 2 = 3

MAIN:  1    2    0
MAIN:  1 + 2 = 3

MAIN:  end of program
```

Block data and entry

C has no counterpart to Fortran block data subprograms or entry points into subprograms. Fortran defines a block data subprogram as a special means to initialize variables and arrays in common blocks. Because C has no sequel to the Fortran common block, it therefore needs no special means to initialize such variables and consequently has no structure to equal the exact functionality of a Fortran block data subprogram. This does not mean that C has no facility to establish initial values for variables used throughout an entire C program, but only that it has no special structure like a Fortran block data subprogram. As an example, this Fortran program uses a block data subprogram to initialize a single variable in common whose value is then displayed in a subprogram:

```
        program main
        common / area / fvar
        call subprogram
        stop
        end
        subroutine subprogram
        common / area / fvar
c       Display as: Variable = 4.5
        write ( 6,1 ) fvar
    1   format ( 1H , 'Variable = ', f3.1 )
        return
        end
        block data initialize
        common / area / fvar
        data fvar / 4.5 /
        end
```

The C counterpart is as follows:

```
        #define cvar 4.5
        main ( )
    {
        void subprogram ( );
        subprogram( );
        return;
    }
        void subprogram ( )
    {
/*      Display as: Variable = 4.5 */
        printf ( "Variable = %3.1f \ n", cvar );
        return;
    }
```

Because the variable cvar was initialized before the main statement, its value—4.5—is available to any subprogram throughout the C example program.

C has no counterpart to the Fortran entry statement. Each C subprogram has one and only one entry point. With significant programming effort, a Fortran "entry-like" scheme could be devised in C using non-local transfers of control statements (i.e., the longjmp library function and setjmp macro) or creating new routines for each entry point as is done in the Fortran entry statement section of Chapter 5. Either construct could prove difficult to debug and/or maintain and might not be as valuable in use as to justify preserving in new or translated C code.

Functions and subroutines

Fortran external functions and subroutines correspond to C user-written function. A Fortran external function has as its counterpart the C function that returns a value to the calling procedure. That returned value is associated with the name of the function. A Fortran subroutine has as its counterpart the C function that does not return a value to the calling procedure. In the example program (FIG. 2-1 and FIG. 2-2), the function func takes two arguments, adds them, and returns the result to the calling program as the value of the function. Neither input arguments are changed within the function named func. In the example (FIG. 2-1 and FIG. 2-2), the subprogram rout takes three arguments. The first two arguments provide input to subprogram rout and the third and final argument returns the output of subprogram rout to the calling program. Neither input arguments are changed, but the output argument—xroutv—is modified in the subprogram rout.

Statement functions

Fortran statement functions correspond to C macros. A C macro is defined early in a program and then, every time it appears in the program, its value is substituted at that point. C's mechanism to establish a macro is the #define statement, which can serve various purposes. In FIG. 2-2, the C function sfun is specified in the first line of the source code in a #define function.

Statement functions are treated again in greater detail in Chapter 5.

Intrinsic functions

Fortran provides around forty intrinsic functions, the majority of which have a mathematical nature and the remainder being character-oriented. C also has a set of intrinsic functions that match most of those from Fortran. TABLE 2-1 shows the correspondence between Fortran intrinsic functions and C functions. In some cases, the C counterpart to a Fortran intrinsic function is a formal C intrinsic function; in other cases, the C counterpart is formally a C library function. Because the C library is an

Table 2-1   Correspondence of Fortran and C Intrinsic Functions.

Description	Fortran	C
Absolute value: real	abs	
Arccosine: real	acos	
Truncation: real	aint	
Natural logarithm: real	alog	
Common logarithm: real	alog10	
Choosing largest value: integer/real	amax0	
Choosing largest value: real/real	amax1	
Choosing smallest value: integer/real	amin0	
Choosing smallest value: real/real	amin1	
Remaindering: real	amod	
Nearest whole number: real	anint	
Arcsine: real	asin	
Arctangent: real	atan	
Arctangent: quotient of reals	atan2	
Type conversion: integer to character	char	
Cosine: real	cos	
Hyperbolic cosine: real	cosh	
Absolute value: double	dabs	fabs
Arccosine: double	dacos	acos
Arcsine: double	dasin	asin
Arctangent: double	datan	atan
Type conversion: integer/real to double	dble	double
Cosine: double	dcos	cos
Hyperbolic cosine: double	dcosh	cosh
Positive difference: double	ddim	
Exponential: double	dexp	exp
Positive difference: real	dim	
Truncation: double	dint	ceil
Natural logarithm: double	dlog	log
Common logarithm: double	dlog10	log10
Choosing largest value: double/double	dmax1	
Choosing smallest value: double/double	dmin1	
Remaindering: double	dmod	fmod
Nearest whole number: double	dnint	floor
Double precision product	dprod	
Transfer of sign: double	dsign	
Sine: double	dsin	sin
Hyperbolic sine: double	dsinh	sinh
Square root: double	dsqrt	
Tangent: double	dtan	tan
Arctangent: quotient of doubles	dtan2	atan2
Hyperbolic tangent: double	dtanh	tanh
Exponential: real	exp	
Type conversion: integer to real	float	float
Absolute value: integer *	iabs	abs/labs
Type conversion: character to integer	ichar	
Positive difference: integer	idim	
Type conversion: double to integer	idint	int
Nearest integer: double	idnint	
Type conversion: real to integer	ifix	int
Index of substring	index	strstr

Table 2-1   Continued.

Description	Fortran	C
Transfer of sign: integer	isign	
Length of character entity	len	sizeof
Lexically greater than or equal	lge	strncmp
Lexically greater than	lgt	strncmp
Lexically less than or equal	lle	strncmp
Lexically less than	llt	strncmp
Choosing largest value: integer/integer	max0	
Choosing largest value: real/integer	max1	
Choosing smallest value: integer/integer	min0	
Choosing smallest value: real/integer	min1	
Remaindering: integer *	mod	%
Nearest integer: real	nint	
Transfer of sign: real	sign	
Sine: real	sin	
Hyperbolic sine: real	sinh	
Type conversion: double to real	sngl	float
Square root: real	sqrt	
Tangent: real	tan	
Hyperbolic tangent: real	tanh	

* C counterparts to the Fortran i abs function differ in terms of their arguments: abs takes a "short" integer argument, and labs takes a "long" integer argument (see Chapter 3). The C counterpart to the Fortran mod function, the percent sign, is the remaindering mathematical operator rather than an intrinsic function.

integral part of ANSI standard C, the distinction between a C intrinsic versus a C library function is not a major issue. Fortran functions dealing with the complex numbers are not listed in TABLE 2-1 because C has no counterpart to Fortran's complex numbers.

Most Fortran mathematical intrinsic functions are defined for real numbers and for double precision numbers. C defines its corresponding functions only for double precision numbers. This difference can easily be overcome by "casting" real numbers in C to double precision when the intrinsic function is invoked. For example, the following Fortran program uses type-specific intrinsic functions to determine the absolute value of Fortran double precision and single precision variables:

```
        program main
        double precision  fdx
        real              frx
        fdx = -1.23d0
        frx = -4.56
c       Display as: 1.23 4.56
        write ( 6,1 ) dabs ( fdx ), abs ( frx )
  1     format ( 1H , f4.2, 1x, f4.2 )
```

```
          stop
          end
```

The identical code in C is as follows:

```
          #include <math.h>
          main ( )
      {
          double      cdx;
          float       crx;
          cdx = -1.23;
          crx = -4.56F;
          Display as: 1.23 4.56 */
          printf ("%4.2f %4.2f \ n",fabs(cdx),fabs((double)crx));
          return;
      }
```

uses the type-specific absolute value intrinsic function fabs for the double variable and, after "casting" the float variable to a type with greater precision with the prefix (double), also uses fabs for the absolute value of the float variable.

This C example introduces the #include programming device. It instructs the C compiler to include the file named in the #include statement at the point in the C program where the #include statement appears. The math.h file used in this C example is defined as a part of the ANSI standard and is supplied with each C compiler. It contains formal declarations for each of the C mathematical library functions, definitions for mathematical domain and range error codes, and the value to be returned by a C mathematical library function if the result exceeds the capacity of C variable of data type double. There are several such "header" files defined as part of the ANSI standard for C. A C programmer can create a private collection of variable definitions, user-written functions, error handling routines, etc., and have such files incorporated into programs with the #include statement. A file named in an #include statement may itself incorporate a second #include file, and this form of "nesting" can extend to a depth of eight files. The concept of including a source file into another source file with the #include statement is covered in detail in Chapter 7.

There are four exceptions to the otherwise straightforward comparison of Fortran intrinsic functions to their C counterparts: remaindering, location of a substring, lexical comparison of strings, and length of a character entity. Fortran computes remainders using the type-specific modulus functions dmod and mod, such as

```
          program main
          double precision  fdx
          integer           fix
          fdx = 11.0d0
          fix = 22
c         Display as: 1.0 2
          write ( 6,1 ) dmod ( fdx,10 ), mod ( fix,20 )
```

```
1   format ( 1H , f3.1, 1x, i1 )
    stop
    end
```

C provides a library function, fmod, that behaves exactly like the Fortran dmod intrinsic function, such as

```
        #include <math.h>
        main ( )
    {
        double  cdx = 11.0;
        int     cix = 22;
        cdx = fmod ( cdx, 10.0 );
        cix = cix % 20;
/*      Display as: 1.0 2 */
        printf ( "%1.1f %d \ n", cdx, cix );
        return;
    }
```

but uses a remainder operator—the percent sign—to compute the remainder for integers. For remaindering, the only difference between the methods established in Fortran and those in C is whether an intrinsic function, a library function, or an operator is used depending on the data type of the variable.

Secondly, Fortran provides an intrinsic function to determine the location of a substring within another string as

```
        program main
        character*20 fca
        character*6  fcb
        fca = 'The first, #1 string'
        fcb = 'string'
c       Display as: 15
        write ( 6,1 ) index ( fca, fcb )
1       format ( 1H , i2 )
        stop
        end
```

The Fortran intrinsic function index returns the character position in the first string where the second string begins. In the example, the characters in the Fortran variable fcb occur in the Fortran variable fca starting in the 15th character position. The C version of this example includes several new programming constructs, such as

```
        #include <stddef.h>
        #include <string.h>
        main ( )
    {
        char    *cca = "The first, #1 string";
        char    *ccb = "string";
        char    *ccc;
```

```
        size_t   cid = 0;
        if ( ( ccc = strstr ( cca, ccb ) ) != NULL )
            cid = ( ccc - cca ) + 1;
/*      Display as: 15 */
        printf ( "%d \ n", cid );
        return;
}
```

Character strings in C are often referenced by their memory address in the host computer system. In the example, the value of the entity referenced by *cca is the memory address at which the literal "The first, #1 string" is stored. The entity *ccb is described as a pointer to the character variable ccb. The value of the pointer is the memory address at which the value of the variable ccb resides. C library function strstr determines the memory address at which the literal in ccb can be found in the string named by cca and returns the result as a pointer to the character variable ccc.

In the example, ccc marks the memory address of the beginning of matching characters between string cca and ccb. Likewise, cca marks the beginning address of the string cca. Subtracting the address at which the match begins from the address at which the string begins gives the character position in cca where the two strings cca and ccb start to be the same. In the example, if no match is found, the variable cid would remain zero. If a match is found, the C character position of the match is computed by evaluating the difference in two memory addresses. The variable cid is declared as a special data type, size_t, which is defined to be "large enough" to hold the difference between the smallest and largest possible memory address on the host computer system. The C character position differs from Fortran by one because the initial position in a C string is zero, whereas the initial position in a Fortran string is one. Uses of pointers, pointer arithmetic, and differences between Fortran and C array and string implementations are further described in Chapter 6.

A third area of difference is in the lexical comparison of strings. Both Fortran and C provide means to determine how two strings stand in alphabetical relation to each other. The two example programs that follow produce these four lines of output:

```
aaa  LLE  aaa
aaa  LGE  aaa
aaa  LLT  zzz
zzz  LGT  aaa
```

Fortran provides this facility in four lexical relational operators:

```
program main
character*3 fca, fcb, fcc
fca = 'aaa'
fcb = fca
fcc = 'zzz'
```

```
      if ( lle ( fca, fcb ) ) write ( 6,1 ) fca, fcb
1     format ( 1H , a3 , ' LLE ', a3 )
      if ( lge ( fca, fcb ) ) write ( 6,2 ) fca, fcb
2     format ( 1H , a3 , ' LGE ', a3 )
      if ( llt ( fca, fcc ) ) write ( 6,3 ) fca, fcc
3     format ( 1H , a3 , ' LLT ', a3 )
      if ( lgt ( fcc, fcb ) ) write ( 6,4 ) fcc, fcb
4     format ( 1H , a3 , ' LGT ', a3 )
      stop
      end
```

C combines the functionality of the four Fortran lexical relational operators into one library function:

```
#include <string.h>
main ()
{
    char    *cca = "aaa";
    char    *ccb;
    char    *ccc = "zzz";
    size_t  n = 3;
    ccb = cca;
    if ( ( strncmp ( cca, ccb, n ) ) <= 0 )
        printf ( "%s LLE %s \n", cca, ccb );
    if ( ( strncmp ( cca, ccb, n ) ) >= 0 )
        printf ( "%s LGE %s \n", cca, ccb );
    if ( ( strncmp ( cca, ccc, n ) ) < 0 )
        printf ( "%s LLT %s \n", cca, ccc );
    if ( ( strncmp ( ccc, ccb, n ) ) > 0 )
        printf ( "%s LGT %s \n", ccc, ccb );
    return;
}
```

The third argument, n, in the strncmp library function limits the number of bytes to be compared. If n is less than the length of the string to be searched, then only the first n characters would be examined. If n is larger than the length of the string to be searched, then the examination would terminate at the end of the string to be searched.

Finally, a fourth area of significant difference between Fortran intrinsic functions and their C counterparts concerns determining the length of a character variable. Fortran provides the intrinsic function len as

```
      program main
      character*20 fca
c     Display as: 20
      write ( 6,1 ) len ( fca )
1     format ( 1H , i2 )
      stop
      end
```

The C version is

```
        main ( )
    {
        char cca[20];
/*      Display as: 20 */
        printf ( "%d \ n", sizeof ( cca ) );
        return;
    }
```

and uses the C library function sizeof in a manner almost exactly like Fortran's len intrinsic function.

3
Data types

Most Fortran data types have direct counterparts in the C programming language. Both languages provide character storage, several integer valued data types, and floating point representation. Neither complex or logical Fortran data types directly appear in the C programming language. C does allow certain data types to be qualified, which provides more selectivity than Fortran in controlling the numerical range and storage allocation of variables. A correspondence of Fortran and C data types is shown in TABLE 3-1.

Data type declarations

Fortran and C variables inherit a particular data type either through explicit declarations or implicit assignment. The symbolic name of a Fortran variable is from one to six characters in length, starts with a letter, and can contain a combination of digits and either upper- or lowercase letters where case is not significant. C variable names are from one to 31 characters in length, start with a letter, and can contain a combination of digits, the underscore character, and a combination of upper- or lowercase letters where case is significant. By default, Fortran variables that start with any of the letters I through N are assigned an integer data type; otherwise, variables are assigned a real data type. In using the initial letter of a variable name to denote a particular data type, a Fortran variable does not have to be declared before it is used. Regardless of the initial letter of name of a variable, the Fortran statements `character`, `integer`, or `real` can be used to explicitly state the data type of a variable. The data type of a C variable must be declared before it is used. This requirement to declare the data type of all C variables is very different from Fortran, even though

**Table 3-1 Correspondence
of Fortran and C Data Types.**

Fortran type	C type
character	char
	signed char
	unsigned char
complex	(not applicable)
double precision	double
	long double
integer	int
	long
	long int
	short
	short int
	signed
	signed int
	signed long
	signed long int
	signed short
	signed short int
	unsigned
	unsigned int
	unsigned long
	unsigned long int
	unsigned short
	unsigned short int
logical	(not applicable)
real	float

explicitly declaring a data type for all Fortran variables is good programming practice. Through implicit and explicit type declarations, both Fortran and C provide means to specify and control data storage.

Character data type

Fortran and C have similar data types to represent character data. C allows the character data type to be qualified as signed or unsigned. Fortran character data correspond to C's char or unsigned char character data. In other words, all printable characters are mapped into a numerical range from zero to 127 such as is returned by Fortran's ichar function. In Fortran, a single character variable is declared, initialized, and displayed as follows:

```
      character fa
      fa = 'A'
      write ( 6,1 ) fa
    1 format ( 1H , a )
```

The C counterpart to that Fortran code fragment is as follows:

```
char ca;
ca = 'A';
printf ( "%c\n", ca );
```

For the moment, you should accept that the C function called printf will display the single character held in the C variable ca. Chapters 5 and 8 will present C file input/output in detail. Longer strings of characters are declared in Fortran as follows:

```
      character*6 fa
      fa = 'ABCDEF'
c     Display as: ABCDEF
      write ( 6,1 ) fa
    1 format ( 1H , a6 )
```

The length of the string is arbitrary. In C, that same declaration is as follows:

```
    char *ca;
    ca = "ABCDEF";
/*  Display as: ABCDEF */
    printf ( "%s\n", ca );
```

Here, a string length limit of at least 509 characters is supported. In C, a character string is defined as an array of characters. In the char statement, the asterisk that precedes the name of the variable ca establishes an array that can be referred to through a pointer. Arrays and pointers in C are presented in Chapter 6.

Complex data type

C provides no native support for a data type like the complex data type from Fortran. Binary arrays that pair two floating point numbers to represent the real and imaginary parts of a complex number can easily be constructed in C. Unlike Fortran, however, C has no predefined operators to perform arithmetic operations on such structures. The section in Chapter 5 for Fortran's complex statement has further suggestions.

Double precision data type

Extended precision floating point numbers are represented as double precision (or real*8) in Fortran and as double and long double in C. There is a direct correspondence among double precision, real*8, and double. Depending on the implementation of a C compiler, the long double data type can have greater precision than double. In Fortran, extended precision floating point numbers are declared, initialized, and displayed as follows:

```
      double precision fx
      real*8 fy
      fx = 1.23d0
      fy = 456.0d0
c     Display as:.123E+001 456.0
      write ( 6,1 ) fx, fy
    1 format ( 1H , e9.3e3, 1x, f5.1 )
```

The C counterpart to that Fortran code fragment is as follows:

```
      double cx;
      long double cz;
      cx = 1.23;
      cz = 456.0L;
/*    Display as: 1.23e+000 456.0 */
      printf ( "%8.2e %5.1Lf \ n", cx, cz );
```

Fortran variables such as fx and fy usually have internal representations accurate to approximately 14 digits. By default, both C variables such as cx and cz have internal representations accurate to at least 10 digits. Although there is a direct correspondence between variables fx and cx, differences exist between variables fy and cz. In Fortran, double precision and real*8 are synonymous, so variables fx and fy are the same type. In C, the double data type, represented by the variable cx, is the direct counterpart. Long double variables, such as cz, can be represented with greater accuracy than double variables, such as cx. Any given implementation of a C compiler can increase the 10 digit default limit provided that the accuracy of long double variables is at least, if not more than, the accuracy of double variables. TABLE 3-2 shows the range of values for C data types.

Integer data type

Integer valued variables can be declared in three ways in Fortran and 17 ways in C. In Fortran, integers are declared, initialized, and displayed as follows:

```
      integer*2 fi
      integer*4 fj
      integer   fk
      fi = 12
      fj = 34
      fk = 56
c     Display as: 123456
      write ( 6,1 ) fi, fj, fk
    1 format ( 1H , 3i2 )
```

Fortran variable fi ranges from −32,767 to 32,767; and variables fj and fk range approximately two billion above and below zero. Variable fk

Table 3-2   Range of Values for C Data Types.

C Type	Minimum Value	Maximum Value
char (printable)	' ' = 32	'~' = 126
signed char	– 127	127
unsigned char	0	255
double (10 digits)	10 ** –37	10 ** 37
long double (10 digits)	10 ** –37	10 ** 37
int	–32767	32767
short	–32767	32767
short int	–32767	32767
signed	–32767	32767
signed int	–32767	32767
signed short	–32767	32767
signed short int	–32767	32767
unsigned	0	65535
unsigned int	0	65535
unsigned short	0	65535
unsigned short int	0	65535
long	–2147483647	2147483647
long int	–2147483647	2147483647
signed long	–2147483647	2147483647
signed long int	–2147483647	2147483647
unsigned long	0	4294967295
unsigned long int	0	4294967295
float (10 digits)	10 ** –37	10 ** 37

is declared according to 1978 ANSI standard Fortran. Variables fi and fj are not declared in a standard-conforming way, but integer*2 and integer*4 statements are common Fortran extensions. The C counterpart to that Fortran code fragment is as follows:

```
       int           ci   =  1;
       short         cj   =  2;
       signed        ck   =  3;
       unsigned      cl   =  4U;
       long          cm   =  5L;
       unsigned long cn   =  6UL;
/*     Display as: 123456 */
       printf ( "%d%hd%d%u%ld%lu \ n", ci,cj,ck,cl,cm,cn );
```

C variables ci, cj, and ck are most like the Fortran variable fi with a range of – 32,767 to 32,767. C variable cl is also similar to the Fortran variable fi, except that its range lies in the positive numbers from zero to 65,535. C variable cm corresponds exactly with Fortran variables fj and fk. Lastly, C variable cn is like Fortran variables fj and fk, except that its range lies in the positive numbers from zero to slightly over four billion. C integer data types permit several different declarations to specify variables with identical numerical ranges. Individual implementations of C can differ, but a guiding principal is that the short integer data type supports 16 bit integers, the int data type is the "natural" size (often 16 bit integers) for the target computer system, the long data type supports at least 32 bits, and the unsigned data type qualifier shifts the numerical range of the underlying data type into the positive numbers.

Logical data type

C provides no native support for a data type like the logical data type from Fortran. Arrays of bit fields that gang multiple integers to represent the series of logical variables could be constructed in C. Unlike Fortran, however, C has no predefined operators to manipulate, compare, and perform input/output on such structures such as provided for by Fortran. The entry for Fortran's logical statement in Chapter 5 has further suggestions.

Real data type

Single precision floating point numbers are represented as real in Fortran and as float in C. In Fortran, single precision floating point numbers are declared, initialized, and displayed as follows:

```
      real*4 fx
      real    fy
      fx  =  7.0
      fy  =  8.0
c     Display as: 7.0 8.0
      write ( 6,1 ) fx, fy
    1 format ( 1H , f3.1, 1x, f3.1 )
```

Typically, Fortran floating point variables have an internal representation accurate to six digits. Variable fy is declared according to 1978 ANSI standard Fortran. Variable fx is not declared in a standard-conforming way, but the real*4 statement is a common Fortran synonym for real. The C counterpart to that Fortran code fragment is as follows:

```
    float cx;
    float cy;
    cx   =   7.0F;
    cy   =   8.0F;
/*    Display as: 7.0 8.0 */
    printf ( "%3.1f %3.1f \n", cx, cy );
```

By default, C single precision floating point variables have an internal representation accurate to at least 10 digits. Floating point constants with the F suffix are considered to be single precision: without the F suffix, such a constant defaults to the extended precision data type double.

Numerical range

C compilers can choose to implement a wider numerical range than that described in this chapter. This affects the accuracy, minimum value, and maximum value of floating point data types. By default, the accuracy of both double and long double are at least 10 digits. As C is defined, nothing prevents a compiler developer from establishing the accuracy of the float data type at 10 digits, double at 16 digits, and long double at 20 digits. Figure 3-1 is a C program that will display the range of values for C data types in a format like TABLE 3-2 for any ANSI C compiler.

3-1 C program to calibrate Table 3-2 for your compiler.

```
#include <float.h>
#include <limits.h>
main ( void )
{
  char       space             = ' ';
  char       tilde             = '~';
  unsigned   uchar__min        = 0u;
  unsigned   uint__min         = 0u;
  unsigned   long int ulong__min = 0ul;
  printf  ( "Figure 3-2. Range of values for C data types. \n\n" );
  printf  ( "C Type                  Minimum Value Maximum Value\n\n" );
  printf  ( "char (printable)        '%c' = %d\t'%c   ' = %d\n",\
                                      space, space, tilde, tilde   );
  printf  ( "signed char             %d\t\t%d\n",     SCHAR__MIN, SCHAR__MAX  );
  printf  ( "unsigned char           %u\t\t%u\n\n" , uchar__min, UCHAR__MAX  );
  printf  ( "double (%d digits)      10 ** %d\t10 ** %d \n", DBL__DIG,\
                                      DBL__MIN__10__EXP, DBL__MAX__10__EXP   );
  printf  ( "long double (%d digits) 10 ** %d\t10 ** %d\n\n", DBL__DIG,\
                                      DBL__MIN__10__EXP, DBL__MAX__10__EXP   );
  printf  ( "int                     %d\t\t%d\n",     INT__MIN, INT__MAX   );
  printf  ( "short                   %hd\t\t%hd\n",   SHRT__MIN, SHRT__MAX  );
  printf  ( "short int               %hd\t\t%hd\n",   SHRT__MIN, SHRT__MAX  );
  printf  ( "signed                  %d\t\t%d\n",     INT__MIN, INT__MAX   );
  printf  ( "signed int              %d\t\t%d\n",     INT__MIN, INT__MAX   );
  printf  ( "signed short            %d\t\t%d\n",     SHRT__MIN,  SHRT__MAX  );
  printf  ( "signed short int        %d\t\t%d\n",     SHRT__MIN,  SHRT__MAX  );
  printf  ( "unsigned                %u\t\t%u\n",     uint__min,  UINT__MAX  );
  printf  ( "unsigned int            %u\t\t%u\n",     uint__min,  UINT__MAX  );
  printf  ( "unsigned short          %u\t\t%u\n",     uint__min,  UINT__MAX  );
  printf  ( "unsigned short int      %u\t\t%u\n",     uint__min,  UINT__MAX  );
  printf  ( "long                    %ld\t%ld\n",     LONG__MIN, LONG__MAX  );
  printf  ( "long int                %ld\t%ld\n",     LONG__MIN, LONG__MAX  );
  printf  ( "signed long             %ld\t%ld\n",     LONG__MIN, LONG__MAX  );
  printf  ( "signed long int         %ld\t%ld\n",     LONG__MIN, LONG__MAX  );
  printf  ( "unsigned long           %lu\t\t%lu\n",   ulong__min, ULONG__MAX  );
  printf  ( "unsigned long int       %lu\t\t%lu\n",   ulong__min, ULONG__MAX  );
  printf  ( "float (%d digits)       10 ** %d\t10 ** %d\n", FLT__DIG,\
                                      FLT__MIN__10__EXP, FLT__MAX__10__EXP   );
}
```

Storage allocation

Fortran and C provide a type qualifier that will preserve the initial value of a variable. The Fortran `parameter` statement and the C const statement inform a compiler that the value of the named variable will not change during the course of program execution. In the following Fortran program,

```
      program main
      real          fx
      parameter (  fx = 123.0  )
      real          fy
      fy = fx
c     Display as: 123.0 123.0
      write ( 6,1 ) fx, fy
    1 format ( 1H , f5.1, 1x, f5.1 )
      stop
      end
```

variable `fx` is initialized to 123.0 in the `parameter` statement and can never again appear on the left-hand side of any assignment operator. In the fifth line of that example, the value of the parameter variable `fx` is assigned to the variable `fy`. A Fortran compiler would flag as a fatal error if that fifth line read `fx = fy` because the value of a parameter variable, once set, cannot be altered. An equivalent C program is as follows:

```
      const float cx = 123.0F;
      main ( )
   {
      float cy;
      cy = cx;
/*    Display as: 123.0 123.0 */
      printf ( "%5.1f %5.1f \n", cx, cy );
      return;
   }
```

The float data type for the variable cx is qualified with the const token to indicate that its value, 123.0, will not be modified in the program. A C compiler would flag as a fatal error if that fifth line read cx = cy because the value of a const variable, once set, cannot be altered. C also provides a volatile qualifier that specifies the reverse of the const qualifier. Whereas a const variable cannot be changed, a volatile variable changes often. A C compiler is expected to immediately retrieve or store the value of a volatile variable at the precise point in a program that such a variable is referred to or assigned a value. Both const and volatile variables allow some measure of control over program optimization: const signals that optimization can be attempted, and volatile forces optimization to be deferred.

4
Operators

There are five broad groups of operators in both Fortran and C: arithmetic, character, relational, logical, and bitwise (see TABLE 4-1). Fortran and C have an identical basic set of operators, but C provides extensions with some convenient new arithmetic operators and fully supported bitwise operators.

When several operators appear in an expression, Fortran and C have identical rules of precedence and associativity for common operators. Precedence determines the order in which a mix of operators in a single statement are executed, such as multiplication and division before addition and subtraction. Associativity determines the order in which two or more of the same operator in a single statement are executed, such as from left to right across the statement or from right to left. It is common practice in Fortran programs for the programmer to establish an explicit order of evaluation with the liberal use of parentheses to group parts of an expression. All ANSI C compilers and many earlier C compilers will not rearrange expressions in the presence of parentheses. However, the original definition of the C language permitted a compiler to regroup multiple occurrences of addition and multiplication operators regardless of the placement of parentheses.

Arithmetic operators

Fortran and C share an almost identical set of arithmetic operators. All five Fortran arithmetic operators are used in the following program:

```
program main
real fx
real fy
```

```
        fx = 4.56
        fy = 1.23
        write ( 6,1 ) fx ** 2.0
    1   format ( 1H ,'Exponentiation ', f5.2 )
        write ( 6,2 ) fx * fy
    2   format ( 1H ,'Multiplication ', f5.2 )
        write ( 6,3 ) fx / fy
    3   format ( 1H ,'Division       ', f5.2 )
        write ( 6,4 ) fx + fy
    4   format ( 1H ,'Addition       ', f5.2 )
        write ( 6,5 ) fx - fy
    5   format ( 1H ,'Subtraction    ', f5.2 )
        stop
        end
```

This display is produced:

Exponentiation	20.79
Multiplication	5.61
Division	3.71
Addition	5.79
Subtraction	3.33

The same display results from this C program:

```
    #include <math.h>
    main ( )
{
    float cx = 4.56F;
    float cy = 1.23F;
    printf ( "Exponentiation  %5.2f \ n", pow ( cx, 2.0F ) );
    printf ( "Multiplication  %5.2f \ n", cx * cy );
    printf ( "Division        %5.2f \ n", cx / cy );
    printf ( "Addition        %5.2f \ n", cx + cy );
    printf ( "Subtraction     %5.2f \ n", cx - cy );
    return;
}
```

Note that C does not have an exponential operator; but a standard mathematical library function, pow, is available to accomplish the same results.

C provides nine arithmetic operators that have no direct counterpart in Fortran. Four of these new operators provide a convenient syntax for assigning a new value to a variable as a function of its old value. Fortran statements like

```
    fx = fx + fy
```

can be written in C for addition and the three other primary arithmetic operators (i.e., division, multiplication, and subtraction) as

```
    cx + = cy;
```

Table 4-1   Fortran and C Operators.

Operator type and description	Fortran	C
Arithmetic operators		
Exponentiation *	**	pow( )
Division	/	/, / =
Multiplication	*	*, * =
Subtraction (or negation)	−	−, − = ,--
Addition (or identity)	+	+, + = , + +
Modulus	mod( )	%, % =
If/else		?:
Character operator		
Concatenation **	//	strcat( )
Relational operators		
Less than	.LT.	<
Less than or equal to	.LE.	< =
Equal to	.EQ.	= =
Not equal to	.NE.	! =
Greater than	.GT.	>
Greater than or equal to	.GE.	> =
Logical operators		
Logical negation	.NOT.	
Logical conjunction	.AND.	&&
Logical inclusive disjunction	.OR.	¦¦
Logical equivalence	.EQV.	
Logical nonequivalence	.NEQV.	
Bitwise operators		
One's complement		~
Bitwise left shift		< <, < < =
Bitwise right shift		> >, > > =
Bitwise AND	.AND.	&, & =
Bitwise exclusive OR		^
Bitwise OR	.OR.	¦, ¦ =

* C has no operator for exponentiation: a library function, pow, is in the C standard mathematical library to raise a number to a power.

** C has no operator for string concatenation: a library function, strcat, is in the C standard string library to perform string concatenation.

Two other operators allow a compact syntax for changing the value of a variable by one. Fortran statements like

```
fx = fx + 1
fi = fi - 1
```

can be written in C as

```
cx =  + + cx;
ci =  − − ci;
```

A pair of operators provide for computations comparable to the Fortran mod intrinsic function. The ninth new operator is a single-line shorthand for the Fortran if ... then/else construct. Figure 4-1 demonstrates all nine C operators with a C program that generates the results shown in FIG. 4-2. A line-for-line Fortran translation of that program is listed in FIG. 4-3. There are superfluous lines in both example programs: variables ci and fi, respectively, exist only to record the initial value of the change variable, ck and fk, and are not otherwise required.

4-1 Additional C arithmetic operators.

```
int ci, cj, ck;

main ( )
{

void reset ( );
reset ( );

cj  = ck;
ck = ci;
printf ( "%d division/assign %d = %d \ n", cj, ci, ck   );
reset ( );

ci   = ck;
ck * = cj;
printf ( "%d multiply/assign %d = %d \ n", ci, cj, ck   );
reset ( );

ci  = ck;
ck  − = cj;
printf ( "%d subtraction/assign %d = %d \ n", ci, cj, ck   );
reset ( );

ci  = cj;
ck  = − − cj;
printf ( "%d decremented = %d \ n", ci, ck   );
reset ( );

ci  = ck;
ck + = cj;
printf ( "%d addition/assign %d = %d \ n", ci, cj, ck   );
reset ( );

ci  = cj;
ck  = + + cj;
printf ( "%d incremented = %d \ n", ci, ck   );
reset ( );

printf ( "%d modulus %d = %d \ n", ck, cj, ck%cj   );
reset ( );
```

4-1 Continued.

```
ci  = ck;
ck %= cj;
printf ( "%d modulus/assign %d = %d \ n", ci, cj, ck  );
reset ( );

ck = (  ci != cj  ) ? 4 : 5;
printf ( "  if/else operator result = %d \ n", ck  );
reset ( );

return;
}

void reset ( )
{
  ci  = 1;
  cj  = 2;
  ck  = 3;
  return;
}
```

4-2 Output of additional C operators program.

```
3 division/assign 1 = 3
3 multiply/assign 2 = 6
3 subtraction/assign 2 = 1
2 decremented = 1
3 addition/assign 2 = 5
2 incremented = 3
3 modulus 2 = 1
3 modulus/assign 2 = 1
  if/else operator result = 4
```

4-3 Additional C operators program in Fortran.

```
program main
integer fi, fj, fk
common / area / fi, fj, fk

call  reset
fj = fk
fk = fk / fi
write ( 6,1 ) fj, fi, fk
1 format ( 1H , il , 'division/assign ', il , ' = ', il )
call reset

fi = fk
fk = fk • fj
write ( 6,2 ) fi, fj, fk
2 format ( 1H , il , 'multiply/assign ', il , ' = ', il )
call reset
```

4-3 Continued.

```
   fi  = fk
   fk  = fk - fj
   write ( 6,3 ) fi, fj, fk
 3 format ( 1H , i1, 'subtraction/assign ', i1, ' = ', i1 )
   call reset

   fi  = fj
   fk  = fj - 1
   write ( 6,4 ) fi, fk
 4 format ( 1H , i1, 'decremented = ', i1 )
   call reset

   fi  = fk
   fk  = fk + fj
   write ( 6,5 ) fi, fj, fk
 5 format ( 1H , i1, 'addition/assign ', i1, ' = ', i1 )
   call reset

   fi  = fj
   fk  = fj + 1
   write ( 6,6 ) fi, fk
 6 format ( 1H , i1, 'incremented = ', i1 )
   call reset

   write ( 6,7 ) fk, fj, mod( fk,fj)
 7 format ( 1H , i1, 'modulus ', i1, ' = ', i1 )
   call reset

   fi  = fk
   fk  = mod( fk,fj)
   write ( 6,8 ) fi, fj, fk
 8 format ( 1H , i1, 'modulus/assign ', i1, ' = ', i1 )
   call reset

   if ( fi .ne. fj ) then
        fk = 4
   else
        fk = 5
   end if
   write ( 6,9 ) fk
 9 format ( 1H , 'if/else operator result = ', i1 )
   call reset

   stop
   end

   subroutine reset
   integer fi, fj, fk
   common / area / fi, fj, fk
   fi  = 1
   fj  = 2
   fk  = 3
   return
   end
```

Character operators

The Fortran concatenation operator allows a programmer to generate a single long string from several components, as in the following program:

```
      program main
      character*5  fca
      character*5  fcb
      character*15 fcd
      fca = 'aaaaa'
      fcb = 'bbbbb'
      fcd = fca / / fcb / / 'ccccc'
      write ( 6,1 ) fcd
1     format ( 1H , 'Concatenation ', a15 )
      stop
      end
```

This display is produced:

Concatenation aaaaabbbbbccccc

The same display results from this C program:

```
      #include <string.h>
      main ( )
{
      char cca[5]   = "aaaaa";
      char ccb[5]   = "bbbbb";
      char ccd[15]  = " ";
      strcat ( ccd,  cca    );
      strcat ( ccd,  ccb    );
      strcat ( ccd, "ccccc" );
      printf ( "Concatenation %s \ n", ccd );
      return;
}
```

Note that C does not have a concatenation operator; but a standard string library function, strcat, is available to accomplish the same result.

Relational operators

There are six relational operators in Fortran to compare the relative values of variables. The following Fortran program demonstrates these operators:

```
      program main
      real  fx
      real  fy
      real  fz
      fx =   4.56
      fy =   1.23
      fz =   fy
      if ( fy .lt. fx ) write ( 6,1 ) fy, fx
```

```
1    format ( 1H , f4.2, ' .LT. ', f4.2 )
     if ( fy .le. fz ) write ( 6,2 ) fy, fz
2    format ( 1H , f4.2, ' .LE. ', f4.2 )
     if ( fy .eq. fz ) write ( 6,3 ) fy, fz
3    format ( 1H , f4.2, ' .EQ. ', f4.2 )
     if ( fy .ne. fx ) write ( 6,4 ) fy, fx
4    format ( 1H , f4.2, ' .NE. ', f4.2 )
     if ( fx .gt. fy ) write ( 6,5 ) fx, fy
5    format ( 1H , f4.2, ' .GT. ', f4.2 )
     if ( fy .ge. fz ) write ( 6,6 ) fy, fz
6    format ( 1H , f4.2, ' .GE. ', f4.2 )
     stop
     end
```

It produces this display:

```
1.23  .LT.  4.56
1.23  .LE.  1.23
1.23  .EQ.  1.23
1.23  .NE.  4.56
4.56  .GT.  1.23
1.23  .GE.  1.23
```

That same demonstration program in C is as follows:

```
main ( )
{
float cx = 4.56F;
float cy = 1.23F;
float cz = cy;
if ( cy < cx )
printf ( "%4.2f .LT. %4.2f \ n", cy, cx );
if ( cy < = cz )
printf ( "%4.2f .LE. %4.2f \ n", cy, cz );
if ( cy = = cz )
printf ( "%4.2f .EQ. %4.2f \ n", cy, cz );
if ( cy != cx )
printf ( "%4.2f .NE. %4.2f \ n", cy, cx );
if ( cx > cy )
printf ( "%4.2f .GT. %4.2f \ n", cx, cy );
if ( cy > = cz )
printf ( "%4.2f .GE. %4.2f \ n", cy, cz );
return;
}
```

The program uses relational operators to compare floating point values; double precision, integer, or individual characters declared using C's int data type could also have been used.

Logical operators

There are six logical operators in Fortran to compare values of Fortran logical data type variables. Four of these six operators function solely with Fortran logical data type variables. The remaining two operators—.and. and .or.—are used to combine the comparison of several variables, such as in the following:

```
      program main
      real  fx
      real  fy
      real  fz
      fx =  4.56
      fy =  1.23
      fz =  3.33
      if (  fx .gt. fz .and.
     -         fy .lt. fz       ) write ( 6,1 ) fy, fz, fx
    1 format ( 1H ,'.AND. ',f4.2,' < ',f4.2,' < ',f4.2 )
      if (  fz .gt. fy .or.
     -         fz .gt. fx       ) write ( 6,2 ) fz, fy, fx
    2 format ( 1H ,'.OR. ',f4.2,' > ',f4.2,' or ',f4.2 )
      stop
      end
```

It generates these two lines of output:

```
.AND.  1.23 < 3.33 < 4.56
 .OR.  3.33 > 1.23 or 4.56
```

The C counterpart to such a program is as follows:

```
      main ()
   {
      float cx = 4.56F;
      float cy = 1.23F;
      float cz = 3.33F;
      if ( cx > cz && cy < cz )
      printf (  ".AND. %4.2f < %4.2f < %4.2f \ n",
            cy, cz, cx );
      if ( cz > cy || cz > cx )
      printf (  " .OR. %4.2f > %4.2f or %4.2f \ n",
            cz, cy, cx );
      return;
   }
```

Like in Fortran, the two C logical operators are in constant use to build compound tests so as to isolate circumstances in which a program needs to take special action.

Bitwise operators

Fortran has no operators specifically designed to manipulate the bits of a variable. Modern Fortran compilers regularly allow two logical operators, .and. and .or., to accept integer arguments for the purpose of handling bit level activity. In addition, these compilers often extend ANSI standard Fortran by including functions to perform bit shift operations. Bit level operators are fully specified in ANSI standard C. Figure 4-4 demonstrates the syntax of all six C bitwise operators and produces the display shown in FIG. 4-5.

4-4 C bitwise operators.

```
#include <stdio.h>
int ci, cj, ck;
char *co;
main ( )
{
void showresult ( );
ci  =  29452;

printf ( " \ nOne's complement \ n" );
ck  =  ~ci;
cj  =  0;
co  =  "~";
showresult( );

printf ( " \ nBitwise left shift \ n" );
cj  =  5;
ck  =  ci < < cj;
co  =  "<<";
showresult( );

printf ( " \ nBitwise right shift \ n" );
cj  =  7;
ck  =  ci > > cj;
co  =  ">>";
showresult( );

printf ( " \ nBitwise AND \ n" );
cj  =  9913;
ck  =  ci & cj;
co  =  "& ";
showresult( );

printf ( " \ nBitwise exclusive OR \ n" );
ck  =  ci ^ cj;
co  =  "^ ";
showresult( );

printf ( " \ nBitwise OR \ n" );
ck  =  ci | cj;
```

4-4 Continued.

```
co = "¦";
showresult( );

printf ( "\n" );
return;
}

void showresult ( )
{
void showbits ( );
printf ( "Decimal %16d %2s %16d = %16d\n", ci, co, cj, ck );
printf ( "Binary " );
showbits ( ci );
printf ( "%2s ", co );
showbits ( cj );
printf ( " = " );
showbits ( ck );
printf ( "\n" );
return;
}

void showbits ( int number )
{
int i;
unsigned int window = 32768;
for ( i = 1; i < = 16; i + + ) {
    putchar ( ( number & window ) ? '1' : '0' );
    window > > = 1;
}
putchar ( ' ' );
return;
}
```

4-5 Results of C bitwise operator demonstration program.

One's complement

Decimal	29452	~		0	=	−29453
Binary	0111001100001100	~	0000000000000000	=	1000110011110011

Bitwise left shift

Decimal	29452	<<		5	=	24960
Binary	0111001100001100	<<	0000000000000101	=	0110000110000000

Bitwise right shift

Decimal	29452	>>		7	=	230
Binary	0111001100001100	>>	0000000000000111	=	0000000011100110

Bitwise AND

Decimal	29452	&		9913	=	8712
Binary	0111001100001100	&	0010011010111001	=	0010001000001000

4-5 Continued.

Bitwise exclusive OR

Decimal	29452	^	9913	=	21941	
Binary	0111001100001100	^	0010011010111001	=	0101010110110101	

Bitwise OR

Decimal	29452	|	9913	=	30653	
Binary	0111001100001100	|	0010011010111001	=	0111011110111101	

5
Concordance

Fortran programs are written using forty-seven distinct statements. This chapter has a separate section for each Fortran statement. Each statement is presented in the same fashion: Fortran syntax, primary C counterpart, other C statements of interest, example Fortran program, example program output, and example C program. Not suprisingly, several Fortran statements have no single C counterpart. In such cases, the example C program was written to parallel the example Fortran program as closely as possible and to produce similar results.

Assign

Fortran	`assign LABEL to VARIABLE`
C Primary	`# #`, `#define`
C Secondary	`goto`

Fortran's `assign` statement associates a statement label with the name of an integer variable. The label must refer to another executable statement in the same program unit in which the `assign` statement appears. Once a statement label has been assigned to a variable, that variable can be used in any of the various forms of Fortran's go to statements or as labels for `format` statements. The following Fortran program uses the `assign` statement in both modes:

```
      program main
      integer label
      integer formatnumber
      assign 2 to label
      assign 5 to formatnumber
      go to label
      write ( 6,1 )
    1 format ( 1H , 'This will be skipped.' )
      stop
    2 continue
      write ( 6,3 )
    3 format ( 1H , 'This will be displayed ( 1 of 2).' )
      write ( 6,formatnumber )
    4 format ( 1H , 'This will NEVER be displayed.' )
    5 format ( 1H , 'This will be displayed ( 2 of 2).' )
      stop
      end
```

The program generates this display:

```
This will be displayed (1 of 2).
This will be displayed (2 of 2).
```

A C program that accomplishes the same function is as follows:

```
    main( )
  {
    #define LABEL lab2
    #define DISPLAY4 printf ( "This will NEVER be "
                              "displayed. \ n" )
    #define DISPLAY5 printf ( "This will be displayed "
                              "(2 of 2). \ n" )
    #define DISPLAY(x) DISPLAY##x
    goto LABEL;
    printf ( "This will be skipped. \ n" );
    return;
```

```
lab2:
        printf ( "This will be displayed (1 of 2). \ n" );
        DISPLAY(5);
        return;
    }
```

This C program illustrates several C language features: labels, manifest constants, and function macros. Fortran uses labels for a number of features such as flow control, do loops, and format statements. C counterparts to such Fortran constructs do not use labels. Most C programs have no labels. When it adds clarity to the intent of a program, the C goto statement can be used to modify the flow of control. It takes one argument that is the name of the label to which control will pass. In this example, the label is itself a variable.

The first three uses of the C #define statement establish three manifest constants. When a variable appears in a such a #define statement, it is initialized with the string that follows on that line. At compile time, that variable will be replaced with the string wherever the variable appears in that program unit. In the example program, the line goto LABEL is interpreted by the compiler as if it had been written as goto lab2. Note that it is customary, but not required, to write manifest constants in uppercase.

The last #define statement establishes a function macro. When invoked, its single argument will be concatenated onto the end of the string DISPLAY through the use of the ## token-pasting operator. In the example, the line DISPLAY(5) is interpreted by the compiler as if it was written as DISPLAY5, which in turn is replaced by the line

```
printf ( "This will be displayed (2 of 2). \ n" )
```

Function macros are discussed again in this chapter in the section on Fortran's function statement.

Backspace

Fortran	backspace UNIT
	backspace (UNIT, iostat=VAR, err=LAB)
C Primary	fseek, ftell
C Secondary	%n, do:while, exit, fclose, fopen, for, perror

The backspace statement allows a record in a sequential file to be re-processed. It re-positions the file pointer to the beginning of the preceding record. The following Fortran program creates a file, writes five records into that file, reads the file forwards, and then, using the backspace statement, reads the file backwards.

```
        program main
        integer output, error, records, input
        character*24 line
        input = 7
        output = 8
        open ( unit=output,    access='SEQUENTIAL',
     -         file='backs.dat',form='FORMATTED',
     -         iostat=error,   status='NEW' )
        if ( error .ne. 0 ) then
            write ( 6,1 )
1           format ( 1H , 'Open of [backs.dat] for ',
     -                    'output failed!' )
            go to 15
        end if
        records = 0
        do 3 i = 1, 5, 1
            records = records + 1
            write ( output,2 ) records
2           format ( 'Record_number_', i1, '_read.' )
3       continue
        close ( unit=output, iostat=error, status='KEEP' )
        if ( error .ne. 0 ) then
            write ( 6,4 )
4           format ( 1H , 'Close of [backs.dat] after',
     -                    'output failed!' )
            go to 15
        end if
        open ( unit=input,     access='SEQUENTIAL',
     -         file='backs.dat',form='FORMATTED',
     -         iostat=error,   status='OLD' )
        if ( error .ne. 0 ) then
            write ( 6,5 )
5           format ( 1H , 'Open of [backs.dat] for ',
     -                    'input failed!' )
            go to 15
        end if
        write ( 6,6 )
6       format ( / 1H , 'Read the file forwards.' )
```

44

```
      do 9 i = 1, 5, 1
         read ( input,7 ) line
 7       format ( a24 )
         write ( 6,8 ) line
 8       format ( 1H , a24 )
 9    continue
      write ( 6,10 )
10    format ( / 1H , 'Read the file backwards.' )
      do 13 i = 1, records, 1
         backspace ( unit=input, iostat=error )
         if ( error .ne. 0 ) then
             write ( 6,11 )
11           format ( 1H , 'Backspace of [backs.dat] ',
      -                   'failed!' )
             go to 15
         end if
         read ( input,7 ) line
         write ( 6,8 ) line
         backspace ( unit=input, iostat=error )
         if ( error .ne. 0 ) then
             write ( 6,12 )
12           format ( 1H , 'Backspace of [backs.dat] ',
      -                   'failed!' )
             go to 15
         end if
13    continue
      close ( unit=input, iostat=error, status='KEEP' )
      if ( error .ne. 0 ) then
          write ( 6,14 )
14        format ( 1H , 'Close of [backs.dat] after ',
      -                 'input failed!' )
15    continue
      stop
      end
```

The program generates this display:

```
Read the file forwards.
Record_number_1_read.
Record_number_2_read.
Record_number_3_read.
Record_number_4_read.
Record_number_5_read.

Read the file backwards.
Record_number_5_read.
Record_number_4_read.
Record_number_3_read.
Record_number_2_read.
Record_number_1_read.
```

A C program that accomplishes the same function is as follows:

```c
#include <stdio.h>
#include <stdlib.h>
#include <stddef.h>
main( )
{
FILE  *output;
int    error;
int    records;
int    i;
FILE  *input;
char  *line;
int    bytes;
int    items;
long   position;
if (( output = fopen ( "backs.dat", "wa" )) = = NULL) {
    perror ( " Open of [backs.dat] for output "
            "failed!" );
    exit ( EXIT_FAILURE );
}
records = 0;
for ( i = 0; i < 5; i+ + ) {
    records = + +records;
    fprintf ( output, "Record_number_%i_read. \ n",
                    records );
}
if ( ( error = fclose ( output ) ) == EOF ) {
    perror ( "Close of [backs.dat] after output "
            "failed! \ n" );
    exit ( EXIT_FAILURE );
}
if ( ( input = fopen ( "backs.dat", "r" )) == NULL ) {
    perror ( "Open of [backs.dat] for input "
            "failed!" );
    exit ( EXIT_FAILURE );
}
printf ( " \ nRead the file forwards. \ n" );
for ( i = 0; i < records; i+ + ) {
    items = fscanf ( input, "%s%n", line, &bytes );
    printf ( "%s \ n", line );
}
printf ( " \ nRead the file backwards. \ n" );
if ( ( position = ftell ( input ) ) == -1L ) {
    perror ( "Can't determine position in "
            "[backs.dat]! \ n" );
    exit ( EXIT_FAILURE );
}
do
{
```

```
        position = (position > bytes) ? position-bytes : 0;
        if ( fseek ( input, position, SEEK_SET) != 0 ) {
            perror ("Backspace of [backs.dat] failed!\n");
            exit ( EXIT_FAILURE );
            }
        items = fscanf ( input, "%s%n", line, &bytes );
        printf ( "%s\n", line );
        position = --position;
    } while ( position > 0 );
    if ( ( error = fclose ( input ) ) == EOF ) {
        perror ( "Close of [backs.dat] after input "
                "failed!\n" );
        exit ( EXIT_FAILURE );
    }
    exit ( EXIT_SUCCESS);
}
```

Both example programs open a file for output, initialize the file with data, close the file, re-open the file for input, and read the file sequentially forward and then in reverse. Fortran's backspace statement is defined only for sequential access files. Specifying an access mode of SEQUEN-TIAL and repeating the default form of FORMATTED in the Fortran open statement corresponds to the C library function fopen invoked with an access mode of wa.

Error detection in the Fortran open statement is handled with the iostat construct. This corresponds to C's comparison of the fopen function return value to the ANSI standard C constant, NULL, as defined in the file stddef.h. Error messages have to be created by the user in Fortran as in format statements 2, 4, 5, 11, 12, and 14. The C example program adds specific error messages to the standard C error messages. Such standard error messages would follow user-defined strings given as arguments to the perror function. On error, the Fortran example program branches unconditionally to the end for a single exit point at label 15. Under similar conditions, the C example program stops at once by invoking the exit function with an argument set to the ANSI standard C constant, EXIT-_FAILURE, as defined in the file stdlib.h. Certainly, the Fortran example could have been coded with a stop statement wherever the go to 15 statement appeared. Conversely, the C program could have been coded with a goto some_label where that label was near the end of the program instead of multiple occurrences of the exit (EXIT_FAILURE) line of code. The example programs were written as they appear because both demon-strate common programming styles in Fortran versus C.

Once the file has been opened, it is populated with five records. C's for loop construct uses an index (the variable i) that is initialized to zero, is incremented (the i++ token) at the bottom of the loop, and tested (the i < 5 token) at the top of the loop until the test fails. Fortran's write to a file is matched by C's fprintf library function. Because the file was opened for output, it needs to be released and then re-opened for input. Fortran's close and open statements here are matched by C's fclose and fopen library functions. Note that errors are detected in the C fclose library function by comparing the return value to the ANSI standard C constant EOF as defined in the file stdio.h.

Reading the file in C uses the fscanf library function. This function returns the number of fields successfully read into the variable items as well as the number of bytes successfully read using the %n format into the variable bytes. Although the Fortran backspace statement shields the user from needing to know the length of each record, such information is critical to the C library functions ftell and fseek used to emulate Fortran's backspace statement. The number of bytes written to the file is reported by the C library function ftell and recorded in the variable position.

The file is then read by backing up over each record using the fseek library function until the beginning of the file is encountered. C's do:while construct instructs the program to execute the body of the loop until the file is positioned before the beginning of the file. File position is manipulated by C's fseek function invoked to reset the file pointer using the SEEK_SET argument as defined in the file stdio.h. The file pointer is reset to the number of bytes from the beginning of the file as recorded in the variable position. Immediately before fseek is used, a new file position is calculated. This new file position is based on the number of characters read from the file on the prior call to fscanf.

In the C example program, a record is read and then the file pointer is returned to the beginning of that record. This greatly differs from Fortran's backspace statement, which sets the file pointer to the beginning of the preceding record. Therefore, as coded, the C example program is appropriate only for circumstances when file has fixed length records. For variable length records, a scheme would have to be devised of keeping track of the actual length of each record (i.e., in an array) that would then be incorporated into the calculation of where each record would begin in the file.

Block Data

Fortran	block data NAME
C Primary	#define, #undef
C Secondary	void

The block data statement begins a program unit in which variables stored in common areas are initialized. ANSI Fortran restricts which Fortran statements can appear in a block data program unit to those statements closely associated with giving a variable its initial value. The following Fortran program is an example of the block data statement:

```
program main
common / area / fvar
call subprogram
stop
end
subroutine subprogram
common / area / fvar
write ( 6,1 ) fvar
1 format ( 1H , 'Variable = ', f3.1 )
return
end
block data initialize
common / area / fvar
data fvar / 4.5 /
end
```

The program generates this display:

Variable = 4.5

A C program that accomplishes the same function is as follows:

```
#define cvar 4.5
main ( )
{
void subprogram ( );
subprogram( );
return;
}
void subprogram ( )
{
printf ( "Variable = %3.1f \ n", cvar );
return;
}
```

Because the variable cvar appeared in a #define statement before the beginning of the program, its value is a constant and is available to any program unit (i.e., main and subprogram). The #define statement establishes cvar as a compile-time constant. If the value of cvar had to change frequently, then instead of the #define statement, the following line should be used in its place:

```
float cvar = 4.5F;
```

This declares cvar as a single precision floating point variable and initializes it to 4.5. Having placed the statement before the beginning of the program, this value of 4.5 for the variable cvar is available to any program unit. If the value of cvar changed infrequently within a single source code file, it could be "undefined" and then reset, such as

```
#undef cvar
#define cvar 1.2
```

This technique should be used with caution, however, because the new value is in effect only for the remainder of the source code file in which it appears. A final note about the C example program concerns the use of the void qualifier. When the subprogram function was declared and when it appeared in the source code file, it was qualified with the term void. This qualifier instructs the compiler that the function does not return a value.

Call

Fortran	call NAME
	call NAME (ARGUMENTS)
C Primary	NAME ( )
C Secondary	&, strcpy, void

Nearly every Fortran program is structured in the same fashion: a main program that selectively invokes subroutines and/or functions. In Fortran, a subroutine is invoked by the call statement, which specifies by name the subroutine to exercise and if necessary passes values to and from the subroutine through an argument list enclosed in parentheses. As an example, the following program calls a single subroutine that modifies three global variables held in a common area and also changes each of the three local variables named in the argument list:

```
      program main
      character*3   globalc, localc
      integer       globali, locali
      real          globalr, localr
      common / area / globalc, globali, globalr
      data          globalc / 'abc'   /
      data          globali / 123     /
      data          globalr / 4.5     /
      localc = 'xyz'
      locali = 678
      localr = 9.0
      write ( 6,1 )  globalc, globali, globalr,
     -               localc,  locali,  localr
    1 format ( 1H ,  'MAIN Global : ', a3, i5, f5.1,
     -                      ' Local : ', a3, i5, f5.1 )
      call sub ( localc, locali, localr )
      write ( 6,1 ) globalc, globali, globalr,
     -               localc,  locali,  localr
      stop
      end
      subroutine sub ( localc, locali, localr )
      character*3   globalc, localc
      integer       globali, locali
      real          globalr, localr
      common / area / globalc, globali, globalr
      write ( 6,1 )  globalc, globali, globalr,
     -               localc,  locali,  localr
    1 format ( 1H ,  'SUB Global : ', a3, i5, f5.1,
     -                ' Local      : ', a3, i5, f5.1 )
      globalc = 'ABC'
      globali = globali  * 10
      globalr = globalr  * 10.0
      localc  = 'XYZ'
      locali  = locali   * 10
      localr  = localr   * 10.0
```

```
   write ( 6,1 ) globalc, globali, globalr,
-             localc, locali, localr
   return
   end
```

The program generates this display:

MAIN	Global:	abc	123	4.5	Local :	xyz	678	9.0
SUB	Global:	abc	123	4.5	Local :	xyz	678	9.0
SUB	Global:	ABC	1230	45.0	Local :	XYZ	6780	90.0
MAIN	Global:	ABC	1230	45.0	Local :	XYZ	6780	90.0

A C program that accomplishes the same function is as follows:

```
   char *globalc = "abc";
   int   globali = 123;
   float globalr = 4.5F;
   main( )
{
   char *localc  = "xyz";
   int   locali  = 678;
   float localr  = 9.0F;
   void  sub ( char *localc,int *locali,float *localr );
   printf ( "MAIN   Global: %3s %5i %5.1f "
                 "Local : %3s %5i %5.1f \ n",
                 globalc, globali, globalr,
                 localc, locali, localr );
   sub ( localc, &locali, &localr );
   printf ( "MAIN   Global: %3s %5i %5.1f "
                 "Local : %3s %5i  %5.1f \ n",
                 globalc, globali, globalr,
                 localc, locali, localr );
   return;
}
   void sub ( char *localc, int *locali, float *localr )
{
   printf ( "SUB   Global: %3s A%5i %5.1f "
                 "Local : %3s %5i %5.1f \ n",
                 globalc, globali, globalr,
                 localc, *locali *localr );
   strcpy ( globalc, "ABC" );
   globali  = globali * 10;
   globalr  = globalr * 10.0;
   strcpy ( localc, "XYZ" );
   *locali  = *locali * 10;
   *localr  = *localr * 10.0;
   printf ( "SUB   Global: %3s %5i %5.1f "
                 "Local : %3s %5i %5.1f \ n",
```

```
                    globalc, globali, globalr,
                    localc, *locali, *localr );
         return;
     }
```

In both programs, three global and three local variables are declared. Global and local variables of types integer, floating point, and character are initialized. In the C example program, the subprogram sub is then specified in a function prototype statement. In the function prototype statement, the void qualifier informs the compiler that sub does not return a value, and the prototype argument list is declared to hold three elements that are pointers to character, integer, and floating point variables. ANSI C requires that each function be introduced with a function prototype statement.

Both programs display the value of each variable as initialized in the main program. When the subprogram is invoked in the C example, the & operator is used to pass the address of the two numeric arguments. In other words, &locali is the address of the int variable locali, and &localr is the address of the float variable localr. Note that the char variable *localc is itself a pointer. Pointers are required here because the function sub is designed to change the value of all three of its arguments. There is a valuable side effect of enforcing this "call by value" structure of C: it forces a programmer to specify as pointers any argument whose value might change in the function. Once sub gains control, the value of its arguments are displayed. Global and local numeric arguments are multiplied by ten. Global and local character variables are given new values with the strcpy function. Before returning, the sub function displays the new values of each global and local variable. The main program completes execution by showing the final values of all variables.

Character

Fortran	character*length VARIABLE
	character VARIABLE*length
	character*(*) VARIABLE
C Primary	char
C Secondary	%*s, size_t, strcat, strcpy, strlen

Character data handling separates ANSI 66 Fortran from ANSI 77 Fortran. The newer standard supports a character data type, character input/output formats, and a limited set of character-related intrinsic functions. Most implementations of ANSI 77 Fortran provide access to a library that includes subroutines for character string manipulation such as copying, searching, justifying, and trimming. However, these subroutines are not in the ANSI standard and vary from system to system. The following Fortran example program uses only ANSI standard statements to create global and local character variables—strings and arrays—and access these variables in whole and in part:

```
      program main
      character*3   gwhole
      character                    lwhole*3
      character     gparts*1(3)
      character*1                  lparts(3)
      character                    expandable*14
      character                    single
      integer                      numeric
      common / area / gwhole,      gparts
      gwhole     = 'abc'
      gparts(1)  = 'd'
      gparts(2)  = 'e'
      gparts(3)  = 'f'
      lwhole     = 'uvw'
      lparts(1)  = 'x'
      lparts(2)  = 'y'
      lparts(3)  = 'z'
      expandable = 'ghijklmnop'
      write ( 6,1 ) gwhole, gparts, expandable,
     -              lwhole, lparts
    1 format ( 1H , 'MAIN ', a3,1x, 3a1,1x, '[',a,']',1x,
     -                a3,1x, 3a1 )
      call sub ( lwhole, lparts, expandable )
      write ( 6,1 ) gwhole, gparts, expandable,
     -              lwhole, lparts
      gwhole(2:2)     = 'b'
      gparts(2)(1:1) = 'e'
      lwhole(2:2)     = 'v'
      lparts(2)(1:1) = 'y'
      write ( 6,1 ) gwhole, gparts, expandable,
     -              lwhole, lparts
      single  = 'a'
      numeric = ichar ( single )
```

```
      write ( 6,2 ) single, char ( numeric ), numeric
 2  format ( 1H , 'MAIN Single character ', '[',a,']'
   -              ' numeric value is: ', a, ' => ', i3.3 )
    stop
    end
    subroutine sub  ( lwhole, lparts, expandable )
    character*3   gwhole
    character                         lwhole*3
    character       gparts*1(3)
    character*1                       lparts(3)
    character*(*)                              expandable
    integer                           length
    common / area / gwhole,           gparts
    length = len ( expandable )
    write ( 6,1 ) gwhole, gparts, expandable(1:length),
   -              lwhole, lparts
 1  format ( 1H , 'SUB ', a3,1x, 3a1,1x, '[',a,']',1x,
   -              a3,1x, 3a1 )
    expandable = 'GHIJK' // 'LMNOP'
    expandable(1:length) = expandable(1:10) // 'QRST'
    write ( 6,1 ) gwhole, gparts, expandable(1:length),
   -              lwhole, lparts
    gwhole      = 'ABC'
    gparts(1)   = 'D'
    gparts(2)   = 'E'
    gparts(3)   = 'F'
    lwhole      = 'UVW'
    lparts(1)   = 'X'
    lparts(2)   = 'Y'
    lparts(3)   = 'Z'
    write ( 6,1 ) gwhole, gparts, expandable(1:length),
   -              lwhole, lparts
    return
    end
```

The program generates this display:

```
MAIN   abc   def   [ghijklmnop ]        uvw   xyz
SUB    abc   def   [ghijklmnop ]        uvw   xyz
SUB    abc   def   [GHIJKLMNOPQRST]     uvw   xyz
SUB    ABC   DEF   [GHIJKLMNOPQRST]     UVW   XYZ
MAIN   ABC   DEF   [GHIJKLMNOPQRST]     UVW   XYZ
MAIN   AbC   DeF   [GHIJKLMNOPQRST]     UvW   XyZ
MAIN   Single character [a] numeric value is: a = > 097
```

A C program that accomplishes the same function is as follows:

```
char  *gwhole      = "abc";
char  *gparts[3]   = { "d", "e", "f" };
main( )
{
char  *lwhole      = "uvw";
```

55

```c
char   *lparts[3]     = { "x", "y", "z" };
char   *expandable = "ghijklmnop";
char   single;
int    numeric;
void sub ( char *lwhole, char *lparts[3],
           char *expandable );
printf ( "MAIN %3s %s%s%s [%-14s] %3s %s%s%s \ n",
         gwhole, gparts[0], gparts[1], gparts[2],
         expandable,
         lwhole, lparts[0], lparts[1], lparts[2] );
sub ( lwhole, lparts, expandable );
printf ( "MAIN %3s %s%s%s [%-14s] %3s %s%s%s \ n",
         gwhole, gparts[0], gparts[1] gparts[2],
         expandable,
         lwhole, lparts[0], lparts[1], lparts[2] );
gwhole[1]  = 'b';
gparts [1]  =  "e";
lwhole [1]  = 'v';
lparts [1]  =  "y";
printf ( "MAIN %3s %s%s%s [%-14s] %3s %s%s%s \ n",
         gwhole, gparts[0], gparts[1], gparts[2],
         expandable,
         lwhole, lparts[0], lparts[1], lparts[2] );
single    = 'a';
numeric  =  single;
printf ( "MAIN Single character [%c] numeric value",
              single );
printf ( " is: %c = > %3.3i \ n", numeric, numeric );
return;
}

#include < stddef.h >
void sub ( char *lwhole, char *lparts[3],
           char *expandable )
{
size__t length;
printf ( "SUB %3s %s%s%s [% – 14s] %3s %s%s%s \ n",
         gwhole, gparts[0], gparts[1], gparts[2],
         expandable,
         lwhole, lparts[0], lparts[1], lparts[2]);
length = strlen ( expandable );
strcpy ( expandable, "GHIJK"    );
strcat ( expandable, "LMNOP", 5 );
strcat ( expandable, "QRST", 4    );
length = strlen ( expandable );
printf ( "SUB %3s %s%s%s [%*s] %3s %s%s%s \ n",
         gwhole, gparts[0], gparts[1], gparts[2],
         length, expandable,
         lwhole, lparts[0], lparts[1], lparts[2] );
strcpy ( gwhole, "ABC" );
gparts [0]  =  "D";
```

```
gparts [1]  =  "E";
gparts [2]  =  "F";
strcpy ( lwhole, "UVW" );
lparts  [0]  =  "X";
lparts  [1]  =  "Y";
lparts  [2]  =  "Z";
printf ( "SUB %3s %s%s%s [%*s] %3s %s%s%s \ n",
        gwhole, gparts[0], gparts[1], gparts[2],
        length, expandable,
        lwhole, lparts[0], lparts[1], lparts[2] );
        return;
}
```

Both programs declare two global variables: gwhole, a character string; and gparts, an array of character strings. Local variants—lwhole and lparts—are also created. A function prototype statement for the single function called sub appears and indicates that the function will take three character arguments and will not return a value. The value of all variables are displayed in the main program after initialization.

When the function sub is invoked, it immediately shows the value of all variables. Then, the length of the string expandable is measured by the ANSI standard C function strlen. This is the actual length of the string—10 characters at this point, which is not the same as the Fortran len function, which returns the declared length of the string (14 in the Fortran example program). Note that the strlen function returns the length of its string argument in the variable length. Length is declared as a special type, size_t, which is defined in the standard C file stddef.h to be a whole number capable of holding a value up to as large as the type unsigned long (i.e., about 4.3 billion). The standard C function strcpy reinitializes the variable expandable to GHIJK, and the two subsequent calls to the standard C function strcat add on more letters to the end of the string expandable just like the Fortran character concatenation operator //. The value of all variables are displayed, including the full 14-character string expandable in uppercase. A new format is introduced to print the expandable string: the asterisk in the %*s format uses the value of the length variable as the width of the field in which to display the string. Both gwhole and lwhole are reinitialized to uppercase versions using the standard C function strcpy. An uppercase letter is moved into each element of gparts and lparts, and the value of all variables is displayed.

On return to the main program, the second letter in both the gwhole and lwhole strings and the second element in the gparts and lparts array of strings are replaced with lowercase letters. Finally, the values of all variables are displayed. The last section of the C example program demonstrates the C counterparts to the Fortran ichar and char intrinsic functions. The assignment of the value of the char variable single to the int variable numeric is comparable to the Fortran ichar function. Using a %c format in the last printf statement for the int variable numeric is comparable to the Fortran char function.

Close

Fortran	close (NUMBER) close (unit=NUMBER, status=KEYWORD) close (NUMBER,iostat=NUMBER,err=LABEL)
C Primary	fclose
C Secondary	exit, FILE, fopen, if/else, perror, remove, strcmp

The close statement terminates access to a file from a program. A file can be closed and retained with the status keyword KEEP or closed and erased with the status keyword DELETE. In either case, the Fortran programmer can provide error handling with the iostat variable and/or by branching to the labelled statement specified after the err keyword. Shown here is a Fortran program that opens a file, populates the file with five lines of text, and then closes and retains the file.

```
      program main
      integer      output, error, records
      character*6  status
      output = 8
      status = 'KEEP'
      open ( unit=output,     access='SEQUENTIAL',
    -        file='close.dat', form='FORMATTED',
    -        iostat=error,     status='NEW' )
      if ( error .ne. 0 ) then
          write ( 6,1 )
1         format ( 1H , 'Open of [close.dat] for output ',
    -                   'failed!' )
          go to 6
      end if
      records = 0
      do 3 i = 1, 5, 1
         records = records + 1
         write ( output,2 ) records
2        format ( 'Record number ', i1, ' written.' )
3     continue
      write ( 5,4 ) status
4     format ( 1H , a, ' the [close.dat] file.' )
      close ( unit=output, iostat=error, status=status )
      if ( error .ne. 0 ) then
          write ( 6,5 )
5         format ( 1H , 'Close of [close.dat] after ',
    -                   'output failed!' )
          go to 6
      end if
6     continue
      stop
      end
```

The program creates this file:

Record number 1 written.
Record number 2 written.

Record number 3 written.
Record number 4 written.
Record number 5 written.

It also generates this display:

KEEP the [close.dat] file.

A C program that accomplishes the same function is as follows:

```c
#include <stdio.h>
#include <stdlib.h>
#include <stddef.h>
main( )
{
FILE   *output;
int     error;
int     records;
int     i;
char   *status = "KEEP";
if (( output = fopen ( "close.dat", "w" )) = = NULL ) {
    perror ( "Open of [close.dat] for output"
            "failed!" );
    exit ( EXIT_FAILURE );
}
records = 0;
for ( i = 0; i < 5; i++ ) {
    records = ++records;
    fprintf ( output, "Record number %i written. \ n",
            records );
}
if ( ( strcmp ( status, "KEEP" ) ) = = 0 ) {
    printf ( "%s the [close.dat] file. \ n", status );
    if ( ( error = fclose ( output ) ) = = EOF )
        perror ("Close of [close.dat] after output "
            "failed! \ n");
        exit ( EXIT_FAILURE );
}
else
    printf ( "%s the [close.dat] file. \ n", status );
    if ( ( error = remove ( "close.dat" ) ) != 0 )
        perror ("Close of [close.dat] after output "
            "failed! \ n");
        exit ( EXIT_FAILURE );
    exit ( EXIT_SUCCESS);
}
```

Both programs open a file called close.dat. The Fortran program explicitly declares the file to be a new file and will error the file that already exists. The C program opens the file in w mode that will create the file if it does not exist or open and immediately truncate the file if it already exists.

The C counterpart to the Fortran unit number, iunit, is declared as a special type, FILE. This type is defined in the C standard file stdio.h and is described as a pointer to that stream of bytes that constitute a file. Note that the programmer does not set the unit number in C; the C standard function fopen establishes a value for iunit that is unique across all files open in a program. Should an error occur on opening the file, the C standard function perror will prefix the standard error message with the string given as the argument to perror. Such an error is considered fatal in this example program, and the C standard function exit is declared with the argument EXIT_FAILURE. EXIT_FAILURE and its counterpart EXIT_SUCCESS are established in the C standard file stdlib.h and are set to an implementation-defined value that will signal the host operating system that the program did or didn't detect a fatal error. Once the file is open, five records are written into it. The C standard function strcmp is used to compare the value of the string status to the keyword KEEP. If the file is to be retained, it is simply closed using the C standard function fclose. Otherwise, the file is deleted with the C standard function remove. In either case, the action to be taken—KEEP or not—is displayed, and both the fclose and remove functions are tested for an error return.

Common

Fortran	common / NAME / VARIABLES
C Primary	struct
C Secondary	strcpy

Most Fortran programs establish one or more common areas. It is the preferred means to provide a single definition of variables that makes the value of those variables accessible across multiple program units. As shared data storage, common can be constructed as simply or as complicated as the programmer desires. The following Fortran program declares two common areas, initializes the variables in them, and changes the value of some common variables in a subroutine:

```
      program main
      character*3  achar, bchar
      integer      aint,  bint
      real         areal, breal
      common / a / achar, aint, areal
      common / b / bchar, bint, breal
      achar = 'abc'
      aint  = 123
      areal = 4.5
      bchar = 'xyz'
      bint  = 678
      breal = 9.1
      write ( 6,1 ) achar, aint, areal, bchar, bint, breal
 1    format ( 1H , 'MAIN common /a/ ', a3,1x, i3,1x, f3.1,
     -                    ' common /b/', a3,1x, i3,1x, f3.1 )
      call sub
      write ( 6,1 ) achar, aint, areal, bchar, bint, breal
      stop
      end
      subroutine sub
      character*3  achar, bchar
      integer      aint,  bint
      real         areal, breal
      common / a / achar, aint, areal
      common / b / bchar, bint, breal
      write ( 6,1 ) achar, aint, areal, bchar, bint, breal
 1    format ( 1H , 'SUB common /a/ ', a3,1x, i3,1x, f3.1,
     -                    'common /b/ ', a3,1x, i3,1x, f3.1 )
      achar = 'ABC'
      aint  = 123
      areal = 5.4
      bchar = 'XYZ'
      bint  = 678
      breal = 1.9
      write ( 6,1 ) achar, aint, areal, bchar, bint, breal
      return
      end
```

The program generates this display:

```
MAIN   common /a/ abc    123 4.5  common /b/ xyz    678 9.1
SUB    common /a/ abc    123 4.5  common /b/ xyz    678 9.1
SUB    common /a/ ABC    123 5.4  common /b/ XYZ    678 1.9
MAIN   common /a/ ABC    123 5.4  common /b/ XYZ    678 1.9
```

A C program that performs the same function is as follows:

```c
char    *achar  = "abc";
int     aint    = 123;
float   areal   = 4.5F;
struct common {
                char    *bchar;
                int     bint;
                float   breal;
              };
struct common B = { "xyz", 678, 9.1F };
main( )
{
void sub ( );
printf ( "MAIN   common /a/ %s %i %3.1f "
                "common /b/ %s %i %3.1f \ n",
                achar,    aint,   areal,
                B.bchar,  B.bint, B.breal );
sub( );
printf ( "MAIN   common /a/ %s %i %3.1f "
                "common /b/ %s %i %3.1f \ n",
                achar,    aint,   areal,
                B.bchar,  B.bint, B.breal );
return;
}
void sub ( )
{
printf ( "SUB   common /a/  %s %i %3.1f "
                "common /b/ %s %i %3.1f \ n",
                achar,    aint,   areal,
                B.bchar,  B.bint, B.breal );
strcpy ( achar, "ABC" );
aint    = 123;
areal   = 5.4F;
strcpy ( B.bchar, "XYZ" );
B.bint  = 678;
B.breal = 1.9F;
printf ( "SUB   common /a/ %s %i %3.1f "
                "common /b/ %s %i %3.1f \ n",
                achar,    aint,   areal,
                B.bchar,  B.bint, B.breal );
return;
}
```

Both common areas hold a character string, an integer, and a floating point number. In Fortran, both common areas are declared in an identical fashion. In the C example program, variables in the first common area are declared individually before the main statement, which guarantees that their value will be accessible across all program units. Variables in the second common area are encapsulated in a data structure called common. The first struct statement defines a class of structure named common to contain a character string, an integer, and a floating point number. The second struct statement declares B to be a structure of class common. Because B is declared before the main statement, it is globally accessible. Values for each variable are displayed in the main program before and after the single function sub is invoked. Elements of what was in the first Fortran common area are referenced as if they were individual variables. Elements of what was in the second Fortran common area are referenced by the structure name, B, with a suffix that specifies which element is being referenced (i.e., B.bchar). In the single function, sub, values for each variable are displayed before and after any changes. The two character strings are re-initialized to uppercase letters with the C standard function strcpy, and the two floating point variables are changed by reversing the order of their individual digits.

If common is used in a Fortran program simply to allow the value of a set of variables to be globally accessible, then declaring variables before the main statement either individually or as part of a C structure works just fine. If common is manipulated in a Fortran program to align certain variables in complex ways, or if a particular common area is not declared identically throughout a program, then the best technique is to establish a large shared data area such as a single long character string and then manage it through specific user-designed code.

Complex

Fortran	complex VARIABLE
C Primary	struct
C Secondary	none

The complex data type in Fortran is an ordered pair of real numbers, the first of which is defined to be the "real" part and the second defined to be the "imaginary" part. The following Fortran program declares a complex variable and a complex array and performs a single complex addition.

```
      program main
      complex a, b( 3 ), c
      a     = ( 1.0, 2.0 )
      b(1)  = ( 3.0, 4.0 )
      b(2)  = ( 5.0, 6.0 )
      b(3)  = ( 7.0, 8.0 )
      c     = ( 0.0, 0.0 )
      write ( 6,1 ) a, b, c
    1 format ( 1H , 5 ( f3.1, ',', f3.1, 3x ) )
      c = a + b( 2 )
      write ( 6,1 ) a, b, c
      stop
      end
```

The program generates this display:

```
1.0,2.0  3.0,4.0  5.0,6.0  7.0,8.0   .0  .0
1.0,2.0  3.0,4.0  5.0,6.0  7.0,8.0  6.0,8.0
```

A C program that accomplishes the same function is as follows:

```
main( )
{
struct complex
            { double real;
              double imaginary;
            };
struct complex  a    = { 1.0, 2.0 };
struct complex  b[3] = { 3.0 ,4.0, 5.0, 6.0, 7.0, 8.0};
struct complex  c    = { 0.0, 0.0 };
printf ( "%3.1f,%3.1f   %3.1f,%3.1f   %3.1f,%3.1f" \
      "   %3.1f,%3.1f   %3.1f,%3.1f\n",
            a.real,    a.imaginary,
         b[0].real,b[0].imaginary,
         b[1].real,b[1].imaginary,
         b[2].real,b[2].imaginary,
            c.real,    c.imaginary );
c.real      = a.real      + b[1].real;
c.imaginary = a.imaginary + b[1].imaginary;
printf ( "%3.1f,%3.1f   %3.1f,%3.1f %3.1f,%3.1f" \
      "   %3.1f,%3.1f    %3.1f,%3.1f\n",
            a.real,    a.imaginary,
```

```
            b[0].real,b[0].imaginary,
            b[1].real,b[1].imaginary,
            b[2].real,b[2].imaginary,
               c.real,     c.imaginary );
    return;
}
```

C has no direct support for Fortran `complex` numbers. The C example program illustrates one way to build a data structure like a Fortran `complex` number and to explicitly program the rules for `complex` number addition. Reference to both elements of the single complex variable is accomplished by adding the .real or .imaginary suffix to the variable name. Reference to any element of the complex array is accomplished by extending the structure name to include the element number (i.e., b[1]) and adding the .real or .imaginary suffix.

Continue

Fortran   LABEL continue

C Primary   ;, continue

C Secondary   for

A major function of the Fortran continue is to mark the end of a do loop. It is also used as the target for a go to statement. Finally, a plain continue statement can appear wherever an executable statement can appear and in such circumstances has no effect. The following Fortran program demonstrates all three uses:

```
      program main
      integer i
      do 3 i = 1, 3, 1
        if ( i .eq. 2 ) go to 2
          write ( 6,1 ) i
1         format ( 1H , 'DO loop index I = ', i1 )
2       continue
3 continue
      continue
      stop
      end
```

The program generates this display:

```
DO loop index I = 1
DO loop index I = 3
```

A C program that accomplishes the same function is as follows:

```
    main( )
{
    int i;
    for ( i = 1; i < = 3; + +i ) {
      if ( i = = 2 )
          continue;
      else
          printf ( "DO loop index I = %i \ n", i );
    }
    ;
    return;
}
```

The body of both programs is a loop in which the index ranges from one to three. Within the loop, the value of the index is printed except when the index has the value two. In Fortran, checking to see if the loop index equals two eventually will cause a transfer of control to the first continue statement and the do loop terminates at the second continue statement. In C, when the loop index equals two, the continue statement following the conditional if statement forces control to the bottom of the for loop, which is the first right curly brace (i.e., }). Finally, in Fortran, a stand-alone continue statement directly above the stop statement has no effect. Similarly, in C, the semicolon directly above the return statement has no effect.

Data

Fortran	data VARIABLE / VALUE /
	data ARRAY / VAL1, VAL2, ..., VALN /
	data (A(I),I=1,3) / VAL1, VAL2, VAL3 /
C Primary	=, {}
C Secondary	none

The `data` statement is the means to initialize a variable or an array. It can be thought of as a mass assignment operator and is very often used to initialize large arrays to zero or blank. The following Fortran program demonstrates several variants of the data statement.

```
      program main
      character  carray(3),  csingle*3
      integer    iarray(3),  isingle, i
      real       rarray(3),  rsingle
      data carray                / 'a', 'b', 'c' /
      data csingle               / 3Hefg /
      data iarray                / 1, 2, 3 /
      data isingle               / 4 /
      data ( rarray(i), i = 1, 3 ) / 5.0, 6.0, 7.0 /
      data rsingle               / 8.0 /
      write ( 6,1 ) carray, csingle,
     -              iarray, isingle,
     -              rarray, rsingle
    1 format ( 1H , 3a1, 1x, a3, 4i2, 4f4.1 )
      stop
      end
```

The program generates this display:

abc efg 1 2 3 4 5.0 6.0 7.0 8.0

A C program that accomplishes the same function is as follows:

```
main( )
{
    char    carray[4] =  { 'a', 'b', 'c', '\0' };
    char   *csingle   =   "efg";
    int     array[3]  =  { 1, 2, 3 };
    int     isingle   =   4;
    float   rarray[3] =  {5.0F, 6.0F, 7.0F };
    float   rsingle   =   8.0F;
    printf ("%s %s %d %d %d %d %3.1f %3.1f %3.1f %3.1f\n",
    carray,                    csingle,
    iarray[0], iarray[1], iarray[2], isingle,
    rarray[0], rarray[1], rarray[2],rsingle );
    return;
}
```

Both programs initialize character, integer, and floating point arrays and variables. In the C example program, single variables are simply assigned a value, whereas values for each element of the arrays are listed within pairs of curly braces (see also Chapter 6). Note that unless otherwise initialized, all static numeric variables and arrays are initialized to zero, and all static pointers are initialized to null. This means that any variable, array, or pointer having static storage (i.e., is globally accessible across all program units) are pre-initialized. Conversely, all automatic variables, arrays, and pointers (i.e., local to a program unit) are not pre-initialized and must be explicitly given a value.

Dimension

Fortran   dimension A (SIZE1, SIZE2, ..., SIZE7)

C Primary   [ ]

C Secondary   for

Arrays are one of the few "data structures" available to the Fortran programmer. Single-dimensioned arrays (vectors) and two dimensional arrays (matrices or tables) are very common. Arrays of larger dimensions are supported but are used to a lesser extent. The following Fortran program establishes a character array and an integer array, initializes them, and displays their value.

```
      program main
      character*3   carray(3)
      integer       iarray(3,3), i, j
      data carray / 'abc', 'efg', 'ijk' /
      data iarray / 1, 4, 7,
     -              2, 5, 8,
     -              3, 6, 9 /
      do 2 i = 1, 3, 1
      write ( 6,1 ) carray(i), ( iarray(i,j), j = 1, 3 )
    1 format ( 1H , a3, 3i2 )
    2 continue
      stop
      end
```

The program generates this display:

```
abc  1 2 3
efg  4 5 6
ijk  7 8 9
```

A C program that accomplishes the same function is as follows:

```
        main( )
{
        char *carray[ ]    = { "abc", "efg", "ijk" };
        int    iarray[3] [3]  = { 1, 2, 3,
                                  4, 5, 6,
                                  7, 8, 9 };
        int    i, j;
        for  ( i = 0; i < 3; i + + ) {
            printf ( "%s", carray[i] );
            for ( j = 0; j < 3; j + + ) {
                printf ( " %d", iarray[i][j] );
            }
            printf ( " \ n" );
        }
        return;
}
```

Both programs establish and initialize a character array: `carray` in Fortran is an array of three-character variables, and carray in C is an array of character strings each initialized with three characters. Both programs establish and initialize a 3-by-3 integer valued table called iarray. There is a major difference between Fortran and C in terms of multidimensional array storage. Tables in Fortran are stored in column-major order. Tables in C are stored in row-major order. Fortran allows array indices to vary between a lower and upper limit that the programmer can set. For example, a ten element Fortran array can have an index that can range from -4 to 5 if it was declared as

```
dimension array(-4:5)
```

C does not directly support such a feature.

Furthermore, default array indices in Fortran range from 1 to the number of elements in the array, while in C such indices range from 0 to one less than the number of elements in the array. In other words, in C, declaring an array as vector[3] establishes the following three elements: vector[0], vector[1], and vector[2]; and declaring an array as table[5] [10] defines fifty elements ranging from table[0] [0] to table[4] [9]. Arrays can also be declared without setting a size (i.e., int row[ ]). The actual length would then be established when the array is initialized. The character array carry in the C example program is exactly such an array: it is declared without a specific length but inherits a length of three when the three elements within the initialization braces are processed. Also, elements of an array can be accessed through a pointer so that the last element of an array list[10] can be referenced as list[9] or *(list + 9), although the former is more common. Lastly, character arrays need to be declared with one more element than would normally be needed to accommodate the end-of-string marker called the null character (i.e., the "\0" character), which means that a string of a proper size to hold the word Fortran needs to be declared char language[8]. Chapter 6 presents additional details on the differences between arrays in Fortran and C.

Do

Fortran	do LABEL VARIABLE = N1, N2, N3
C Primary	for
C Secondary	continue, break, do/while, while

Along with the if statement, the Fortran do statement is likely to be one of the most frequently used statements in the language. It is regularly used to traverse an array applying a series of formula to each element in turn. The following Fortran program exercises the do loop construct with increasing, decreasing, and real indices.

```
      program main
      integer i
      integer total
      real    x
      write ( 6,1 )
  1   format (/ 1H , 'First loop ... increasing integer' /)
      do 3 i = 1, 5, 1
      if ( mod( i,2 ) .eq. 0 ) go to 3
      write ( 6,2 ) i
  2   format ( 1H , 'i index = ', i1 )
  3   continue
      write ( 6,4 )
  4   format (/ 1H , 'Second loop ... decreasing integer' /)
      do 6 i = 5, 1, -2
      write ( 6,5 ) i
  5   format ( 1H , 'i index = ', i1 )
  6   continue
      write ( 6,7 )
  7   format ( / 1H , 'Third loop ... increasing real' / )
      do 9 x = 1.0, 2.0, 0.5
      write ( 6,8 ) x
  8   format ( 1H , 'x index = ', f3.1 )
  9   continue
      write ( 6,10 )
 10   format (/ 1H , 'Fourth loop ... sum integers (0,10)'/)
      total = 0
      do 11 i = 0, 10, 1
      total = total + i
 11   continue
      write ( 6,12 ) total
 12   format ( 1H , 'total = ', i2 )
      stop
      end
```

The program generates this display:

```
First loop ... increasing integer
i index  = 1
i index  = 3
i index  = 5
```

Second loop ... decreasing integer

i index = 5

i index = 3

i index = 1

Third loop ... increasing real

x index = 1.0

x index = 1.5

x index = 2.0

Fourth loop ... sum integers (0,10)

total = 55

A C program that accomplishes the same function is as follows:

```
main( )
{

int    i;
float   total;
float   x;
printf ( " \nFirst loop ... increasing integer \n \n" );
for  ( i = 1; i < = 5; i + + ) {
     if ( (i%2) == 0 ) continue;
     printf ( "i index = %d \n", i );
}
printf ( " \nSecond loop ... decreasing integer \n \n" );
for  ( i = 5; i > = 1; i - = 2 ) {
     printf ( "i index = %d \n", i );
}
printf ( " \nThird loop ... increasing real \n \n" );
for  ( x = 1.0F; x < = 2.0F; x + = 0.5F ) {
     printf ( "x index = %3.1f \n", x );
}
printf (" \nFourth loop ... sum integers (0,10) \n \n" );
for  ( i = 0, total = 0; i < 11; i + + ) total + = i;
printf ( "for alternative ... total = %d \n", total );
total = 0;
i = 0;
do
{
   total + = i;
} while ( + + i < 11 );
printf ( "do/while alternative ... total = %d \n",
                                  total );

total = 0;
i = 0;
while ( i < 11 ) {
     total + = i;
     i + + ;
}
```

72

```
        printf ( "while alternative  ...    total = %d \ n",
                                    total );
        return;
        }
```

It displays these results of three alternatives for the fourth loop:

```
    for alternative  ...total = 55
    do/while alternative  ...  total = 55
    while alternative  ...total = 55
```

The Fortran and C version of the first three loops are very similar. The last Fortran loop is programmed in several ways in the C example program. The first is a "one-line do loop" in which the index and the variable to hold the sum are initialized in the first argument and the sum is performed after the last argument. The second is the C do/while construct in which the content of the loop is executed until the loop index reaches eleven. The third and final loop is a while loop in which the body of the loop executes while the loop index is less than eleven.

Note that during the execution of the full for loop, the do/while loop, or the full while loop, the loop can be escaped for a particular value of the index or some datum with a continue statement or stopped with the break statement. For example, in the following C program, each loop is fully executed twice once for an index value of one and the final time for an index value of three:

```
        main( )
{
        int i;
        for (   i = 1; i < = 5; i + + ) {
                if ( i == 2 ) continue;
                if ( i > 3 ) break;
                printf ( "for loop %i \ n", i );
        }
        i = 1;
        do
        {
                if ( i == 2 ) continue;
                if ( i > 3 ) break;
                printf ( "do/while loop %i \ n", i );
        } while ( + + i < = 5 );
        i = 0;
        while ( i < = 5) {
                i + + ;
                if ( i == 2 ) continue;
                if ( i > 3 ) break;
                printf ( "while loop %i \ n", i );
        }
        return;
}
```

The Fortran counterpart to this C example program would have a single do loop. Early in the loop, there would be test of the value of the index; and when it was equal to two, control would transfer to the terminal continue of the do loop. In the middle of the loop would be a second test of the value of the index; when it was greater than three, control would transfer to a `continue` statement beyond the end of the terminal `continue` of the do loop.

Double precision

Fortran	double precision VARIABLE
C Primary	double
C Secondary	none

Fortran offers two forms of floating point support: real and double precision. ANSI 77 Fortran states that double precision offers "greater" precision than real but does not specify any measure of precision for either. The following Fortran program creates a double precision variable, array, and function and exercises these three constructs.

```
      program main
      double precision variable
      double precision array(3)
      double precision farg
      double precision fvalue
      double precision fname
      variable = 1.0d0
      array(1) = 2.0d0
      array(2) = 3.0d0
      array(3) = 4.0d0
      farg     = array(3)
      fvalue   = fname ( farg )
      write ( 6,1 ) variable, array, fvalue
    1 format ( 1H , 5f4.1 )
      stop
      end
      double precision function fname ( farg )
      double precision farg
      fname = farg + 1.0d0
      return
      end
```

The program generates this display:

1.0 2.0 3.0 4.0 5.0

A C program that accomplishes the same function is as follows:

```
    main( )
{
    double variable   = 1.0;
    double array[3]   = { 2.0, 3.0, 4.0 };
    double farg       = array[2];
    double fvalue;
    double fname ( double farg );
    fvalue = fname ( farg );
    printf ( "%3.1f %3.1f %3.1f %3.1f %3.1f \n",
            variable,array[0],array[1],array[2],fvalue );
    return;
}
```

```
        double fname ( double farg )
{
        return farg + 1.0;
}
```

Both programs initialize the variable, each array element, and the function argument in very much the same way. Note that C requires the type of the function and its argument to be declared in the main program in a function prototype statement, while Fortran only requires the function—not the argument—to be declared. Fortran specifies that double precision constants should use the "d" exponent (i.e., 1.0d0) and that real constants have no designated exponent. Conversely, C specifies that double constants have no designated exponent but that float constants should use an "F" suffix (i.e., 2.0F).

Else

Fortran   else

C Primary   else

C Secondary   { }, = =, if

A major advantage of the ANSI 77 Fortran standard over the ANSI 66 standard was the specification of an "if...then...else" construct. Without it, even moderately complicated control structures became a jumble of go to statements. The following Fortran program includes three forms of if statements—single outcome, dual outcome, and compound:

```
      program main
      integer i, j
      i = 1
      j = 1
      if ( i .eq. 1 ) then
         write ( 6,1 )
1        format ( 1H , 'This line will print (#1).' )
      else
      endif
      if ( i .eq. 1 ) then
         write ( 6,2 )
2        format ( 1H , 'This line will print (#2).' )
      else
         write ( 6,3 )
3        format ( 1H , 'This line will NOT print (#2).' )
      endif
      if ( i .eq. 1 ) then
         write ( 6,4 )
4        format ( 1H , 'This line will print (#3a).' )
         if ( j .eq. 1 ) then
            write ( 6,5 )
5           format ( 1H , 'This line will print (#3b).' )
         else
            write ( 6,6 )
6           format ( 1H , 'This line will NOT print (#3b).')
         endif
      else
         write ( 6,7 )
7        format ( 1H , 'This line will NOT print (#3a).' )
      endif
      stop
      end
```

The program generates this display when the variables i and j are both equal to one:

    This line will print (#1).
    This line will print (#2).
    This line will print (#3a).
    This line will print (#3b).

Under other conditions, the program would produce the following results:

Var		Print (or not) specific messages					
i j	will 1	will 2	not 2	will 3a	not 3a	will 3b	not 3b
1 1	print	print		print		print	
1 2	print	print		print			print
2 1			print		print		
2 2			print		print		

A C program that accomplishes the same function is as follows:

```
main( )
{
    int i = 1;
    int j = 1;
    if ( i == 1 )
        printf ( "This line will print (#1). \n" );
    if ( i == 1 )
        printf ( "This line will print (#2). \n" );
    else
        printf ( "This line will NOT print (#2). \n" );
    if ( i == 1 ) {
        printf ( "This line will print (#3a). \n" );
        if ( j == 1 )
            printf ( "This line will print (#3b). \n" );
        else
            printf ( "This line will NOT print (#3b). \n" );
    }
    else
        printf ( "This line will NOT print (#3a). \n" );
    return;
}
```

The first if has a single outcome because no action is associated with its corresponding else statement. The second if has two outcomes depending on the value of the decision variable i, and both the Fortran and C code are very similar in design. The third if is compound: the outer part—3a—turns on the value of the decision variable i, and the inner part—3b—depends on the value of the decision variable j. In the Fortran example program, both parts of this compound if are written with indentation to illustrate the effect of the two if. . .then statements. In the C example program, both parts of the compound if are likewise written with indentation, but the curly braces surrounding the full contents of the outer if are critical. Only these braces associate the last else statement with the beginning of the outer if statement.

Else If

Fortran   else if (CONDITION) then

C Primary   else if

C Secondary none

Three-way decision paths are not an uncommon requirement of a program. They cover situations in which a program must take one action if a key decision variable has a particular value, another action if not, and a third action to cover error conditions. In Fortran, those three paths are provided by the if statement, the else if statement, and the else statement, respectively. The following Fortran program exercises these three statements:

```
      program main
      integer i
      do 4 i = 1, 3, 1
      if ( i .eq. 1 ) then
         write ( 6,1 ) i
   1     format ( 1H , 'SELECTED: i = ', i1 )
      else if ( i .eq. 2 ) then
            write ( 6,2 ) i
   2            format ( 1H , 'SELECTED: i = ', i1 )
      else
         write ( 6,3 ) i
   3     format ( 1H , 'PASSED (print only on last cycle): "
      -                'i = ', i1 )
      endif
   4 continue
      stop
      end
```

The program generates this display:

```
SELECTED: i = 1
SELECTED: i = 2
PASSED (print only on last cycle): i = 3
```

A C program that accomplishes the same function is as follows:

```
      main( )
   {
      int i;
      for ( i = 1; i < = 3; i + + ) {
      if ( i == 1 )
        printf ( "SELECTED: i = %d \ n", i );
      else if ( i == 2 )
            printf ( "SELECTED: i = %d \ n", i );
      else
         printf ( "PASSED (print only on last cycle): "
                "i = %d \ n", i );
```

```
        }
    return;
}
```

Both Fortran and C provide very similar code constructs to implement the else if statement. In fact, replacing the Fortran do loop with a C for loop and the Fortran write and format statements with C's printf completes nearly all of the translation between the two example programs.

End

Fortran	end
C Primary	exit
C Secondary	abort, EXIT__SUCCESS, return

Terminating every program unit in a Fortran program is the end statement. It is preceded by a stop in the main program and by a return in functions and subroutines. The following Fortran program demonstrates the end statement:

```
      program main
      integer i
      integer farg
      integer fvalue
      integer fname
      i = 1
      farg = i
      fvalue = fname ( farg )
      write ( 6,1 ) i, fvalue
1     format ( 1H , i1 , 1x, i1 )
      stop
      end
      integer function fname ( farg )
      integer farg
      fname = farg + 1
      return
      end
```

The program generates this display:

1 2

A C program that accomplishes the same function is as follows:

```
      #include <stdlib.h>
      main( )
{
      int i = 1;
      int farg = i;
      int fvalue;
      int fname ( int farg );
      fvalue = fname ( farg );
      printf ( "%d %d \ n", i, fvalue );
      exit ( EXIT__SUCCESS );
}
      int fname ( int farg )
{
      return farg + 1;
}
```

Note that in the C main program, the effect of the Fortran stop-and-end statement pair is accomplished with C's exit statement. In C, the exit statement not only terminates the program but flushes all file buffers, closes all files, and transmits the value of its argument to the host operating system. That argument typically takes on the value EXIT_SUCCESS or EXIT_FAILURE, which are defined in the C standard file stdlib.h. EXIT_SUCCESS communicates a successful program completion to the host operating system, and EXIT_FAILURE communicates program failure to the host operating system. An alternative to the exit statement is the C abort function call, which terminates a program immediately without necessarily flushing file buffers and/or closing files. Lastly, a C main program does not have to invoke the exit function: it can use the return statement, with or without an argument, in its place. In fact, the closing right curly brace, in the absence of a return statement, will perform the same as a return statement without an argument.

End If

Fortran　　　end if

C Primary　　}

C Secondary　==, { }, if

A major advantage of the ANSI 77 Fortran standard over the ANSI 66 standard was the specification of the "if...then" and the "if...then...else" constructs. The end if Fortran statement terminates the if part of both forms of "if...then" constructs. Without these kinds of constructs, even moderately complicated control structures became a jumble of go to statements. The following Fortran program includes three forms of if statements—single outcome, dual outcome, and compound:

```
      program main
      integer i, j
      i = 1
      j = 1
      if ( i .eq. 1 ) then
         write ( 6,1 )
1        format ( 1H , 'This line will print (#1).' )
      endif
      if ( i .eq. 1 ) then
         write ( 6,2 )
2        format ( 1H , 'This line will print (#2).' )
      else
         write ( 6,3 )
3        format ( 1H , 'This line will NOT print (#2).' )
      endif
      if ( i .eq. 1 ) then
         write ( 6,4 )
4        format ( 1H , 'This line will print (#3a).' )
         if ( j .eq. 1 ) then
            write ( 6,5 )
5           format ( 1H , 'This line will print (#3b).' )
         else
            write ( 6,6 )
6           format ( 1H , 'This line will NOT print (#3b).')
         endif
      else
         write ( 6,7 )
7        format ( 1H , 'This line will NOT print (#3a).' )
      endif
      stop
      end
```

The program generates this display when the variables i and j are both equal to 1:

This line will print (#1).
This line will print (#2).
This line will print (#3a).
This line will print (#3b).

Under other conditions, the program would produce the following results:

Var   Print (or not) specific messages

i j	will 1	will 2	not 2	will 3a	not 3a	will 3b	not 3b
1 1	print	print		print		print	
1 2	print	print		print			print
2 1			print		print		
2 2			print		print		

A C program that accomplishes the same function is as follows:

```
        main( )
    {
        int i = 1;
        int j = 1;
        if ( i == 1 )
            printf ( "This line will print (#1). \n" );
        if ( i == 1 )
            printf ( "This line will print (#2). \n" );
        else
            printf ( "This line will NOT print (#2). \n" );
        if ( i == 1 ) {
            printf ( "This line will print (#3a). \n" );
            if ( j == 1 )
                printf ( "This line will print (#3b). \n" );
            else
                printf ( "This line will NOT print (#3b). \n" );
        }
        else
            printf ( "This line will NOT print (#3a). \n" );
        return;
    }
```

The first if has a single outcome because no action is associated with its corresponding else statement. The second if has two outcomes depending on the value of the decision variable i, and both the Fortran and C code are very similar in design. The third if is compound: the outer part—3a—turns on the value of the decision variable i, and the inner part—3b—depends on the value of the decision variable j. In the Fortran example program, both parts of this compound if are written with indentation to illustrate the effect of the two if. . .then statements. In the C example program, both parts of the compound if are likewise written with indentation, but the curly braces surrounding the full contents of the outer if are critical. Only these braces associate the last else statement with the beginning of the outer if statement.

Endfile

Fortran	endfile (unit=VAR, iostat=VAR, err=LAB) endfile NUMBER
C Primary	none
C Secondary	break, exit, fclose, feof, fflush, fgetc, fopen, fprintf, fputc, fscanf, L__tmpnam, remove, rename, perror, tmpnam

When necessary, files can be truncated with the endfile Fortran statement. Although the endfile statement can be applied to any file type, it is much more common to use this statement with sequential rather than direct access files. The following Fortran program creates a file, populates it with five records, and then truncates the file after the third record:

```
      program main
      integer output, error, records, input
      character*24 line
      input = 7
      output = 8
      open ( unit=output,        access='SEQUENTIAL',
    -        file='endfile.dat', form='FORMATTED',
    -        iostat=error,       status='NEW' )
      if ( error .ne. 0 ) then
          write ( 6,1 )
1         format ( 1H , 'Open of [endfile.dat] for ',
    -                  'output failed!' )
          go to 20
      end if
      records = 0
      write ( 6,2 )
2     format ( / 1H , 'Write five records to output file.' )
      do 5 i = 1, 5, 1
          records = records + 1
          write ( output,3 ) records
3         format ( 'Record number ', i1, ' read.' )
          write ( 6,4 ) records
4         format ( 1H , 'Record number ', i1, ' written.' )
5     continue
      close ( unit=output, iostat=error, status='KEEP' )
      if ( error .ne. 0 ) then
          write ( 6,6 )
6         format ( 1H , 'Close of [endfile.dat] after ',
    -                  'output failed!' )
          go to 20
      end if
      open ( unit=input,         access='SEQUENTIAL',
    -        file='endfile.dat', form='FORMATTED',
    -        iostat=error,       status='OLD' )
      if ( error .ne. 0 ) then
          write ( 6,7 )
```

```
  7       format ( 1H , 'Open of [endfile.dat] for ',
      -                  'input failed!' )
          go to 20
      end if
      write ( 6,8 )
  8   format ( / 1H , 'Read three records (out of five).' )
      do 11 i = 1, 3, 1
          read ( input,9 ) line
  9       format ( a24 )
          write ( 6,10 ) line
 10       format ( 1H , a24 )
 11   continue
      write ( 6,12 )
 12   format ( / 1H , 'Truncate the file.' )
      endfile ( unit=input, iostat=error )
      if ( error .ne. 0 ) then
          write ( 6,13 )
 13       format ( 1H , 'Truncation of [endfile.dat] ',
      -                  'failed!' )
          go to 20
      end if
      write ( 6,14 )
 14   format ( / 1H , 'Rewind the file.' )
      rewind ( unit=input, iostat=error )
      if ( error .ne. 0 ) then
          write ( 6,15 )
 15       format ( 1H , 'Rewind of [endfile.dat] failed!' )
          go to 20
      end if
      write ( 6,16 )
 16   format (/ 1H ,'Read until EOF (i.e., three records).')
      do 17 i = 1, 32767, 1
          read ( input,9,end=18 ) line
          write ( 6,10 ) line
 17   continue
 18   continue
      close ( unit=input, iostat=error, status='KEEP' )
      if ( error .ne. 0 ) then
          write ( 6,19 )
 19       format ( 1H , 'Close of [endfile.dat] after ',
      -                  'input failed!' )
          go to 20
      end if
 20   continue
      stop
      end
```

The program creates this data file:

```
Record_number_1_read.
Record_number_2_read.
Record_number_3_read.
```

It also generates this display:

```
Write five records to output file.
Record number 1 written.
Record number 2 written.
Record number 3 written.
Record number 4 written.
Record number 5 written.

Read three records (out of five).
Record number 1 read.
Record number 2 read.
Record number 3 read.
```

Truncate the file.

Rewind the file.

```
Read until EOF (i.e., three records).
Record number 1 read.
Record number 2 read.
Record number 3 read.
```

A C program that accomplishes the same function is as follows:

```
#include <stdio.h>
#include <stdlib.h>
#include <stddef.h>
main( )
{
FILE  *output;
int    error;
int    records;
int    i;
FILE  *input;
char  *line;
int    bytes;
int    items;
long   position;
long   characters;
int    c;
```

```
FILE   *temp;
char    tempfile[L_tmpnam];
if (( output = fopen ("endfile.dat","w")) == NULL ) {
     perror ( "Open of [endfile.dat] for "
               "output failed!" );
     exit ( EXIT_FAILURE );
}
printf ( " \ nWrite five records to output file. \ n" );
records = 0;
for ( i = 0; i < 5; i++ ) {
     records = ++records;
     fprintf ( output, "Record_number_%i_read. \ n",
               records );
     printf ("Record number %d written. \ n",records);
}
if ( ( error = fclose ( output ) ) == EOF ) {
     perror ( "Close of [endfile.dat] after "
               "output failed! \ n" );
     exit ( EXIT_FAILURE );
}
if ((input = fopen ( "endfile.dat", "r" )) == NULL) {
     perror ( "Open of [endfile.dat] for "
               "input failed!" );

     exit ( EXIT_FAILURE );
}
printf ( " \ nRead three records (out of five). \ n" );
position = 0;
for ( i = 0; i < 3; i++ ) {
     items = fscanf ( input, "%s%n", line, &bytes );
     printf ( "%s \ n", line );
     position += bytes;
}
printf ( " \ nTruncate the file at byte number %ld. \ n",
          position );
if (( temp = fopen (tmpnam(tempfile),"w")) == NULL ) {
     perror ( "cannot open a temporary file! \ n" );
     exit ( EXIT_FAILURE );
}
printf ( "... temporary file [%s] is open ... \ n",
          tempfile );
rewind ( input );
for (characters=0;characters<=position;characters++) {
     c = fgetc ( input );
     fputc ( c, temp );
}
printf ( "... %ld bytes transferred ... \ n",
          position );
```

```c
    if ( ( error = fclose ( input ) ) == EOF ) {
        perror ( "Close of [endfile.dat] after "
                "copy failed! \ n" );
        exit ( EXIT_FAILURE );
    }
    if ( ( error = remove ( "endfile.dat" ) ) != 0 ) {
        perror ("Remove of [endfile.dat] failed]! \ n");
        exit ( EXIT_FAILURE );
    }
    printf ( "... original [endfile.dat] "
            "file removed ... \ n" );
    if ( ( error = fflush ( temp ) ) != 0 ) {
        perror ( "cannot flush "
                "temporary file buffer! \ n" );
        exit ( EXIT_FAILURE );
    }
    if ( ( error = fclose ( temp ) ) == EOF ) {
        perror ( "cannot close temporary file! \ n" );
        exit ( EXIT_FAILURE );
    }
    if (( error = rename (tempfile,"endfile.dat")) != 0 ) {
        perror ( "Rename of temp to "
                "[endfile.dat] failed! \ n" );
        exit ( EXIT_FAILURE );
    }
    printf ("... [%s] file renamed to "
            "[endfile.dat] ... \ n",tempfile );
    if (( input = fopen ("endfile.dat","r") ) == NULL ) {
        perror ( "Open of [endfile.dat] for "
                "input failed!" );
        exit ( EXIT_FAILURE );
    }
    printf (" \ nRead until EOF (i.e., three records). \ n");
    for ( i = 0; i < 32767; i++ ) {
        items = fscanf ( input, "%s%n", line, &bytes );
        if ( ( error = feof ( input ) ) == 0 )
            printf ( "%s \ n", line );
        else
            break;
    }
    if ( ( error = fclose ( input ) ) == EOF ) {
        perror ( "Close of [endfile.dat] after "
                "input failed! \ n" );
        exit ( EXIT_FAILURE );
    }
    exit ( EXIT_SUCCESS);
}
```

The C code generates this display:

```
Write five records to output file.
Record number 1 written.
Record number 2 written.
Record number 3 written.
Record number 4 written.
Record number 5 written.

Read three records (out of five).
Record__number__1__read.
Record__number__2__read.
Record__number__3__read.

Truncate the file at byte number 65.
. . . temporary file [NAME] is open . . .
. . . 65 bytes transferred . . .
. . . original [endfile.dat] file removed . . .
. . . [NAME] file renamed to [endfile.dat] . . .

Read until EOF (i.e., three records).
Record__number__1__read.
Record__number__2__read.
Record__number__3__read.
```

Both programs create the primary data file called endfile.dat in such a way that the file is certain to be empty (i.e., Fortran's open status=NEW and C's fopen keyword w). If the file could not be opened by the C example program, the perror function will prefix the standard C error message with the user-specified string given as perror's argument. Then the C example program would terminate and inform the host operating system (through the EXIT__FAILURE argument to the exit function) that the program did not complete normally.

Five records are written into the file. C uses the fprintf library function to write into a file; the syntax of this statement is almost identical to the printf library function that has been used throughout C example programs in this chapter.

The file is then closed, re-opened for input, and positioned to the end of the third record. In the C program example, the fscanf standard function is used to read the file. As it reads each line, it updates two variables: items records the number of variables read, and bytes records the number of bytes read. The variable position keeps a running total of the number of bytes that comprise that first three lines of the file.

The remaining part of the Fortran example program is straightforward: the file is truncated with the endfile statement, repositioned to the beginning of the file by the rewind statement, and the file is read and displayed to the end-of-file mark (i.e., three records).

C has no direct counterpart to the Fortran endfile statement. Where the Fortran program was able to deal only with the file being truncated, the C program has to shorten the file by copying a portion of the original file to a temporary file and renaming that temporary file. The temporary file is actually a permanent file created by the fopen C standard function. It is temporary in the sense that its name is generated by the C standard function tmpnam, which makes up a name from one to L_tmpnam characters in length. After being rewound, the input file is read, byte-by-byte, from the beginning to the end of the third record and then written to the temporary file. (Incidentally, processing a file byte-by-byte with the fgetc and fputc C standard functions occurs often in C programs.) The original file is then deleted with the remove C standard function. All data is then force-written to the temporary file with the fflush C standard function, the file is closed with fclose, given the name of the original input file by the rename function, and opened for input with the fopen function.

Reading the file line-by-line to the end is accomplished by the fscanf and feof C standard functions: fscanf reads one record at a time from a file, and feof checks to see if the file has reached the end-of-file mark. Finally, in both example programs, the file is closed.

Emulating the Fortran endfile statement in the manner of the C example program is not very convenient, but no specific C statement exists that will truncate a file at an arbitrary point.

Entry

Fortran	entry NAME (ARGUMENTS)
C Primary	none
C Secondary	&, void

Subroutines and functions can be written with multiple entrances and multiple exits. Over the years, it has become common in Fortran programming practice to design code so that each subprogram has one entrance and one exit. However, the entry statement can be used to provide several ways into a subprogram. The following Fortran program uses one additional entry point for a subroutine and a function:

```fortran
      program main
      integer i
      integer j
      integer entryb
      integer funb
      do 2 i = 1, 2, 1
          if ( i .eq. 1 ) then
              call entrya ( i, j )
          else
              j = entryb ( i )
          endif
          write ( 6,1 ) i, j
1         format ( 1H , 'Index i = ', i1, ' and j = ', i1 )
2     continue
      stop
      end
      subroutine suba ( i, j )
      integer i, j
      j = i + 1
      entry entrya ( i, j )
      j = i + 2
      return
      end
      integer function funb ( i )
      integer i, entryb
      funb = i + 3
      entry entryb ( i )
      entryb = i + 4
      return
      end
```

The program generates this display:

```
Index i = 1 and j = 3
Index i = 2 and j = 6
```

A C program that accomplishes the same function is as follows:

```c
      main()
      {
```

```c
        int i;
        int j;
        void    suba      ( int i, int *j );
        void    entrya    ( int i, int *j );
        int     funb      ( int i );
        int     entryb    ( int i );
        for (  i = 1; i < = 2; i++  ) {
            if ( i == 1 ) {
                entrya ( i, &j );
            }
            else
                j = entryb ( i );
            printf ( "Index i = %i and j = %i \ n", i, j );
        }
        return;
    }
        void suba ( int i, int *j )
    {
     *j = i + 1;
        entrya ( i, j );
        return;
    }
        void entrya ( int i, int *j )
    {
     *j = i + 2;
        return;
    }
        int funb ( int i )
    {
        return i + 3;
    }
        int entryb ( int i )
    {
        return i + 4;
    }
```

No C statement directly corresponds to the Fortran entry statement. In the C example program, two Fortran subprograms (each with an entry statement) had to be expanded into four separate functions. C's counterpart to the Fortran subroutine suba had to include an explicit call to a separate function, entrya, in order to emulate the first entry statement in the Fortran example program. Fortran's function funb had to be rewritten as a C function with the same name to handle the main role of the original function; and a second C function, entryb, had to be created to perform the role of the second entry statement in the Fortran example program. These two example programs come as close as possible to being complimentary, given the fact that C has no statement matching the Fortran entry statement.

Equivalence

Fortran   equivalence (VARIABLE, ARRAY(element))
                equivalence (A(elementI) ,B(elementJ))

C Primary   *, &, #define, union

C Secondary none

Programmers have gone to great lengths to reduce the physical memory requirements of their programs. In some circumstances, data storage has to be kept to a minimum in order to allow the program to run in a restricted execution environment. Even in large, virtual memory based execution environments, programs are made as small as possible to improve performance. A specific Fortran statement—equivalence—is often used to help reduce a program's physical memory requirements. The following Fortran program uses the equivalence statement:

```
      program main
      integer     i, iarray(3), jarray(2)
      real        r, x
      equivalence ( i,          iarray(1) )
      equivalence ( iarray(2), jarray(1) )
      equivalence ( r,          x          )
      i         = 1
      iarray(2) = 2
      jarray(2) = 3
      r         = 4.56
      write ( 6,1 ) i, iarray, jarray, r, x
  1   format ( 1H , i2
     -           / 1H , 3i2
     -           / 1H , 2x, 2i2
     -           / 1H , 1x, f5.2, 1x, f5.2 )
      stop
      end
```

The program generates this display:

```
   1
 1 2 3
   2 3
 4.56  4.56
```

A C program that accomplishes the same function is as follows:

```
#define i  iarray[0]
main ()
{
    int    iarray[3] = { 1, 2, 3 };
    int   *jarray;
    union { float r; float x; } real;
    printf ( " %i \ n", i );
    printf ( " %i %i %i \ n",
             iarray[0], iarray[1], iarray[2] );
```

```
        jarray = &iarray[1];
        printf ( " %i %i \ n",
                jarray[0], jarray[1] );
        real.r = 4.56F;
        printf ( " %5.2f %5.2f \ n", real.r, real.x );
        return;
}
```

Three different kinds of equivalence statements are demonstrated in the example programs. In the first equivalence statement, the simple variable i is paired with the first element of the iarray array showing how a variable can overlay an arbitrary element of an array. In the C example program, this is accomplished by the #define statement, which tells the compiler to replace the string i with iarray[0] wherever it occurs. Here, Fortran allows a variable to "overlay" the memory location of an array element, and C establishes a synonym linking two variable names.

In the second equivalence statement, two arrays are tied together: jarray overlaps the last two elements of iarray. In the C example program, iarray is defined as a three-element array, and jarray is only defined as a pointer. Just before jarray is printed, it is initialized to the memory address of the second element of iarray with the statement jarray = &iarray[1]. Recall that a pointer is a variable that holds the memory address of a data object. In this case, jarray is a pointer to the memory address of an integer data object because it was declared with the statement int *jarray. When the & operator is used in the jarray = &iarray[1] assignment statement, it calculates the memory address of the second element of the iarray array. Then that memory address is assigned to jarray. Once the first element of jarray is linked to the second element of iarray, all other elements of both arrays are likewise aligned so that iarray[2] is the same as jarray[1]. Here, Fortran and C truly establish two variables that occupy the same memory locations.

In the third and last equivalence statement, two floating point variables—r and x—are joined. In the C example program, this is accomplished with the union statement. A union is similar to C's struct data structure that has been used often in this chapter; but where elements of a struct are aligned sequentially in storage, elements of a union overlay each other in storage. By that definition, both real.r and real.x are different names for the same storage location.

Fortran and C both have mechanisms to permit two variables to occupy the identical storage location. Fortran programmers have used the equivalence statement in hundreds of ways to reduce programs' memory requirements. C's tools—#define statements, pointers, and unions—can go a long way to provide the Fortran programmer with tools to establish an equivalence among variables. Also, Chapter 6 introduces C's ability to dynamically allocate memory for arrays of arbitrary data type and dimensions.

External

Fortran	external SUBPROGRAM_NAME
C Primary	none
C Secondary	abs

ANSI standard Fortran defines the syntax of the language and the names and specifications for a series of support functions (i.e., abs, sqrt, sin, etc.). Many Fortran compilers extend the ANSI standard defined support functions with additional tools to facilitate certain ways of manipulating data. Therefore, a program that uses a particular name for a user-written subprogram on one computer system may find that that name conflicts with a system-supplied support function on another computer system. To guard against that possibility, the user-written subprogram can be named in a Fortran external function to explicitly inform the compiler that the user-written subprogram should be invoked rather than the system-supplied support function. The following Fortran program explicitly declares a user-written subroutine, a user-written function, and redefines a system-supplied support function:

```
      program main
      integer i
      integer j
      integer fun
      integer iabs
      external sub, fun, iabs
      do 2 i = 1, 3, 1
      if ( i .eq. 1 ) call sub ( i, j )
      if ( i .eq. 2 ) j = fun ( i )
      if ( i .eq. 3 ) j = iabs ( i )
      write ( 6,1 ) i, j
  1   format ( 1H , 'Index i = ', i1, ' j = ', i1 )
  2   continue
      stop
      end
      subroutine sub ( i, j )
      integer i, j
      j = i + 3
      return
      end
      integer function fun ( i )
      integer i
      fun = i + 4
      return
      end
      integer function iabs ( i )
      integer i
      iabs = i + 5
      return
      end
```

The program generates this display:

Index i = 1 j = 4
Index i = 2 j = 6
Index i = 3 j = 8

A C program that accomplishes the same function is as follows:

```
        main( )
    {
        int i;
        int j;
        void   sub ( int i, int *j );
        int    fun ( int i );
        int    abs ( int i );
        for ( i = 1; i < = 3; i++ ) {
            if ( i == 1 )
                sub ( i, &j );
            if ( i == 2 )
                j = fun ( i );
            if ( i == 3 )
                j = abs ( i );
        printf ( "Index i = %i j = %i \ n", i, j );
        }
        return;
    }
        void sub ( int i, int *j )
    {
      *j = i + 3;
        return;
    }
        int fun ( int i )
    {
        return i + 4;
    }
        int abs ( int i )
    {
        return i + 5;
    }
```

Declaring sub and fun as external subprograms in the Fortran example program guarantees that if the host computer system has functions by those names, the user-written versions will be executed. That same effect is achieved by declaring those two subprograms after all #include statements, if any, in the C example program.

Both programs redefine the respective Fortran- and C-supplied functions that compute the absolute value of an integer. The user-supplied Fortran iabs function and C abs function do not return the absolute value of their argument but return the value of their argument incremented by five.

Format

Fortran	format (SPECIFICATIONS)
C Primary	printf
C Secondary	#define, fprintf, fscanf, scanf, sizeof, sprintf, sscanf, va_end, va_list, va_start, vfprintf, vprintf, vsprintf

A large percentage of the source code in any given Fortran program is dedicated to preparing and formatting data for input and output. Fortran's primary mechanism to edit and lay out data for input and output is the format statement. The following Fortran program exercises a wide variety of format specifications:

```
      program main
      character*5      fc
      double precision fd
      real             fe
      real             ff
      real             fg
      integer          fi
      character*37     format14
      integer          ichar0
      fc = 'abcde'
      fd = 1.23d0
      fe = 4.56
      ff = 7.89
      fg = 10.11
      fi = 1213
      format14 = '( 1H , 7x, a__, 1x, f10.__, 1x, i10.__ )'
      write ( 6,1 ) fc, fc, fc, fc
1     format ( 1H ,' [', a, ']','  [', a4, ']',
     -            ' [', a5, ']',' [', a6, ']' )
      write ( 6,2 ) fd, fd, fd
2     format ( 1H , d10.3, 1x, sp, d10.3, s, 1x, 3p, d10.2 )
      write ( 6,3 ) fe, fe, fe, fe
3     format ( 1H , e10.3, 1x, sp, e10.3, s, 1x, 3p, e10.2,
     -         0p, 1x, e10.3e2 )
      write ( 6,4 ) ff, ff, ff
4     format ( 1H , f10.2, 1x, sp, f10.2, s, 1x, 3p, f10.2 )
      write ( 6,5 ) fg, fg, fg, fg
5     format ( 1H , 4x, g10.3, 1x, sp, g10.3, s, 1x, 3p,
     -         g10.2, 0p, 1x, g10.3e2 )
      write ( 6,6 )
6     format ( 1H ,'1st string', 1x, 10h2nd string )
      write ( 6,7 )
7     format ( 1H ,'single space' )
      write ( 6,8 )
8     format ( 1H ,'NO ADVANCE (overprint)' )
      write ( 6,9 )
9     format ( 1H+, 'no advance' )
      write ( 6,10 )
```

```
10  format ( 1H0, 'double space' )
    write ( 6,11 )
11  format ( 1H1, 'new page (top of form)' )
    write ( 6,12 ) fi, fi, fi
12  format ( 1H , i10, 1x, sp, i10, s, 1x, i10.5 )
    write ( 6,13 )
13  format (      tr16, 'twenty', tl14, 'ten' )
    ichar0 = ichar ( '0' )
    format14( 13:13 ) = char ( ichar0 + 3 )
    format14( 24:24 ) = char ( ichar0 + 4 )
    format14( 35:35 ) = char ( ichar0 + 5 )
    write ( 6,format14 ) fc, ff, fi
    stop
    end
```

The program generates this display:

```
  [abcde]        [abcd]      [abcde]      [ abcde]
.123D+01     +.123D+01     123.D-02
.456E+01     +.456E+01     456.E-02    .456E+01
    7.89         +7.89     7890.00
    10.1         +10.1        10.         10.1
1st string 2nd string
single space
no advance (overprint)

double space
new page (top of form)
    1213         +1213       01213
     ten        twenty
     abc        7.8900       01213
```

A C program that accomplishes the same function is as follows:

```
    main ( )
{
    char       cc[5] = "abcde";
    double     cd;
    float      ce;
    float      cf;
    float      cg;
    int        ci;
    int        i;
    int        j;
    int        k;
    cd  = 1.23;
    ce  = 4.56F;
    cf  = 7.89F;
    cg  = 10.11F;
    ci  = 1213;
```

```
            printf ( "    [%s]      [%.4s]  [%.5s]  [%6.5s]\n",
                  cc, cc, cc, cc );
            printf ( "%10.2e % + 10.2e %10.2e \n", cd, cd, cd );
            printf ( "%10.2E % + 10.2E %10.2E %10.2E \n",
                  ce, ce, ce, ce );
            printf ( "%10.2f % + 10.2f %10.2f \n",
                  cf, cf, 1000.0F*cf );
            printf ( "%10.2g % + 10.2g %10.2g %10.2g \n",
                  cg, cg, cg, cg );
            printf ( "1st string 2nd string \n" );
            printf ( "single space \n" );
            printf ( "NO ADVANCE (overprint) \r" );
            printf ( "no advance \n" );
            printf ( " \ndouble space \n" );
            printf ( " \fnew page (top of form) \n" );
            printf ( "%10i % + 10i %10.5i \n", ci, ci, ci );
            printf ( "                    twenty \r    ten \n" );
            i  = 3;
            j  = 4;
            k  = 5;
            printf ( "      %.*s %10.*f %10.*i \n",
                  i, cc, j, cf, k, ci );
            return;
      }
```

The program generates this display:

```
         [abcde]         [abcd]      [abcde]       [ abcde]
     1.23e+000     +1.23e+000   1.23e+000
     4.56E+000     +4.56E+000   4.56E+000   4.56E+000
          7.89         +7.89     7890.00
            10           +10          10            10
     1st string 2nd string
     single space
     no advance (overprint)

     double space
     new page (top of form)
          1213         +1213      01213
           ten        twenty
           abc        7.8900      01213
```

Each of the fourteen format statements in the Fortran example program demonstrate a new feature of editing data for output.

Character data are manipulated in the first format with the a format specification. Several variations appear that force the display of a five character string into fields of different widths. If the Fortran field width is less than the string length, it is left-justified and truncated; and if the width is more than the string length, it is right-justified and blank-padded on the left. C's %width.precision syntax does the same thing. If the width is not specified, then the field is left-justified and the string is truncated; if the precision and width is given, then the string is right-justified in a field as long as the specified width.

A very significant difference appears at the end of the first C printf specification: the \n string. Fortran generates a line feed at the end of every format specification. There is no way within the bounds of ANSI standard Fortran to stop that line feed from occurring. C, on the other hand, never automatically generates a line feed at the end of a printf specification: the programmer explicitly forces a line feed at a particular point in a printf specification by including the \n string. In effect, Fortran controls the final line feed in a format specification, while in C the programmer controls any and all line feeds in a printf specification. This extra control is very valuable because the programmer can build a complicated print or display line from many small printf statements, each being extended until finally the line feed character is specified.

Floating point data can be processed by several Fortran and C output specifications. The second Fortran format employs the double precision format specifier, sign control, and scaling. C's matches Fortran's d format with an e specifier and can explicitly ask for the sign to be printed with the addition symbol flag, as in the %+10.2e specifier. Sign printing control in C is on a per field basis, rather than like Fortran's sign printing, where sp or ss would start a certain way of handling signs for one or more variables processed in a format statement and s would have to be used to revert to default processing.

The third Fortran format uses the e format specifier, which is most closely aligned with C's E printf specifier. The fourth Fortran format exercises the Fortran f format, which is identical in most respects to the f specifier of C. Floating point data can also be processed by Fortran's and C's g output specifier. Both languages have very detailed rules about the form of g specifier output, given the magnitude of the floating point number and the width and precision of the g field. Some of these rules are covered in Chapter 8.

Literal data are easily printed by both languages. Fortran allows the literal to be enclosed in single quotation marks or following a character count Hollerith prefix, as in the sixth format. C has one method: it encloses literals in double quotation marks.

Line spacing is shown in formats 7, 8, 9, and 10 in the Fortran example program. Single spacing is the default for a Fortran format statement. It's normal, however, to see a single line feed—the \n string—terminating the format specification in a C printf statement. Overprinting is controlled in Fortran with the 1H+ specifier, as seen in the ninth format statement. C allows this practice through the use of the \r specifier: \n implies a carriage return and a line feed, where \r implies just the carriage return. A 1H0 Fortran format specifier forces double spacing, which can be accomplished in C by beginning the format specification with the \n string to force a blank line. Page control is implemented in Fortran with the 1H1 specifier and in C with the \f string.

Integer data are printed in Fortran with the i specifier and in C with either the i or d specifier. The twelfth format demonstrates simple output, signed output, and zero-padded output of an integer. An identical effect is achieved in C with the simple %10i specifier, the addition symbol flag in the %+10i specifier, and explicitly setting a field width and precision value in the %10.5i specifier. There is no difference between the i and d in a C printf statement: two specifiers that accomplish the same thing exist in C due to historical reasons in the development of the language.

Moving data right and left within a single line of output is the function of Fortran's tr and tl specifiers. C has no direct counterpart. The effect of the thirteenth format in the Fortran example program is achieved in the C example program through spacing of the literal string and using the \r specifier (i.e., \r generates a carriage return without a line feed).

Run-time formatting is a method within Fortran to adapt the appearance of a display to conditions encountered during execution. The final format statement in the Fortran example program sets the width of each field when the program is running. The final printf statement in the C example program uses an asterisk to hold the place of the field width and an additional variable (i.e., the i, j, and k variables) to define the field width while the program is running.

C provides an additional feature that inserts a variable name automatically into a display. In Fortran, a variable name can be linked to its value only through the efforts of the programmer, such as in the following:

```
      program main
      integer    i
      integer    j
      character a
      i = 1
      j = 2
      a = 'i'
      write ( 6,1 ) a, i
  1   format ( 1H , a, ' = ', i1 )
      a = 'j'
      write ( 6,1 ) a, j
      stop
      end
```

The program generates this display:

```
    i = 1
    j = 2
```

A C program that accomplishes the same function is as follows:

```
      #define format1(x) printf ( #x" = %d\n", x )
      main( )
    {
```

```
    int   i = 1;
    int   j = 2;
    format1 ( i );
    format1 ( j );
    return;
}
```

The number sign, #, is used in the definition of the format1 statement
function to copy the variable name into the display. Consequently, when
the function is exercised with the variable i or j as its single argument, the
function shows both the variable name and its value.

Fortran `format` statements are used for buffer, file, and terminal
input and output. C uses the same set of specifications described in this
section in nine different functions depending on the nature of the input
and output. These nine functions are as follows:

C function	Input/Output		Buffer, file or terminal		Arguments
fprintf		output	file		fixed
fscanf	input		file		fixed
printf		output		terminal	fixed
scanf	input			terminal	fixed
sprintf		output	buffer		fixed
sscanf	input		buffer		fixed
vfprintf		output	file		variable
vprintf		output		terminal	variable
vsprintf		output	buffer		variable

The first six functions must have an equal number of format specifiers
and variables. In essence, if a printf statement specifies three integers (i.e.,
"%i %i %i \ n"), then the specification must be followed by exactly three
integer variables as arguments to the printf function.

The last three functions can accept a variable number of arguments.
This is particularly important when all or parts of an array are to be displayed. Fortran permits the array name to be given on a `write` statement,
and the associated `format` specification will be executed as many times
as necessary to satisfy the `write` request. The following Fortran example
program demonstrates this:

```
program main
integer    iarray(4)
integer    itable(3,3)
real       farray(4)
real       ftable(3,3)
character  carray(4)
character  ctable(3,3)
data       iarray / 10,20,30,40 /
```

```
      data   itable / 1,2,3,4,5,6,7,8,9 /
      data   farray / 10.0,20.0,30.0,40.0 /
      data   ftable / 1.0,2.0,3.0,4.0,5.0,
     -                6.0,7.0,8.0,9.0 /
      data   carray / 'A','B','C','D' /
      data   ctable / 'a','b','c','d','e',
     -                'f','g','h','i' /
      write ( 6,1 )
   1  format ( 1H )
      write ( 6,2 ) iarray
   2  format ( 1H , 5i5 )
      write ( 6,1 )
      write ( 6,2 ) itable
      write ( 6,1 )
      write ( 6,3 ) farray
   3  format ( 1H , 5f5.1 )
      write ( 6,1 )
      write ( 6,3 ) ftable
      write ( 6,1 )
      write ( 6,4 ) carray
   4  format ( 1H , 5a5 )
      write ( 6,1 )
      write ( 6,4 ) ctable
      stop
      end
```

The program generates this display:

```
   10    20    30    40
    1     2     3     4     5
    6     7     8     9

 10.0  20.0  30.0  40.0

  1.0   2.0   3.0   4.0   5.0
  6.0   7.0   8.0   9.0

   A     B     C     D

   a     b     c     d     e
   f     g     h     i
```

A C program that accomplishes the same function is as follows:

```
       main( )
   {
       #define format1 printf  ( " \ n" )
       void    format2    ( int elements, ... );
       void    format3    ( int elements, ... );
       void    format4    ( int elements, ... );
       int     iarray[4]     = { 10,20,30,40 };
       int     itable[3][3]  = { 1,2,3,4,5,6,7,8,9 };
```

```
float    farray[4]    = { 10.0F,20.0F,30.0F,40.0F };
float    ftable[3][3] = { 1.0F, 2.0F, 3.0F, 4.0F,
                          5.0F, 6.0F, 7.0F, 8.0F,
                          9.0F };
char     carray[4]    = { 'A','B','C','D' };
char     ctable[3][3] = { 'a','b','c','d','e',
                          'f','g','h','i' };
format1;
format2 ( sizeof(iarray)/sizeof(int),    iarray );
format1;
format2 ( sizeof(itable)/sizeof(int),    itable );
format1;
format3 ( sizeof(farray)/sizeof(float),  farray );
format1;
format3 ( sizeof(ftable)/sizeof(float),  ftable );
format1;
format4 ( sizeof(carray)/sizeof(char), carray );
format1;
format4 ( sizeof(ctable)/sizeof(char), ctable );
return;
}

#include < stdarg.h >
void format2 ( int elements, ... )
{

int    i;
va_list begin_array;
va_list arg_pointer;
va_start ( arg_pointer, elements );
begin_array = va_arg ( arg_pointer, va_list );
arg_pointer = begin_array;
for ( i = 1; i < = elements; i + + ) {
    printf ( "%4.0d ", va_arg ( arg_pointer, int ) );
    if ( i%5 == 0 )
        printf ( " \ n" );
}
printf ( " \ n" );
va_end ( arg_pointer );
return;
}

#include < stdarg.h >
void format3 ( int elements, ... )
{

int    i;
va_list begin_array;
va_list arg_pointer;
va_start ( arg_pointer, elements );
begin_array = va_arg ( arg_pointer, va_list );
arg_pointer = begin_array;
for ( i = 1; i < = elements; i + + ) {
    printf ( "%4.1f ", va_arg ( arg_pointer,float ) );
```

```
            if ( i%5 == 0 )
            printf ( " \ n" );
        }
        printf ( " \ n" );
        va__end ( arg__pointer );
        return;

    }
        #include <stdarg.h>
        void format4 ( int elements, ... )
    {
        int    i;
        va__list begin__array;
        va__list arg__pointer;
        va__start ( arg__pointer, elements );
        begin__array = va__arg ( arg__pointer, va__list );
        arg__pointer = begin__array;
        for ( i = 1; i <= elements; i++ ) {
            printf ( "%4c ", va__arg ( arg__pointer, char ) );
            if ( i%5 == 0 )
                printf ( " \ n" );
        }
        printf ( " \ n" );
        va__end ( arg__pointer );
        return;

    }
```

The first C function, format1, is created through the #define statement and generates a blank line. The remaining three C functions all take two arguments: the number of elements in the one-dimensional array or two-dimensional table, and the name of the array or table. The length is calculated through the use of the sizeof function, which returns the length of its argument in bytes. So, in format2, the value of sizeof(iarray)—the number of bytes needed to store the array—divided by the value of sizeof(int)—the number of bytes needed to store just one element of the array—is 4, which is the length of the array.

Each of the remaining three C functions have the same structure. The C standard macro va__start is invoked with the arguments arg__pointer and elements: arg__pointer is a variable with a special data type, va__list, set to point to the beginning of the array or table to be printed, while elements is a count of the number of entries in the array or table. A pointer to the next entry is returned by the first invocation of the va__arg macro: this entry would be the pointer to the first element of the array or table. The for loop is then executed as many times as there are elements in the array or table. Each time, the next element of the array or table is extracted by the va__arg macro and displayed using the printf function in an appropriate format (i.e., d, f, or c depending on int, float, or char data types). A new line is started after each five elements of the array or table are displayed. This matches the five element formats in the Fortran example program (i.e., 5i5,

5f5.1, and 5a5, respectively). A new line is then generated to finish the last line of printed data. Finally, the C standard library function va_end is invoked to facilitate a normal return to the calling program (in this case, the main program).

This section has concentrated on Fortran output to a terminal. Later in this chapter, sections on the read and write Fortran statement will provide examples of input and output to other devices. Furthermore, Chapter 8 will review Fortran format specifiers and C edit specifiers in some additional detail.

Function

Fortran   TYPE function NAME (ARGUMENTS)
C Primary   #define, return
C Secondary   none

Fortran supports two kinds of subprograms: subroutines and functions. Functions, in turn, can be either statement functions or subprogram functions. Both kinds are demonstrated in the following Fortran program:

```
program main
integer i
integer j
integer k
integer l
real      x
real      y
real      fun
state ( jarg, karg ) = i + jarg + karg
i = 1
j = 2
k = 3
l = state ( j, k )
write ( 6,1 ) l, i, j, k
1    format ( 1H , i1, ' = ', 2 ( i1, ' + ' ), i1 )
x = 123.0
y = fun ( x )
write ( 6,2 ) y, x
2    format ( 1H , f5.1, ' = ', f5.1, ' + 333.0' )
stop
end
real function fun ( xarg )
real xarg
fun = xarg + 333.0
return
end
```

The program generates this display:

```
6 = 1 + 2 + 3
456.0 = 123.0 + 333.0
```

A C program that accomplishes the same function is as follows:

```
main ( )
{
    int    i = 1;
    int    j = 2;
    int    k = 3;
    int    l;
    float  x = 123.0F;
    float  y;
    float  fun ( float x );
```

```
#define state(jarg,karg) i + jarg + karg
l = state ( j, k );
printf ( "%i = %i + %i + %i \ n", l, i, j, k );
y = fun ( x );
printf ( "%5.1f = %5.1f + 333.0 \ n", y, x );
return;
}

float fun ( float xarg )
{
    return xarg + 333.0;
}
```

Functions in both languages are very similar in construction. Fortran allows the type of function to be explicitly declared. Before the ANSI C standard was developed, the data type of a C function was declared only when it was not an integer, and arguments were declared in separate lines. For example, a pre-ANSI version of the C example program fun function would be

```
float fun ( xarg )
float xarg;
{
    return xarg + 333.0;
}
```

and the function would have been declared in the main program as

```
float fun ( );
```

Advantages of the current ANSI specification is that the number and type of a function's arguments are known by the compiler, and the first line of the function is a good reminder to the programmer which arguments are input and which are output. A Fortran statement function is available for the duration of the subprogram in which it is defined. In other words, the example program's statement function, state, can be invoked in the main program because it was defined there but not in the function fun. Both Fortran and C allow a local variable to be involved in the specification of the statement function even though that variable does not appear in the argument list. In this case, the local variable i is part of the statement function but is a third variable in addition to the two arguments jarg and karg.

Go To (assigned)

Fortran   go to VARIABLE (LAB, LAB, ..., LAB)

C Primary   switch

C Secondary   ;, #define, case, default

Fortran provides several decision constructs to control the flow of execution in a program. One of these is the assigned go to statement as shown in the following program:

```
      program main
      integer i
      assign 3 to i
      go to i ( 1, 3 )
1     write ( 6,2 )
2     format ( 1H ,'This line will NOT be displayed.' )
      go to 5
3     write ( 6,4 )
4     format ( 1H ,'This line will be displayed.' )
5     continue
      stop
      end
```

The program generates this display:

This line will be displayed.

A C program that accomplishes the same function is as follows:

```
        main( )
    {
        #define i 3
        switch ( i ) {
            case 1: goto lab__1;
            case 3: goto lab__3;
            default: goto lab__5;
        }
lab__1: printf ( "This line will NOT be displayed. \ n" );
        goto lab__5;
lab__3: printf ( "This line will be displayed. \ n" );
lab__5: ;
        return;
    }
```

In the Fortran example program, the variable i in the assigned go to statement was initialized, as required, by an assign statement, and one of the statement labels in the assigned go to statement list was the same as the value of the variable i. In the C example program, the switch construct provided two explicit actions when the variable i was either one or three and provided a "catch all" action—the default specification—when the variable was any other value. You will rarely see the goto statement in a C program: although the statement clearly is part of the language, it appears to be infrequently used in real-world coding practice.

Go To (computed)

Fortran go to (LAB, LAB, ..., LAB), VARIABLE

C Primary goto, switch

C Secondary ;, case, default

Fortran provides several decision constructs to control the flow of execution in a program. One of these is the computed go to statement, as shown in the following program:

```
      program main
      integer i
      i = 2
      go to ( 1, 3 ), i
      go to 5
1     write ( 6,2 )
2     format ( 1H , 'This line will NOT be displayed.' )
      go to 5
3     write ( 6,4 )
4     format ( 1H , 'This line will be displayed.' )
5     continue
      stop
      end
```

The program generates this display:

This line will be displayed.

A C program that accomplishes the same function is as follows:

```
        main( )
    {
        int i = 2;
        switch ( i ) {
                case 1: goto lab__1;
                case 2: goto lab__3;
                default: goto lab__5;
        }
lab__1:   printf ( "This line will NOT be displayed. \ n" );
          goto lab__5;
lab__3:   printf ( "This line will be displayed. \ n" );
lab__5:   ;
          return;
    }
```

In the Fortran example program, the variable i in the computed go to statement was initialized in a simple assignment statement and is used to index into the list of statement labels. In the C example program, the switch construct provided two explicit actions when the variable i was either one or three and provided a "catch all" action—the default specification—when the variable was any other value. The default condition in C's switch construct specifies what action to take if the decision variable i is not one or two: Fortran does not have such a safety net. In Fortran, if the decision variable i is less than one or more than the number of labels given as arguments in the computed go to statement, then execution continues onto the next statement. This particular Fortran example program guards against this problem by having an unconditional go to statement follow the computed go to statement, thus diverting processing around the two write statements. You will rarely see the goto statement in a C program: although the statement clearly is part of the language, it appears to be infrequently used in real-world coding practice.

Go To (unconditional)

Fortran   go to LABEL

C Primary   goto

C Secondary ;

Fortran provides several decision constructs to control the flow of execution in a program. One of these is the unconditional go to statement, as shown in the following program:

```
      program main
      integer i
      i = 1
      if ( i .ne. 0 ) go to 2
      write ( 6,1 )
    1 format ( 1H , 'This line will NOT be displayed.' )
      go to 4
    2 continue
      write ( 6,3 )
    3 format ( 1H , 'This line will be displayed.' )
    4 continue
      stop
      end
```

The program generates this display:

This line will be displayed.

A C program that accomplishes the same function is as follows:

```
        main ( )
    {
        int i = 1;
        if ( i != 0 ) goto lab_2;
        printf ( "This line will NOT be displayed. \n" );
        goto lab_4;
lab_2:  ;
        printf ( "This line will be displayed. \n" );
lab_4:  ;
        return;
    }
```

In the Fortran example program, the variable i in the unconditional go to statement was initialized in a simple assignment statement. Being initialized to a non-zero value, it forces the second of the write statements to be executed. The C example program is constructed in a manner almost identical to the Fortran example program. You will rarely see the goto statement in a C program: although the statement clearly is part of the language, it appears to be infrequently used in real-world coding practice.

If (arithmetic)

Fortran	`if ( EXPRESSION ) LABEL, LABEL, LABEL`
C Primary	if
C Secondary	;, for, goto

Based on the sign of an expression or variable, Fortran can redirect the flow of execution using the arithmetic if statement. The arithmetic if statement branches to three different labels depending on whether the decision expression or variable is negative, zero, or positive. The following Fortran program uses the arithmetic if statement:

```
      program main
      integer i
      do 7 i = -1, 1, 1
      if ( i ) 1, 3, 5
1     continue
      write ( 6,2 ) i
2     format ( 1H , 'Index i is negative ...', i2 )
      go to 7
3     continue
      write ( 6,4 ) i
4     format ( 1H , 'Index i is zero .......', i2 )
      go to 7
5     continue
      write ( 6,6 ) i
6     format ( 1H , 'Index i is positive ...', i2 )
7     continue
      stop
      end
```

The program generates this display:

```
Index i is negative. . .  - 1
Index i is zero . . . . . .   0
Index i is positive . . .   1
```

A C program that accomplishes the same function is as follows:

```
          main ( )
     {
          int i;
          for ( i = - 1; i < = 1; i + + ) {
             if ( i < = 0 ) {
               if ( i == 0 )
                 goto label__3;
               else
                 goto label__1;
             }
           else
             goto label__5;
label__1:         printf ( "Index i is negative . . . %2i \ n", i );
          goto label__7;
```

114

```
label__3:       printf ( "Index i is zero . . . . . . . %2i \ n", i );
                goto label__7;
label__5:       printf ( "Index i is positive . . . %2i \ n", i );
label__7:       ;
          }
       return;
     }
```

Both programs use a loop—do in Fortran and for in C—to generate values of negative one, zero, and one for the decision variable i in sequence. Fortran's arithmetic if statement is a compact way to redirect the flow of execution depending on the value of the decision variable. C's compound if statement is more involved but accomplishes the same result.

You will rarely see the goto statement in a C program: although the statement clearly is part of the language, it appears to be infrequently used in real-world coding practice. The C example program was written with several goto statements to parallel the Fortran example program. It could have been written without goto statement as the following:

```
     main ( )
   {
   int i;
   for ( i = - 1; i < = 1; i + + ) {
     if ( i < = 0 ) {
       if ( i == 0 )
         printf ("Index i is zero . . . . . . . %2i \ n",i);
       else
         printf ("Index i is negative . . . %2i \ n",i);
       }
     else
         printf ( "Index i is positive . . . %2i \ n", i );
     }
   return;
   }
```

Each of the goto statements within the for loop was replaced by the corresponding printf statement.

If (logical)

Fortran
```
if ( EXPRESSION ) go to LABEL
if ( EXPRESSION ) EXPRESSION
```

C Primary   goto, if

C Secondary   == , != , ;

Conditional execution is a major programming design tool in any computer programming language. Both versions of Fortran's logical if statement are regular features of most Fortran programs. The first form of Fortran's logical if statement forces a change in the flow of execution, as in the following example:

```
      program main
      integer i
      i = 1
      if ( i .ne. 1 ) go to 2
      write ( 6,1 ) i
1     format (1H ,'This line will display . . .', i1,' = 1')
2     continue
      write ( 6,3 )
3     format ( 1H , 'End of Logical IF Fortran ',
     -               'statement example.' )
      stop
      end
```

The program generates this display:

This line will display . . . 1 = 1
End of Logical IF Fortran statement example.

A C program that accomplishes the same function is as follows:

```
      main ( )
      {
      int i = 1;
      if ( i != 1 ) goto lab2;
      printf ( "This line will display . . . %i = 1 \n", i );
lab2: ;
      printf ( "End of Logical IF Fortran "
            "statement example. \ n" );
      return;
      }
```

Both the Fortran and C example programs follow an identical template: a decision variable is initialized, checked against a constant with an if statement, a line of text is conditionally displayed, and a final end-of-program line of text is printed. The second form of the Fortran logical if statement conditionally executes any valid Fortran executable statement except do, any other if construction, or end, as in the following example:

```
      program main
      integer i
```

116

```
      integer j
      integer k
      i = 0
      j = 2
      k = 1
      if ( i .eq. 0 ) i = j + k
      write ( 6,1 ) i, j, k
1     format ( 1H , i1, ' = ', i1, ' + ', i1 )
      stop
      end
```

The program generates this display:

```
3 = 2 + 1
```

A C program that accomplishes the same function is as follows:

```
      main ( )
{
    int i   = 0;
    int j   = 2;
    int k   = 1;
    if ( i == 0 )
        i = j + k;
    printf ( "%i = %i + %i\n", i, j, k );
    return;
}
```

Aside from syntactical differences between individual Fortran and C statements, both example programs have the same structure and control flow. Although the indentation of the C if statement is not required, it is very common to see C source code written in a style where indentation is used as a visual reminder of the scope of a control structure.

If ... Then

Fortran	if (expression) then
C Primary	}
C Secondary	== , else

Three-way decision paths are not an uncommon requirement of a program. They cover situations in which a program must take one action if a key decision variable has a particular value, another action if not, and a third action to cover error conditions. In Fortran, those three paths are provided by the if statement, the else if statement, and the else statement, respectively. The following Fortran program exercises these three statements:

```
       program main
       integer i, j
       i = 1
       j = 1
       if ( i .eq. 1 ) then
          write ( 6,1 )
1         format ( 1H , 'This line will print (#1).' )
       else
       endif
       if ( i .eq. 1 ) then
          write ( 6,2 )
2         format ( 1H , 'This line will print (#2).' )
       else
          write ( 6,3 )
3         format ( 1H , 'This line will NOT print (#2).' )
       endif
       if ( i .eq. 1 ) then
          write ( 6,4 )
4         format ( 1H , 'This line will print (#3a).' )
          if ( j .eq. 1 ) then
             write ( 6,5 )
5            format ( 1H , 'This line will print (#3b).' )
          else
             write ( 6,6 )
6            format (1H , 'This line will NOT print (#3b).')
          endif
       else
          write ( 6,7 )
7         format ( 1H , 'This line will NOT print (#3a).' )
       endif
       stop
       end
```

The program generates the following display when the variables i and j are both equal to 1:

This line will print (#1).
This line will print (#2).

This line will print (#3a).
This line will print (#3b).

Under other conditions, the program would produce the following results:

Var   Print (or not) specific messages

i j	will 1	will 2	not 2	will 3a	not 3a	will 3b	not 3b
1 1	print	print		print		print	
1 2	print	print		print			print
2 1			print		print		
2 2			print		print		

A C program that accomplishes the same function is as follows:

```
    main( )
{
    int i = 1;
    int j = 1;
    if ( i == 1 )
        printf ( "This line will print (#1). \n" );
    if ( i == 1 )
        printf ( "This line will print (#2). \n" );
    else
        printf ( "This line will NOT print (#2). \n" );
    if ( i == 1 ) {
        printf ( "This line will print (#3a). \n" );
        if ( j == 1 )
            printf ( "This line will print (#3b). \n" );
        else
            printf ( "This line will NOT print (#3b). \n" );
    }
    else
        printf ( "This line will NOT print (#3a). \n" );
    return;
}
```

The first if has a single outcome because no action is associated with its corresponding else statement. The second if has two outcomes depending on the value of the decision variable i, and both the Fortran and C code are very similar in design. The third if is compound: the outer part—3a—turns on the value of decision variable i, and the inner part—3b—depends on the value of decision variable j. In the Fortran example program, both parts of this compound if are indented to illustrate the effect of the two if ... then statements. In the C example program, both parts of the compound if are likewise indented, but the curly braces surrounding the full contents of the outer if are critical. Only these braces associate the last else statement with the beginning of the outer if statement.

Implicit

Fortran	implicit TYPE (L, L, ..., L)
	implicit TYPE (LETTER-LETTER)
C Primary	none
C Secondary	—, (double), for, sqrt

Fortran variables, arrays, external functions, and statement functions inherit a data type depending on the first letter of their symbolic name: i through n are integers, and the remainder are real. This blanket default typing can be overridden by the Fortran implicit statement. The following Fortran program reverses the sense of the default typing:

```
      program main
      implicit real     ( i - n )
      implicit integer ( a - h, o - z )
      i = 6561.0
      do 2 x = 3, 1, -1
      i = sqrt ( i )
      write ( 6,1 ) x, i
1     format ( 1H , '3 ** ', i1, ' = ', f4.1 )
2     continue
      stop
      end
```

The program generates this display:

```
3 ** 3 = 81.0
3 ** 2 =  9.0
3 ** 1 =  3.0
```

A C program that accomplishes the same function is as follows:

```
      #include <math.h>
      main ()
{
      float i = 6561.0F;
      int   x;
      for ( x = 3; x > = 1; x − − ) {
         i = sqrt ( (double) i );
         printf ( "3 ** %i = %4.1f\n", x, i );
      }
      return;
}
```

Both programs display powers of three by successively taking the square root of the next higher power: Fortran uses the real sqrt function, and C uses the double sqrt function and promotes the float variable i to a double through the cast operator (i.e., (double)). Data typing of variables is automatic in the Fortran example program and is manual in the C example program. Fortran's implicit statement has no counterpart in C, which is understandable because C has no default mapping between a variable name and its data type. Explicit data typing of each variable in C is required.

Inquire

Fortran   inquire (UNIT=NUMBER, OPTIONS)
                 inquire (FILE=NAME, OPTIONS)

C Primary   fopen

C Secondary & &, = =, ! =, fclose, FILE, freopen, NULL

ANSI 77 Fortran has a major advantage over ANSI 66 Fortran in the area of file handling. The first Fortran standard had no real file handling capabilities, whereas the second Fortran standard has a rich collection of language statements to open, close, and query files. The Fortran inquire statement can be invoked for three purposes: to report file attributes, to determine if a file exists, and to ascertain if a file is open to a program. For each purpose, the Fortran inquire statement can query by Fortran file unit number or by file name. Each of these features of the inquire statement are exercised in the following Fortran program:

```
      character  caccess*10
      character  cblank*4
      character  cdirect*7
      logical    lexist
      character  cfile*11
      character  cform*11
      character  cformatted*7
      integer    iiostat
      character  cname*11
      integer    inextrec
      integer    inumber
      logical    lopened
      integer    irecl
      character  csequential*7
      character  cunformatted*7
      integer    iunit=7
      open ( unit=7, file='inquire.dat' )
      write ( 6,1 )
1     format ( / 1H , 'The file [inquire.dat] open ',
     -                'on unit 7.' )
      write ( 6,2 )
2     format ( / 1H , 'INQUIRE by unit number ...' )
      iunit = 7
      cfile = ''
      inquire ( access=caccess,      blank=cblank,
     -          direct=cdirect,      exist=lexist,
     -          form=cform,          formatted=cformatted,
     -          iostat=iiostat,      name=cname,
     -          nextrec=inextrec,    number=inumber,
     -          number=inumber,      opened=lopened,
     -          recl=irecl,          sequential=csequential,
     -          unformatted=cunformatted, unit=iunit )
      write ( 6,3 )  caccess,  cblank,      cdirect, lexist,
     -               cform,       cformatted, iiostat, cname,
```

```fortran
     -              inextrec, inumber,     lopened, irecl,
     -              csequential,           cunformatted
3    format ( /  1H , 'access . . . . . . . . ',a10, 2x,
     -           1H , 'blank . . . . . . . . . ',a4
     -        /  1H , 'direct . . . . . . . . ',a7, 5x,
     -           1H , 'exist . . . . . . . . ',l1
     -        /  1H , 'form . . . . . . . . . . ',a11, 1x,
     -           1H , 'formatted . . . . . ',a7
     -        /  1H , 'iostat . . . . . . . . ',i5.5, 7x,
     -           1H , 'name . . . . . . . . . ',a11, 1x,
     -        /  1H , 'nextrec . . . . . . . ',i5.5, 7x,
     -           1H , 'number . . . . . . . . ',i5.5
     -        /  1H , 'opened . . . . . . . . ',l1, 11x,
     -           1H , 'recl . . . . . . . . . . ',i5.5
     -        /  1H , 'sequential . . . . ',a7, 5x,
     -           1H , 'unformatted . . . ',a7)
     write ( 6,4 )
4    format ( /  1H , 'INQUIRE by file name . . .' )
     iunit = 0
     cfile = cname
     inquire ( access=caccess,     blank=cblank,
     -          direct=cdirect,    exist=lexist,
     -          form=cform,        formatted=cformatted,
     -          iostat=iiostat,    name=cname,
     -          nextrec=inextrec,  number=inumber,
     -          number=inumber,    opened=lopened,
     -          recl=irecl,        sequential=csequential,
     -          unformatted=cunformatted, file=cname )
     write ( 6,3 )  caccess,   cblank,      cdirect, lexist,
     -              cform,      cformatted, iiostat, cname,
     -              inextrec, inumber,     lopened, irecl,
     -              csequential,           cunformatted
     inquire ( file=cname, exist=lexist )
     if ( lexist ) then
         write ( 6,5 ) cname
5        format ( / 1H , 'The file [', a11, '] exists.' )
     else
         write ( 6,6 ) cname
6        format ( / 1H , 'The file [', a11, '] does',
     -                   'NOT exist.' )
     endif
     inquire ( file=cname, opened=lopened )
     if ( lopened ) then
         write ( 6,7 ) cname
7        format ( / 1H , 'The file [', a11, '] is open.' )
     else
         write ( 6,8 ) cname
8        format ( / 1H , 'The file [', a11, '] is ',
     -                   'NOT open.' )
     endif
```

```
        close ( unit=inumber )
        stop
        end
```

The program generates this display:

The file [inquire.dat] open on unit 7.

INQUIRE by unit number . . .

access	SEQUENTIAL	blank	NULL
direct	NO	exist	T
form	FORMATTED	formatted	YES
iostat	00000	name	inquire.dat
nextrec	00001	number	00007
opened	T	recl	00000
sequential	YES	unformatted	NO

INQUIRE by file name . . .

access	SEQUENTIAL	blank	NULL
direct	NO	exist	T
form	FORMATTED	formatted	YES
iostat	00000	name	inquire.dat
nextrec	00001	number	00007
opened	T	recl	00000
sequential	YES	unformatted	NO

The file [inquire.dat] exists.

The file [inquire.dat] is open.

A C program that accomplishes the same function is as follows:

```
        #include < stdio.h >
        main ( )
{
    char *cfile = "inquire.dat";
    FILE *iunitr;
    FILE *iunitrb;
    if ( (( iunitr = fopen (cfile, "r" )) = = NULL ) & &
        (( iunitrb = fopen (cfile, "rb")) = = NULL )       ) {
        printf ( " \ nThe file [%s] does NOT exist. \ n",
            cfile );
    }
    else
        printf ( " \ nThe file [%s] exists. \ n",
            cfile );
        if ( iunitr != NULL )
            fclose ( iunitr );
        if ( iunitrb != NULL )
            fclose ( iunitrb );
```

```
        return;
    }
```

The program generates this display:

The file [inquire.dat] exists.

C's ability to query file attributes and report on the connection of a file to a program is very restricted compared to the capabilities of Fortran's `inquire` statement.

C cannot report file attributes because C does not distinguish between files created in text or binary mode (i.e., Fortran's formatted and unformatted mode, respectively). C allows the programmer to develop whatever file structure is desired and process the resulting file accordingly.

C cannot report if a file is already open to a program because the association between a file and the pointer to the file (i.e., iunitr and iunitrb in the C example program) is managed by C whereas, in Fortran, the association between a file and a unit number (i.e., `iunit` in the Fortran example program) is explicitly managed by the programmer. As such, even though the C standard function fclose will fail if no file is associated with the pointer given as the argument to the fclose function, this pointer will not come into existence unless a file has been successfully opened. Furthermore, the C standard function freopen, which will reopen a file on a different file pointer, will execute without error if the file in question was not already open.

C's standard library fopen function can be used to determine if a file already exists. In the C example program, a file is opened both for input in both text mode and binary mode (i.e., the "r" and "rb" arguments, respectively). If the file could be opened in either or both modes, then the file is declared to exist. Attempting to open a file in both text and binary modes is done purely as a precaution. ANSI C distinguishes between a text file and a binary file in terms of the way a file can be manipulated by certain functions but does not require the host operating system to distinguish between the file modes. Because some host operating systems do and others do not distinguish between text and binary file modes, the C example-program was written to accommodate either condition.

Integer

Fortran	`integer VARIABLE` `integer FUNCTION_NAME`
C Primary	int
C Secondary	long, short, signed, unsigned

Variables, arrays, and functions that deal in whole numbers are defined in Fortran with the `integer` statement. Each use of the `integer` statement is demonstrated in the following program:

```
      program main
      integer variable
      integer array(3)
      integer farg
      integer fvalue
      integer fname
      variable = 1
      array(1) = 2
      array(2) = 3
      array(3) = 4
      farg     = array(3)
      fvalue   = fname ( farg )
      write ( 6,1 ) variable, array, fvalue
1     format ( 1H , 5i4 )
      stop
      end
      integer function fname ( farg )
      integer farg
      fname = farg + 1
      return
      end
```

The program generates this display:

```
1   2   3   4   5
```

A C program that accomplishes the same function is as follows:

```
      main( )
      {
      int variable = 1;
      int array[3]  = { 2, 3, 4 };
      int farg       = array[2];
      int fvalue;
      int fname ( int farg );
      fvalue = fname ( farg );
      printf ( "%3d %3d %3d %3d %3d \ n",
               variable, array[0], array[1], array[2],
               fvalue );
      return;
      }
      int fname ( int farg )
```

```
{
    return farg + 1;
}
```

ANSI 77 Fortran defines a single form of the `integer` data type. Many Fortran compilers support two additional forms: `integer*2` for whole numbers in the range of ± 32,767, and `integer*4` for whole numbers in the range of ± 2,147,484,647. Both additional forms are supported in ANSI C. Fortran's `integer*2` is C's int, short, and signed int data types, and `integer*4` is represented by long and signed long, among others (see FIG. 3-2).

C also provides two new series of types: one for whole numbers in the range of 0 to 65,535 with four different names (i.e., unsigned, unsigned int, unsigned short, and unsigned short int), and the other for whole numbers in the range of 0 to 4,294,967,295 with two different names (i.e., unsigned long and unsigned long int). Chapter 3 presents some additional details about Fortran and C whole number data types.

Intrinsic

Fortran	`intrinsic FUNCTION_NAME`
C Primary	(*function)( )
C Secondary	cos, (double), (float), sin

Fortran has about seventy intrinsic functions (see FIG. 2-4). In order to use any of these intrinsic functions as an argument to a subprogram, the function must be specified in an `intrinsic` statement. All Fortran intrinsic functions can be used as subprogram arguments except those that perform type conversion (such as `int` and `ichar`), those that compare lexical relationships (such as `lge` and `lgt`), and those that choose the largest or smallest in a series (i.e., the `max` and `min` family of intrinsic functions). The following Fortran program alternates between the `sin` and `cos` functions as the argument to a function:

```
      program main
      real trig, radians, sine, cosine
      intrinsic sin, cos
      radians  = 0.5
      sine     = sin ( radians )
      cosine   = cos ( radians )
      write ( 6,1 ) sine, radians, cosine, radians
1     format ( 1H , f7.6, ' = sin (',f2.1,') ',
     -                f7.6, ' = cos (',f2.1,')' )
      sine    = trig ( sin, radians )
      cosine = trig ( cos, radians )
      write ( 6,1 ) sine, radians, cosine, radians
      stop
      end
      real function trig ( result, radians )
      real result, radians
      trig = result ( radians )
      return
      end
```

The program generates this display:

```
.479426 = sin (.5) .877583 = cos (.5)
.479426 = sin (.5) .877583 = cos (.5)
```

A C program that accomplishes the same function is as follows:

```
        #include <math.h>
        main ( )
{
        float radians = 0.5F, sine, cosine;
        float trig ( double (*function)( ), float radians );
        sine    = (float) sin ( radians );
        cosine = (float) cos ( radians );
        printf ( "%7.6f = sin (%2.1f) "
                 "%7.6f = cos (%2.1f) \ n",
                 sine,radians,cosine,radians );
```

```
sine    = trig ( sin, radians );
cosine = trig ( cos, radians );
printf ( "%7.6f = sin (%2.1f) "
         "%7.6f = cos (%2.1f) \ n",
         sine,radians,cosine,radians );
return;
}
float trig ( double (*function)( ), float radians )
{
float result;
result = (float) (*function)(radians);
return result;
}
```

Fortran's intrinsic statement allows a generic function such as trig to be written that can exercise a variety of Fortran intrinsic functions. C's counterpart is to pass a pointer to a function as an argument. In effect, this argument is the base address of the executable code for the function being passed as an argument. In the trig function prototype, the syntax (*function)( ) represents a dummy pointer that is replaced by the actual function name—sin or cos—when the trig function is invoked. Note that the choice of the name "function" in the trig function prototype is arbitrary: any valid C symbolic name would be equally effective. This C example program also demonstrates explicit type conversion through the use of the cast operator such as (float) and (double).

Logical

Fortran	`logical VARIABLE`
	`logical FUNCTION__NAME`
C Primary	typedef
C Secondary	!, #define

Variables, arrays, and functions that deal with logical values are defined in Fortran with the `logical` statement. Each use of the `logical` statement is demonstrated in the following program:

```
      program main
      logical variable
      logical array( 3 )
      logical farg
      logical fvalue
      logical fname
      variable = .TRUE.
      array(1) = .FALSE.
      array(2) = .TRUE.
      array(3) = .FALSE.
      farg     = array(3)
      fvalue   = fname ( farg )
      write ( 6,1 ) variable, array, fvalue
  1   format ( 1H , 514 )
      stop
      end
      logical function fname ( farg )
      logical farg
      if ( .not. farg ) fname = .TRUE.
      return
      end
```

The program generates this display:

```
T  F  T  F  T
```

A C program that performs the same function is as follows:

```
typedef int logical;
#define   FALSE   0
#define   TRUE    1
main ( )
{
logical variable;
logical array[3];
logical farg;
logical fvalue;
logical fname ( logical farg );
char    tf[2] = { 'F', 'T' };
variable = TRUE;
array[0] = FALSE;
```

```
        array[1]  = TRUE;
        array[2]  = FALSE;
        farg      = array[2];
        fvalue    = fname ( farg );
        printf ( "  %c  %c  %c  %c  %c \ n", tf[variable],
                tf[array[0]], tf[array[1]], tf[array[2]],
                tf[fvalue] );
        return;
}
        logical fname ( logical farg )
{
        logical a = FALSE;
        if ( !farg ) a = TRUE;
        return a;
}
```

Both programs produce the same display, but the Fortran example program builds on an existing feature of that language while the C example program creates a new data type and defines two global constants to produce the same result.

C's typedef statement establishes a synonym for a particular storage class. This particularly useful feature of the C language allows a complicated data storage declaration to be written out just once in a typedef statement for repeated use in the remainder of the program. In the example program, the typedef statement establishes the word logical as another name for the int data type. Subsequently, two #define statements establish numeric equivalents for TRUE and FALSE constants, and a tf array is created to hold the letters T and F to fulfill the need to display logical variables and arrays. With this new type definition and given the choice for the TRUE and FALSE constants, Fortran's two standard logical variable expressions

```
if ( .not. logical_variable )
if (       logical_variable )
```

have analogs in C:

```
if (         !logical_variable )
if (         logical_variable )
```

This particular use of the C typedef and #define statements gives the appearance that C directly supports Fortran's logical data type. C does not directly support Fortran's logical data type, but it does have language features that can be used to emulate such a data type.

Open

Fortran	open (UNIT=N, FILE=NAME)
C Primary	fopen
C Secondary	BUFSIZ, exit, fclose, FILE, fread, fscanf, fwrite, __IOFBF, remove, rewind, setvbuf, sizeof, strcpy, strtol, tmpfile, tmpnam

ANSI 77 Fortran has a major advantage over ANSI 66 Fortran in the area of file handling. The first Fortran standard had no real file handling capabilities, whereas the second Fortran standard has a rich collection of language statements to open, close, and query files. The Fortran open statement can be invoked to open new or old files, formatted or unformatted files, sequential or direct access files, and temporary files. The following Fortran program opens a sequential access file, a direct access file, and a temporary file:

```
      character caccess*10
      character cblank*4
      character cfile*8
      character cform*11
      integer   iiostat
      integer   irecl
      character cstatus*7
      integer   iunit
      write ( 6,1 )
1     format ( / 1H, 'Open a default sequential access ',
     -              'method (SAM) file...'                )
      caccess = 'SEQUENTIAL'
      cblank  = 'NULL'
      cfile   = 'open.sam'
      cform   = 'FORMATTED'
      cstatus = 'UNKNOWN'
      irecl   = 0
      iunit   = 7
      open ( access=caccess, blank=cblank,  file=cfile,
     -       form=cform,     iostat=iiostat,
     -       status=cstatus, unit=iunit     )
      write ( 6,2 ) caccess, cblank, cfile,  cform,
     -              iiostat, irecl,  cstatus, iunit
2     format ( / 1H, 'access.........', a10, 2x,
     -           1H, 'blank..........', a4
     -         / 1H, 'file...........', a8,  4x,
     -           1H, 'form...........', a11
     -         / 1H, 'iostat.........', i5.5, 7x,
     -           1H, 'recl...........', i5.5
     -         / 1H, 'status.........', a7,  5x,
     -           1H, 'unit...........', i5.5     )
      close ( unit=iunit )
      write ( 6,3 )
3     format ( / 1H, 'Open a default direct access ',
     -              'method (DAM) file...'           )
```

```
      caccess  = 'DIRECT'
      cblank   = 'n/a '
      cfile    = 'open.dam'
      cform    = 'UNFORMATTED'
      cstatus  = 'UNKNOWN'
      irecl    = 512
      iunit    = 7
      open (  access=caccess,                    file=cfile,
    -         form=cform,      iostat=iiostat, recl=irecl,
    -         status=cstatus, unit=iunit                    )
      write ( 6,2 ) caccess,   cblank,   cfile,    cform,
    -               iiostat,   irecl,    cstatus,  iunit
      close ( unit=iunit )
      write ( 6,4 )
    4 format ( / 1H , 'Open a default temporary file...' )
      caccess  = 'SEQUENTIAL'
      cblank   = 'NULL'
      cfile    = 'n/a       '
      cform    = 'FORMATTED'
      cstatus  = 'SCRATCH'
      irecl    = 0
      iunit    = 7
      open (  access=caccess, blank=cblank,
    -         form=cform,      iostat=iiostat,
    -         status=cstatus, unit=iunit           )
      write ( 6,2 ) caccess,   cblank,   cfile,    cform,
    -               iiostat,   irecl,    cstatus,  iunit
      stop
      end
```

The program generates this display:

Open a default sequential access method (SAM) file . . .

access	SEQUENTIAL	blank	NULL
file	open.sam	form	FORMATTED
iostat	00000	recl	00000
status	UNKNOWN	unit	00007

Open a default direct access method (DAM) file . . .

access	DIRECT	blank	n/a
file	open.dam	form	UNFORMATTED
iostat	00000	recl	00512
status	UNKNOWN	unit	00007

Open a default temporary file . . .

access	SEQUENTIAL	blank	NULL
file	n/a	form	FORMATTED
iostat	00000	recl	00000
status	SCRATCH	unit	00007

A C program that accomplishes the same function is as follows:

```c
#include <stdio.h>
#include <stdlib.h>
main ( )
{
char   fopen_key[4];
FILE *iunit;
printf ( " \nOpen a default sequential access "
     · "method (SAM) file . . . \n" );
strcpy ( fopen_key, "r" );
iunit = fopen ( "open.sam", fopen_key );
if ( iunit == NULL )
    strcpy ( fopen_key, "wa" );
else
     fclose ( iunit );
if (( iunit = fopen ("open.sam",fopen_key)) == NULL ) {
    printf ( ". . . FAILED to open for "
           "%s access. \n", fopen_key );
    exit ( EXIT_FAILURE );
}
else
     printf ( ". . . successfully opened for "
            "%s access. \n", fopen_key );
printf ( " \nOpen a default direct access "
      "method (DAM) file . . . \n" );
strcpy ( fopen_key, "rb + " );
iunit = fopen ( "open.dam", fopen_key );
if ( iunit == NULL )
    strcpy ( fopen_key, "wb + " );
else
     fclose ( iunit );
if (( iunit = fopen ("open.dam",fopen_key)) == NULL ) {
    printf ( ". . . FAILED to open for "
           "%s access. \n", fopen_key );
    exit ( EXIT_FAILURE );
}
else
    printf ( ". . . successfully opened for "
           "%s access. \n", fopen_key );
printf ( " \nOpen a default temporary file . . . \n" );
if ( ( iunit = tmpfile ( ) ) == NULL ) {
    printf ( ". . . FAILED to open temporary"
           "file. \n");
    exit ( EXIT_FAILURE );
}
else
    printf ( ". . . successfully opened"
           "temporary file. \n");
printf ( " \n" );
```

```
        exit ( EXIT_SUCCESS );
    }
```

The program generates this display when executed the first time:

Open a default sequential access method (SAM) file . . .
. . . successfully opened for wa access.

Open a default direct access method (DAM) file . . .
. . . successfully opened for wb+ access.

Open a default temporary file . . .
. . . successfully opened temporary file.

It generates this display when executed a second time:

Open a default sequential access method (SAM) file . . .
. . . successfully opened for r access.

Open a default direct access method (DAM) file . . .
. . . successfully opened for rb+ access.

Open a default temporary file . . .
. . . successfully opened temporary file.

Both programs use a number of features of their respective file opening statements. However, there are differences between Fortran and C in terms of file types, file input and output, and file attribute control.

Sequential access files in Fortran correspond to text files in C and unformatted direct access files correspond to binary files. C's fopen function specifies the mode in which a file is accessed. These modes correspond to the Fortran open statement's sequential and direct access and formatted and unformatted keywords, such as the following:

Access	Form	C Input	C Output
sequential	formatted	r	wa
sequential	unformatted	rb	wab
direct	formatted	r+	w+
direct	unformatted	rb+	wb+

Each input mode—the r access flag—requires that the file already exists. Each output mode—the w access flag—will truncate an existing file or create the file if it does not already exist. For output, both sequential access mode file types are opened with the letter a (for "append"in the C access flag; this forces all writes to occur at the end of the file. Both direct access file types are opened with the plus symbol (for "update") in the C access flag that allows the file to be written to or read from any location in the file. In the C example program, Fortran formatted sequential access and unformatted direct access files are opened as text and binary files, respectively. Executing the program twice demonstrates the difference between opening a file for output versus input.

Regarding the temporary file, Fortran can open any type of file temporarily. This is accomplished in the Fortran open statement by removing the file argument so that the file has no name and using the keyword SCRATCH in the status argument. C's tmpfile function also creates a temporary file, but tmpfile opens a binary file for output (i.e., a wb+ access flag). If a different file type is required as a temporary file, it must be opened explicitly with C's fopen, closed with fclose, and deleted with remove. With such a temporary file, a temporary file name can be generated by using tmpnam( ) as the first argument in the fopen call, and this file name will be unique among all files open to the program.

Fortran allows more precise control over opening an existing file or creating a file. If a program requires a file to exist before being opened, the Fortran open statement can set the status flag to OLD whether or not the file is to be read or written. C's fopen function can force the same requirement if the file is opened with any access flag that includes the letter r. If a program requires that a file be created, the Fortran open statement can set the status flag to NEW and an error will occur if the file already exists. C's fopen function will create a file if the file is opened with an access flag including w but will not error if the file already exists. If the file exists, it will be truncated at its beginning and all of its contents will be lost. To prevent opening an existing file and having it truncated by mistake, the existence of the file can be checked with C's fopen function used to emulate Fortran's inquire statement (see the inquire description earlier in this chapter).

C does not provide as much information about file attributes as does Fortran. In this chapter, the section on the Fortran inquire statement included a Fortran example program that reported a whole series of file attributes, but the corresponding C example program was only able to determine file existence.

Aside from fundamental file attributes such as unit, name, error and access control, the remaining Fortran file attributes establish the record length of direct access files and blank interpretation.

Fortran's direct access files have a fixed record length. That record length is specified as the argument to the recl option in Fortran's open statement. The following Fortran program opens such a file with a record length of 36 bytes, populates it with three records, and then reads back all three records:

```
    program main
    integer  irecl,     irec
    real     rarray(9), xarray(9)
    data     rarray / 0.0, 1.0, 2.0, 3.0, 4.0,
   -                      5.0, 6.0, 7.0, 8.0 /
    irecl = 36
```

```
      open ( unit=7,            file='recl.dat',
  -        access='DIRECT', recl=irecl         )
      write ( 6,1 ) irecl
1     format ( 1H , '[recl.dat] is open with '
  -            'a record length of ', i2, ' bytes.'
  -          / 1H , 'The default record length ',
  -            'is ??? bytes.' )
      do 2 irec = 1, 3, 1
      rarray(1) = float ( irec )
      write ( 7,rec=irec ) rarray
2     continue
      do 4 irec = 1, 3, 1
      read ( 7,rec=irec ) xarray
      write ( 6,3 ) xarray
3     format ( 1H , 9f4.1 )
4     continue
      close ( unit=7 )
      stop
      end
```

The program generates this display:

[recl.dat] is open with a record length of 36 bytes.
The default buffer length is ??? bytes.
1.0 1.0 2.0 3.0 4.0 5.0 6.0 7.0 8.0
2.0 1.0 2.0 3.0 4.0 5.0 6.0 7.0 8.0
3.0 1.0 2.0 3.0 4.0 5.0 6.0 7.0 8.0

A C program that accomplishes the same function is as follows:

```
#include < stdio.h >
main ( )
{
    FILE *n;
      int    irecl = 36, irec;
    struct array { float r[9];   } rarray[1] =
                            { 0.0F, 1.0F, 2.0F,
                              3.0F, 4.0F, 5.0F,
                              6.0F, 7.0F, 8.0F };
    struct array xarray[1];
    char    buffer[36];
    n = fopen ( "recl.dat", "wb + " );
    setvbuf ( n, buffer, __IOFBF, sizeof ( buffer ) );
    printf ( "[recl.dat] is open with "
          "a record length of %2i bytes. \ n", irecl );
    printf ( "The default buffer length is %d bytes. \ n",
          BUFSIZ );
    for ( irec = 1; irec < = 3; irec ++ ) {
        rarray[0].r[0]  = (float) irec;
        fwrite ( rarray, sizeof(struct array), 1, n );
    }
```

```
        fclose ( n );
        n = fopen ( "recl.dat", "rb+" );
        setvbuf ( n, buffer, _IOFBF, sizeof ( buffer ) );
        for ( irec = 1; irec < = 3; irec + + ) {
            fread ( xarray, sizeof ( struct array ), 1, n );
            printf ( " %3.1f %3.1f %3.1f", xarray[0].r[0],
                        xarray[0].r[1], xarray[0].r[2] );
            printf ( " %3.1f %3.1f %3.1f", xarray[0].r[3],
                        xarray[0].r[4], xarray[0].r[5] );
            printf ( " %3.1f %3.1f %3.1f", xarray[0].r[6],
                        xarray[0].r[7], xarray[0].r[8] );
            printf ( " \ n" );
        }
        fclose ( n );
        return;
    }
```

C uses the setvbuf function to establish the record length for the file. ANSI C uses a standard buffer that is BUFSIZ bytes long where BUFSIZ is at least 256 bytes. The C example program uses a buffer, called buffer, that is declared to be 36 bytes long; its length is calculated by the sizeof operator as the last argument to the setvbuf function. By default, ANSI C fully buffers input and output to files, and the example program echos that default with the _IOFBF macro. Other buffering schemes are line-buffered and no buffering (i.e., the _IOLBF and _IONBF macros, respectively).

Blanks in numeric fields in a Fortran formatted file are normally ignored. Trailing and embedded blanks can be interpreted as zeros if Fortran open statement's blank option is set to ZERO. The following Fortran program demonstrates reading the same file under both options:

```
      program main
      integer iarray(4)
      write ( 6,1 )
1     format ( 1H , 'Processing blank=NULL file...' )
      open ( unit=7, file='nz.dat', blank='NULL' )
      read ( 7,2 ) iarray
2     format ( 4i5 )
      close ( unit=7 )
      write ( 6,3 ) iarray
3     format ( 1H , 4 ( 5x, i5 ) )
      write ( 6,4 )
4     format ( 1H , 'Processing blank=ZERO file...' )
      open ( unit=7, file='nz.dat', blank='ZERO' )
      read ( 7,2 ) iarray
      close ( unit=7 )
      write ( 6,3 ) iarray
      stop
      end
```

When using the following input file (the second line is present only to show you the spacing and actually isn't processed),

```
12      34          2 45
12345123451234512345
```

this display is generated:

```
Processing blank=NULL file . . .
    12      34    0      245
Processing blank=ZERO file . . .
12000      340    0     2045
```

A C program that accomplishes the same function is as follows:

```c
#include <stddef.h>
#include <stdlib.h>
#include <stdio.h>
main ( )
{
FILE *n;
char    buffer[20], carray[4][5], number[6];
char    blank = ' ';
int     i, j, k, last, first, index;
long    iarray[4];
printf ( "Processing blank=NULL file . . . \n" );
n = fopen ( "nz.dat", "r" );
fscanf ( n, "%20c \n", buffer );
k = 0;
for ( i=0; i<=3; i++ ) {
    last = 0;
    for ( j=0; j<=4; j++ ) {
        carray[i][j] = buffer[k];
        if ( buffer[k] != blank )
            last = j;
        k += 1;
    }
    first = 0;
    for ( j=last; j>=0; j-- ) {
        if ( carray[i][j] != blank )
            first = j;
    }
    index = 0;
    for ( j=first; j<=last; j++ ) {
        if ( carray[i][j] != blank ) {
            number[index] = carray[i][j];
            index += 1;
        }
    }
}
number[index] = '\0';
```

```
            iarray[i] = strtol ( &number[0], NULL, 10 );
        }
        printf ( "     %5ld    %5ld    %5ld      %5ld \ n",
                iarray[0], iarray[1], iarray[2], iarray[3] );
        printf ( "Processing blank = ZERO file . . . \ n" );
        rewind ( n );
        n = fopen ( "nz.dat", "r" );
        fscanf ( n, "%20c \ n", buffer );
        k = 0;
        last = 4;
        for ( i = 0; i < = 3; i + + ) {
            for ( j = 0; j < = last; j++ ) {
                carray[i][j] = buffer[k];
                k + = 1;
            }
            first = 0;
            for ( j = last; j > = 0; j-- ) {
                if ( carray[i][j] ! = blank )
                    first = j;
            }
            index = 0;
            for ( j = first; j < = last; j++ ) {
                if ( carray[i][j] = = blank ) {
                    number[index] = '0';
                }
                else
                    number[index] = carray[i][j];
            index += 1;
            }
        number[index] = ' \ 0';
        iarray[i] = strtol ( &number[0], NULL, 10 );
        }
        printf ( "     %5ld    %5ld    %5ld      %5ld \ n",
                iarray[0], iarray[1], iarray[2], iarray[3] );
        fclose ( n );
        return;

    }
```

Fortran automatically interprets blanks for the programmer whether blanks are ignored or treated as zero. C requires the programmer to explicitly handle each individual digit of a number to ignore a blank or replace it with zero.

Corresponding to Fortran's NULL case, the C example program extracts each of the four fields from the line that was read, determines the starting and ending character of each field, compresses embedded blanks if they exist, and converts the resulting string to a number with the strtol function. This complex method of handling is necessary to cover the case of embedded blanks because C recognizes blanks as separators between fields. If the file had been read as

```
fscanf ( n, "%ld %ld %ld %ld \ n", iarray[0],
          iarray[1], iarray[2], iarray[3] );
```

then the array would hold the values 12, 34, 2, and 45. Under this format, C interprets the five blanks in columns 11 through 15 and the single blank at column 19 as field separators. If the numbers in the file had been written with a zero in the field of blanks and no embedded blanks, such as

```
12      34   0     245
12345123451234512345
```

and reread with the fscanf statement above, then the array would hold the values 12, 34, 0, and 245.

C does not require complicated coding to process numeric fields in formatted files. Straightforward uses of fscanf are possible if such files include a zero rather than all blanks in each empty field and represent numbers with digit strings that do not have embedded blanks. In the ZERO case, the C example program processes each field in the same way except that it replaces trailing and embedded blanks with zeros.

Parameter

Fortran	parameter (NAME = expression)
C Primary	#define
C Secondary	none

Parameters are Fortran compile-time constants. In essence, once their value is set at the beginning of a source code file, it cannot be changed. As such, parameters are useful in holding the value of natural constants (i.e., pi) and in setting the size of arrays. Furthermore, they can be displayed by any output statement but cannot be read from a file or the terminal, nor can they be assigned a value by any expression. The following Fortran program demonstrates the use of a constant:

```
      program main
      parameter ( n1 = 1 )
      parameter ( n2 = n1 + n1 )
      parameter ( n3 = n1 + n2 )
      parameter ( n4 = n2 * n2 )
      parameter ( n5 = n2 + n3 )
      real        array(n2)
      character   string(n5)
      data        array / 6.0, 7.0 /
      data        string / ',', ' ', '8', '.', '0' /
      write ( 6,1 ) n1, n2, n3, n4, n5, array, string
    1 format ( 1H , 5 ( i1, ',' ), f3.1, ',', f3.1, 5a1 )
      stop
      end
```

The program generates this display:

    1, 2, 3, 4, 5, 6.0, 7.0, 8.0

A C program that accomplishes the same function is as follows:

```
      #define n1 1
      #define n2 n1 +  n1
      #define n3 n1 +  n2
      #define n4 n2 *  n2
      #define n5 n2 +  n3
      main ()
{
      float array[n2]  = { 6.0, 7.0 };
      char  string[n5] = ", 8.0";
      printf ( "%i, %i, %i, %i, %i, %3.1f, %3.1f%s \ n",
               n1, n2, n3, n4, n5,
               array[0], array[1], string );
      return;
}
```

Both example programs set parameters to a simple constant (n1), "compute" a parameter's value using other parameters (n3 and n4), and use parameters to set the size of arrays (n2 and n5). In one way, Fortran parameters are treated as if they were a full-fledged variable in that they must be one of Fortran's data types. C's #define statement actually instructs the compiler to replace the source string with the target string wherever it appears. In other words, with this definition

    #define n6 1 + 5

the compiler would compile this line of code

    printf ("%i\n", n6);

as if it had been written as

    printf ("%i\n", 1 + 5);

In this context, C's #define statement establishes symbolic constants used by the compiler to pre-process the source code file.

Pause

Fortran	pause pause NUMBER pause STRING
C Primary	getchar
C Secondary	none

Fortran allows program execution to be suspended through the use of the pause statement. The following Fortran example program gives an example of pause:

```
        program main
        write ( 6,1 )
1       format ( 1H , 'About to pause without comment ...' )
        pause
        pause 1
        pause 'Two'
        stop
        end
```

The program generates this display:

About to pause without comment . . .

Pause – 1
Two

A C program that accomplishes the same function is as follows:

```
        main ( )
{
    int     i = 1;
    char *s = "Two";
    int     c;
    printf ( " \nAbout to pause without comment . . . " );
    c = getchar( );
    printf ( " \nPause – %d ", i );
    c = getchar( );
    printf ( " \n%s ", s );
    c = getchar( );
    return;
}
```

ANSI C has no special, dedicated mechanism to do what Fortran's pause statement can accomplish. Where the Fortran example program used the pause statement to suspend execution, the C example program used a standard terminal write and read to produce the same effect.

Print

Fortran	print LABEL, VARIABLE
	print *, VARIABLE
C Primary	printf
C Secondary	none

Fortran's print statement is a less-functional write statement. Where the write statement can handle several file types and control error handling, the print statement directs output to one type of device and has no error control. Print statements are bound to display data on the same device as referenced by the read(*... and write(*... statements: this is nearly always the terminal. The following Fortran program demonstrates the print statement:

```
      program main
      character*3 c
      integer    i
      real       x
      c = 'abc'
      i = 123
      x = 4.5
      write ( 6,1 )
    1 format ( 1H , 'PRINT under format control ...' )
      print 2, c, i, x
    2 format ( 1H , a3, i4, f4.1 )
      write ( 6,3 )
    3 format ( 1H , 'PRINT using list-directed',
     -                 'formatting ...' )
      print *, c, i, x
      stop
      end
```

The program generates this display:

```
PRINT under format control . . .
abc 123 4.5
PRINT using list-directed formatting . . .
abc             123            4.500000
```

A C program that accomplishes the same function is as follows:

```
    main ( )
    {
    char *c  =  "abc";
    int    i  = 123;
    float  x  = 4.5F;
    printf ( "PRINT under format control . . . \n" );
    printf ( "%3s %3i %3.1f \n", c, i, x );
    printf ("PRINT using list-directed formatting . . . \n");
```

```
    printf ( "%s          %i        %f \ n", c, i, x );
    return;
}
```

A print statement can display data under format control or with list-directed formatting. In the Fortran example program, the format statement referenced by the first print statement is similar to the corresponding printf statement in the C example program. List-directed output is produced when a print statement references the asterisk as the format. Implementations differ, but it is typical to see five to ten spaces separate each field under this Fortran's list-directed form of print output. The C example program explicitly includes spaces to separate fields in the last printf statement.

Program

Fortran   program NAME

C Primary   main( )

C Secondary   argc, argv

ANSI 77 Fortran introduced a statement to name the main program. Typically, the compiler and/or the host operating system uses the name main to refer to a program, but this can be changed with the program statement. The following Fortran program uses the program statement:

```
      program PROGRAM
      write ( 6,1 )
 1    format ( 1H , 'PROGRAM Fortran statement: ',
     -                'example output . . . PROGRAM.' )
      stop
      end
```

The program generates this display:

PROGRAM Fortran statement: example output . . . PROGRAM.

A C program that accomplishes the same function is as follows:

```
      main ( int argc, char *argv[ ] )
{
      printf (   "PROGRAM Fortran statement: "
                 "example output . . . %s. \ n", argv[0] );
      return;
}
```

These two programs use very different mechanisms to generate the same display. The Fortran example program uses the Fortran program statement to give the main program the name "program." The C example program accesses an array of program arguments to display the first such argument (i.e., argv[0]). This first argument is always the name of the command issued to execute this program. The C example program will produce the example output, provided that it was executed with a command "PROGRAM."

In a larger context, what C offers the programmer is a way to write a main program that accepts a varying number of arguments from the command line. The two arguments to the main statement define the number of arguments—argc—and an array of pointers to the character strings that make up those arguments—argv. The first element of the argument array—argv[0]—is reserved to hold the program name. Each succeeding element holds the next command line argument for the program. A C sample program that echoes command line arguments is as follows:

```
      main ( int argc, char *argv[ ] )
{
      int i;
```

```
        for ( i = 0; i < argc; i++ ) {
            printf ( "\nArgument %2.2i: %s", i, argv[i] );
        }
        printf ( "\n" );
        return;
}
```

If this example program was invoked as follows

    PROGRAM a 2 c 4.56

it would generate this display:

    Argument 00: PROGRAM
    Argument 01: a
    Argument 02: 2
    Argument 03: c
    Argument 04: 4.56

Any data type can be represented in the argv array because the argv array holds each program argument in a character string. Passing numbers as arguments is supported because functions like strtol, strtoul, or strtod can convert a string into a long integer, an unsigned long integer, or a double number.

Read

Fortran	read (NUMBER, LABEL) VARIABLE
	read (UNIT=NUM, REC=NUM, ERR=LAB) VAR
	read (ARRAY, LAB, ERR=LAB) VARIABLE
C Primary	fread, fscanf, fseek, ftell, sscanf
C Secondary	||, ! = , %n, break, fclose, ferror, feof, fopen, sizeof, sscanf, strlen, struct

Fortran file input is accomplished through the use of the read statement. Four distinct file types can be processed by the read statement: formatted sequential access files, list-directed sequential access files, unformatted direct access files, and internal files. Each of these file types will be described in turn.

Formatted sequential access files represent the modern analogue of yesterday's card reader. Such "flat files" are often the means to export data from one application for subsequent input into another application program. The following Fortran program reads a formatted sequential access file and displays what was read:

```
      program main
      integer   i, j, iunit
      real      r
      character c*3
      iunit = 7
      open ( unit=iunit, file='readsf.dat' )
      do 6 j = 1, 3, 1
          read ( iunit,1,err=2,end=7 ) i, r, c
1         format ( i1, 1x, f3.1, 1x, a3 )
          go to 4
2            continue
             write ( 6,3 ) j
3            format ( 1H , 'READ error ... record ',
     -                i1, ' skipped!' )
             go to 6
4         continue
          write ( 6,5 ) j, i, r, c
5         format ( 1H , 'Record ', i5.5, ': ',
     -                i1, 1x, f3.1, 1x, a3 )
6     continue
7     continue
      write ( 6,8 ) j-1
8     format ( 1H , 'EOF reached after record ', i5.5, '.' )
      close ( unit=iunit )
      stop
      end
```

It uses the following data file

```
1  2.0   abc
2  3.0   def
3  xxx   ghi
```

and generates this display:

Record 00001: 1 2.0 abc
Record 00002: 2 3.0 def
READ error ... record 3 skipped!
EOF reached after record 00003.

A C program that accomplishes the same function is as follows:

```c
#include <stdio.h>
main ( )
{
    int      i, j;
    FILE  *iunit;
    float    r;
    char   *c;
    int      items;
    int      bytes;
    iunit = fopen ( "readsf.dat", "r" );
    for ( j = 1; j <= 3; j + + ) {
        items = fscanf ( iunit, "%i %f %s%n \ n",
                          &i, &r, c, &bytes );
        if ( ( items ! = 3 ) ||
            ( bytes ! = 9 )          ) {
            printf ( "READ error ... "
                      "record %i skipped! \ n", j );
        }
        else
            printf ( "Record %5.5i: %1i %3.1f %3s \ n",
                      j, i, r, c );
    }
    printf ( "EOF reached after record %5.5i. \ n", j-1 );
    fclose ( iunit );
    return;
}
```

Both programs open the same data file. By default, Fortran will open the file with the keyword for the access option set to SEQUENTIAL and the keyword for the form option set to FORMATTED. C's fopen function is explicitly told to open the file for input in text mode. Three records are read from the file. Fortran's read statement is programmed here with an error trap that will inform the user, by record number, where the read error occurred. C's fscanf function reports the number of fields read in the items variable and the number of bytes read, through the %n format, into the bytes variable. Error control is maintained by comparing the value of both the items and bytes variable to the known number of fields and bytes per line (i.e., 3 and 9, respectively). When the erroneous third line of the data file is processed, fscanf sets items to 1 to correspond to the successful processing of the first field. However, it does not update the bytes variable because the %n format appears after the field specification for the data element in error. Finally, the number of records processed is reported to the user and the single input file is closed.

List-directed sequential access files are convenient because they bypass the rigid column alignment requirement of formatted files. The following Fortran program reads three records from a file in a list-directed format:

```
      program main
      integer    i, j, iunit
      real       r
      character c*3
      iunit = 7
      open ( unit=iunit, file='reads1.dat' )
      do 6 j = 1, 3, 1
         read ( iunit,*,err=2,end=7 ) i, r, c
         go to 4
2        continue
         write ( 6,3 ) j
3        format ( 1H , 'READ error ... record ',
     -               i1,' skipped!' )
         go to 6
4        continue
         write ( 6,5 ) j, i, r, c
5        format ( 1H , 'Record ', i5.5, ': ',
     -               i1, 1x, f3.1, 1x, a3 )
6     continue
7     continue
      write ( 6,8 ) j-1
8     format ( 1H , 'EOF reached after record ', i5.5, '.' )
      close ( unit=iunit )
      stop
      end
```

It uses this data file

```
1  2.0   'abc'
2  3.0   'def'
3  xxx   'ghi'
```

and generates this display:

```
Record 00001:  1  2.0  abc
Record 00002:  2  3.0  def
READ error ... record 3 skipped!
EOF reached after record 00003.
```

A C program that accomplishes the same function is as follows:

```
#include <stdio.h>
main ()
{
```

```
int        i, j, k;
FILE       *iunit;
float      r;
char       *c;
int        items;
int        bytes;
iunit = fopen ( "readsl.dat", "r" );
for ( j = 1; j < = 3; j + + ) {
    items = fscanf ( iunit, "%i %f %*c%s%n \ n",
                    &i, &r, c, &bytes );
    k = strlen ( c );
    c[k-1] = ' \ 0';
    if ( items ! = 3 )
        printf ( "READ error ... "
                "record %i skipped! \ n", j );
    else
        printf ( "Record %5.5i: %1i %3.1f %s \ n",
                j, i, r, c );
}
printf ( "EOF reached after record %5.5i. \ n", j-1 );
fclose ( iunit );
return;
}
```

Both programs open the same data file. By default, Fortran will open the file with the keyword for the access option set to SEQUENTIAL and the keyword for the form option set to FORMATTED. C's fopen function is explicitly told to open the file for input in text mode. Three records are read from the file. Fortran's read statement is programmed here with an error trap that will inform the user, by record number, where the read error occurred. C's fscanf function reports the number of fields read in the items variable and the number of bytes read, through the %n format, into the bytes variable. Error control is maintained by comparing the value of items variable to the known number of fields (i.e., 3). When the erroneous third line of the data file is processed, fscanf sets items to 1 to correspond to the successful processing of the first field. However, it does not update the bytes variable because the %n format appears after the field specification for the data element in error.

Fortran requires that character data must be enclosed in single quotation marks when read under a list-directed format. The C example program strips the first quotation mark through the use of the %*c format, which ignores one character from the input file. Then, the strlen function is used to determine the length of the string as read from the file. This length will exclude the first quotation mark but include the second quotation mark. After determining the length of the string as read, the second quotation mark is overwritten by the null character (i.e., \ 0), which marks the new end of the string. Finally, the number of records processed is reported to the user and the single input file is closed.

Unformatted direct access files are the only "structured" file directly supported by Fortran. The following Fortran program reads three records and then rereads the first record:

```
program main
integer     i, j, k, iunit
real        r
character  c*3
iunit = 7
open ( unit=iunit, file='readdf.dat',
-         access='direct', recl=11 )
  do 6 j = 1, 4, 1
     k = j
     if ( k .eq. 4 ) k = 1
     read ( iunit,rec=k,err=2 ) i, r, c
     go to 4
2        continue
         write ( 6,3 ) k
3        format ( 1H , 'READ error ... record ',
                  i1, ' skipped!' )
         go to 6
4     continue
      write ( 6,5 ) k, i, r, c
5     format ( 1H , 'Record ', i5.5, ': ',
-                i1, 1x, f3.1, 1x, a3 )
6  continue
   write ( 6,8 ) k
8  format ( 1H , 'Last record read ',
-          'was number ', i5.5, '.' )
   close ( unit=iunit )
   stop
   end
```

It generates this display:

```
Record 00001: 1  2.0  abc
Record 00002: 2  3.0  def
Record 00003: 3  4.0  ghi
Record 00001: 1  2.0  abc
Last record read was number 00001.
```

The input data file to the Fortran example program is the output data file from the Fortran example program used to create a direct access file in this chapter under the write Fortran statement.

A C program that accomplishes the same function is as follows:

```
#include <stdio.h>
main ( )
{
int     j, k;
FILE *iunit;
```

```
struct   binary {  long   i;
                   float  r;
                   char   c[4]; } record[1];
int     items;
int     count = 1;
long    curpos;
int     error;
long    position;
long    bytes   =   12;
iunit   = fopen ( "readdc.dat", "rb" );
bytes   = (long) sizeof ( struct binary );
for ( j = 1; j < = 4; j + + ) {
    k = j;
    if ( k = = 4 )
        k =    1;
    curpos   = ftell ( iunit );
    position = ( k-1 ) * bytes;
    error    = fseek ( iunit, position, SEEK__SET );
    if ( error ! = 0 ) {
        printf ( "FSEEK position error! \ n" );
        break;
    }
    items = fread ( record, sizeof (struct binary),
                    count, iunit            );
    if ( items = = count ) {
        printf ( "Record %5.5i: %ld %3.1f %s \ n",
            k, record[0].i, record[0].r,
            record[0].c              );
    }
    else
        printf ( "READ error ... "
                 "record %i skipped! \ n", k );
}
printf ( "Last record read was number %5.5i. \ n", k );
fclose ( iunit );
return;
}
```

This C example program generated the same display as did the Fortran example program. The input data file to the C program is the output data file from the C program in this chapter used to create a direct access file in the section that covers Fortran's `write` statement.

Both programs opened files that were nearly identical, differing only in the length of each logical record. Fortran wrote eleven bytes into the file for each logical record: four for the `integer` variable, four for the `real` variable, and `three` for the character string. C wrote twelve bytes into the file for each logical record: four for the int variable, four for the float variable, and four for the character string (i.e., three characters plus the null character— \ 0—used to terminate the string). Consequently, direct access files that contain any character data are not interchangeable between Fortran and C unless the null character is handled explicitly. For files written by a Fortran program to be read by a C program, an additional variable needs to be output after each character string. This variable should be defined as

```
character*1 null
```

and initialized as

```
null = char ( 0 )
```

For files written by a C program to be read by a Fortran program, an additional variable defined like the `null` variable above needs to be read and disregarded after processing each character string.

File position in Fortran is specified by the `rec` option on the `read` statement. File position in the C example program needs to be calculated. C's ftell function is used to determine the current position in the input file measured in bytes from the beginning of the file. This could be used to determine if the file was correctly positioned for the next read. The new position is calculated as a function of the desired record number and the number of bytes per logical record. C's fseek function then advances the file pointer the correct number of bytes from the beginning of the file to the new position. If the file cannot be positioned, fseek returns a non-zero error number.

Variable lists for `direct` access input in Fortran are no different from the corresponding lists for `sequential` access input. C's fread function performs unformatted input of an entire logical record at a time where the individual variables are combined into a C struct construct. In the C example program, individual variables i, r, and the c character array are combined into a C struct named binary. One instance of this struct name record[1] is then defined. C's fread function reads all three variables at once into the struct named record. The length of the struct is computed by the sizeof function, and only one instance of record is processed per read because fread's third argument, the variable count, is set to one. If the file can be read, fread returns the number of instances of record processed correctly. If the file cannot be read, fread returns a number that can be used by two other C functions, ferror and feof, to identify the error and/or determine if the end-of file has been reached.

ANSI 77 standard Fortran permits in-memory buffers to be treated as if they were files. The following Fortran program reads such a buffer:

```
program main
integer      i, j
real         r
character    c*3
character*9  buffer(3)
buffer(1) = '1  2.0  abc'
buffer(2) = '2  x.0  def'
buffer(3) = '3  4.0  ghi'
```

```
         read ( buffer(j),1,err=2 ) i, r, c
1        format ( i1, 1x, f3.1, 1x, a3 )
         go to 4
2         continue
          write ( 6,3 ) j
3         format ( 1H , 'READ error ... buffer ',
-                  i1, ( ' skipped!' )
          go to 6
4  continue
   write ( 6,5 ) j, i, r, c
5  format ( 1H , 'Buffer ', i5.5, ': ',
-           i1, 1x, f3.1, 1x, a3 )
6  continue
   write ( 6,8 ) j-1
8  format ( 1H , 'Last buffer processed was ', i5.5, '.' )
   stop
   end
```

The program generates this display:

```
Buffer 00001: 1 2.0 abc
READ error ... buffer 2 skipped!
Buffer 00003: 3 4.0 ghi
Last buffer processed was 00003.
```

A C program that accomplishes the same function is as follows:

```
#include <stdio.h>
#include <stddef.h>
#include <stlib.h>
main ()
{
int      i, j;
float    r;
char     *c;
char     *buffer[3]  =  { "1 2.0 abc",
                          "2 x.0 def",
                          "3 4.0 ghi" };
int      items;
for ( j=0; j<=2; j++ ) {
    items = sscanf ( buffer[j], "%i %f %s",
                                &i, &r, c );
    if ( items !=3 ) {
        printf ( "READ error ... "
                 "buffer %i skipped!\n", j+1 );
    }
    else
        printf ( "Buffer %5.5i: %i %3.1f %3s\n",
                 j+1, i, r, c );
}
```

```
      printf ( "Last buffer processed was %5.5i. \ n", j );
      return;
}
```

Both programs "read" an in-memory character array named buffer. Fortran supports processing such character arrays through the use of the read statement. If an error occurs, the err option on the read statement is exercised, and control passes to series of statements that will display an error message. C's sscanf function reads character strings from an array of pointers to those strings. Values for numeric variables are read through the address—&i and &r, respectively—for those variables. Values for character strings are read through pointers for those variables (i.e., the *c variable). The number of fields correctly read is returned from the sscanf function into the variable items. If three fields are not read, an error message is produced. Finally, both programs report the number of buffers processed.

Real

Fortran	`real VARIABLE`
	`real FUNCTION_NAME`
C Primary	float
C Secondary	F

Variables, arrays, and functions that deal with single precision floating point numbers are defined in Fortran with the `real` statement. Each use of the `real` statement is demonstrated in the following program:

```
      program main
      real variable
      real array(3)
      real farg
      real fvalue
      real fname
      variable = 1.0
      array(1) = 2.0
      array(2) = 3.0
      array(3) = 4.0
      farg     = array(3)
      fvalue   = fname ( farg )
      write ( 6,1 ) variable, array, fvalue
    1 format ( 1H , 5f4.1 )
      stop
      end
      real function fname ( farg )
      real farg
      fname = farg + 1.0
      return
      end
```

The program generates this display:

    1.0 2.0 3.0 4.0 5.0

A C program that accomplishes the same function is as follows:

```
    main( )
    {
    float variable =  1.0F;
    float array[3]  =  { 2.0F, 3.0F, 4.0F };
    float farg      =  array[2];
    float fvalue;
    float fname ( float farg );
    fvalue = fname ( farg );
    printf ( "%3.1f %3.1f %3.1f %3.1f %3.1f \ n",
            variable, array[0], array[1], array[2],
            fvalue );
    return;
    }
    float fname ( float farg )
```

```
{
    return farg + 1.0F;
}
```

ANSI 77 Fortran defines a single form of the `real` data type. Many Fortran compilers support two additional forms: `real*4` as a synonym for the unqualified `real` statement, and `real*8` as a synonym for the `double precision` data type. Fortran's `real` or `real*4` is C's float data type, and `real*8` is represented by C's double and long double (see FIG. 3-2). A major difference between Fortran's `real` and C's float data types is the syntax used to initialize variables. Fortran `real` constants are simple digit strings with a decimal point and/or an explicit E exponent, such as the following:

```
123.0
1.23E2 for 123
1E2 for 100
```

C uses an f or F suffix to distinguish a float from a double floating point constant, such as

```
123.0f or 123.0F
1.23e2F or 1.23E2f for 123
1E2f or 1e2F for 100
```

Chapter 3 presents some additional details about Fortran and C floating point data types.

Return

Fortran	return
	return NUMBER
C Primary	return
C Secondary	&, *

Concluding every subprogram, Fortran's `return` statement comes in two forms. The simple form of the `return` statement has no arguments and transfers control from the subprogram to the calling routine at the point at which the subprogram was invoked. A more complex form takes one argument (which is an index) into a list of statement labels. The list is an argument to the subprogram and directs control to be transferred to one of several alternate returns in the calling routine. The following Fortran program demonstrates both forms of `return` statement:

```
      program main
      integer i, j, k
      integer fun
      i = 1
      call sub ( i, j )
      k = fun ( j )
      write ( 6,1 ) i, j, k
 1    format ( 1H , 3i2 )
      do 6 i = 1, 2, 1
         call alt ( i, *2, *4 )
         go to 4
 2       continue
            write ( 6,3 ) i
 3          format ( 1H , 'Return #', i1,
 -                        ' to label 2 ' )
            go to 6
 4       continue
            write ( 6,5 ) i
 5          format ( 1H , 'Return #', i1,
 -                        ' to label 4 ' )
 6 continue
   stop
   end
   subroutine sub ( i, j )
   integer i, j
   j = i + 1
   return
   end
   integer function fun ( j )
   integer j
   fun = j + 1
   return
   end
   subroutine alt ( i, *, *)
   integer i
```

```
if ( i .eq. 1 ) return 1
if ( i .eq. 2 ) return 2
return
end
```

The program generates this display:

```
1 2 3
Return #1 to label 2
Return #2 to label 4
```

A C program that accomplishes the same function is as follows:

```c
void main ( )
{
int    i = 1,   j, k;
void  sub    ( int i, int *j );
int    fun    ( int j );
int    alt    ( int j );
sub ( i, &j );
k = fun ( j );
printf ( "%i %i %i \ n", i, j, k );
for ( i = 1; i < = 2; i++ ) {
    j = alt ( i );
    if ( j == 1 ) {
        printf ( "Return #%i to label 2 \ n", i );
    }
    else
        printf ( "Return #%i to label 4 \ n", i );
}
return;
}

void sub ( int i, int *j )
{
*j = i + 1;
 return;
}

int fun ( int j )
{
 return j + 1;
}

int alt ( int j )
{
 return j;
}
```

Both programs invoke the subprograms: a subroutine sub, a function fun, and an example of alternate return subroutine alt.

Subprogram sub takes its first argument, i, adds one to it, and returns the result in the second argument, j. In the C version, sub is invoked with the second argument using a &j syntax, and that second argument is declared and manipulated in the function with a *j syntax.

When invoked, the address of the main program variable j is passed to the function through the use of the & operator. On receipt, the second argument of the sub function accepts that address in the form of a pointer to an int data type and manipulates the data element at the address pointed to by that pointer, *j.

The second subprogram, fun, is a function in both the Fortran and C sense. Both versions accept a single argument, add one to it, and send the result back to the main program either as the value of the function name in Fortran or through an argument to the return statement in C.

Alt, the third subprogram, exhibits Fortran's "alternate return" version of the return statement. Depending on the value transferred to the main program by the return statement, one or the other of the display statements will be executed. If alt exits without triggering either of the "alternate return" versions of the return statement, then control will transfer to the statement following the call to this subroutine. The C example program includes a version of the alt subprogram that causes the same result as the Fortran program but uses a hand-coded construct. In other words, C's return statement does not have any formal mechanism to effect a transfer of control like Fortran's alternate return.

Rewind

Fortran	rewind (UNIT=N, IOSTAT=V, ERROR=LAB) rewind NUMBER
C Primary	rewind
C Secondary	&, fclose, FILE, fopen, fprintf, fscanf

A program's position in a file can be reset to the beginning of the file through the use of the rewind statement. It is commonly used to "switch" between writing and reading a sequential file: write to the file, rewind it, and then read from the file. The following Fortran program processes a sequential file in just such a manner:

```
      program main
      integer i
      integer funit
      integer iiostat
      funit = 7
      open ( unit=funit, file='rewind.dat' )
      do 2 i = 1, 3, 1
      write ( funit,1 ) i
   1  format ( i5.5 )
   2  continue
      rewind ( unit=funit, iostat=iiostat )
      if ( iiostat .ne. 0 ) then
           write ( 6,3 ) iiostat
   3       format ( 1H , 'REWIND error ... ',
      -               'IOSTAT = ', i5.5 )
           stop
      else
           write ( 6,4 )
   4       format ( 1H , 'File [rewind.dat] is rewound.' / )
      endif
      do 7 i = 1, 3, 1
         read ( funit,5 ) j
   5     format ( i5 )
         write ( 6,6 ) i, j
   6     format ( 1H , 'Record ', i1, ': ', i5.5 )
   7  continue
      close ( unit=funit )
      stop
      end
```

The program generates this display:

```
File [rewind.dat] is rewound.
Record 1: 00001
Record 2: 00002
Record 3: 00003
```

A C program that accomplishes the same function is as follows:

```c
#include <stdio.h>
main ( )
{
   int      i;
   int      j;
   FILE  *funit;
   funit = fopen ( "rewind.dat", "w+" );
   for ( i = 1; i < = 3; i++ ) {
         fprintf ( funit, "%5.5i \ n", i );
   }
   rewind ( funit );
   printf ( "File [rewind.dat] rewound. \ n \ n" );
   for ( i = 1; i < = 3; i++ ) {
         fscanf ( funit, "%i", &j );
         printf ( "Record %i: %5.5i \ n", i, j );
   }
   i = fclose ( funit );
}
```

Both programs open the file for sequential formatted output, and populate the file with three records. The Fortran example program has several error handling statements following the rewind statement in case the file in question could not be rewound. C's rewind statement has no error control: if for any reason the file cannot be rewound, the program will not be able to receive any notification of this problem. ANSI standard C defines the rewind function as a void function that does not return a value to the calling program. Quite a number of compilers implement this function differently and allow it to return a value—usually defined as a success-/failure indicator—to the calling program.

Finally, both programs read the file and display its contents. In the C example program, the last argument to the fscanf function that reads the file is &j. The address operator, &, is necessary because in reading the file, fscanf will update the value of the variable j, and it can do it only through the address of that variable.

Save

Fortran	save VARIABLE
	save / COMMON__BLOCK__NAME /
	save
C Primary	static
C Secondary	none

Variables local to a subprogram typically do not retain their value after the subprogram completes execution. If the programmer desires them to do so, he/she can explicitly retain them by naming the variables in a save statement. ANSI 77 standard Fortran cautions that variables in named common will not retain their value from subprogram to subprogram unless that common area appears in a save statement in the main program. Most compilers will automatically retain the value of variables in named common, but the save statement is the only definite, standard, and approved method to do so. The following Fortran sample program demonstrates the effect of the save statement:

```
      program main
      integer      i
      integer      globali, locali
      real         globalr, localr
      character*3  globalc, localc
      common / area / globali, globalr, globalc
      save   / area /
      globali = 10
      globalr = 20.0
      globalc = 'ABC'
      locali  = 1
      localr  = 2.0
      localc  = 'abc'
      write ( 6,1 ) locali, localr, localc,
     -              globali, globalr, globalc
 1    format (/ 1H , 2( 1x, i2, 1x, f4.1, 1x, 1H[, a3, 1H] ))
      do 3 i = 1, 2, 1
      write ( 6,2 ) i
 2    format ( / 1H , 'CALL #', i1, ' to subroutine ...' )
      call sub
 3    continue
      write ( 6,4 )
 4    format ( / 1H , 'MAIN regained control ...' )
      write ( 6,1 ) locali, localr, localc,
     -              globali, globalr, globalc
      stop
      end
      subroutine sub
      integer      globali, locali
      real         globalr, localr

      common / area / globali, globalr, globalc
```

```
      save            locali,localr,localc
      write ( 6,1 ) locali, localr, localc,
-                globali, globalr, globalc
 1 format (/ 1H , 2( 1x, i2, 1x, f4.1, 1x, 1H[, a3, 1H]))
  locali = 3
  localr = 4.0
  localc = 'def'
  write ( 6,1 ) locali, localr, localc,
-                globali, globalr, globalc
  return
  end
```

The program generates this display:

```
1    2.0  [abc]  10  20.0  [ABC]

CALL #1 to subroutine ...

0     .0  [   ]  10  20.0  [ABC]
3    4.0  [def]  10  20.0  [ABC]

CALL #2 to subroutine ...

3    4.0  [def]  10  20.0  [ABC]
3    4.0  [def]  10  20.0  [ABC]

MAIN regained control ...

1    2.0  [abc]  10  20.0  [ABC]
```

A C program that accomplishes the same function is as follows:

```
int     globali  = 10;
float   globalr  = 20.0F;
char    *globalc = "ABC";
main ()
{
int     i;
int     locali  = 1;
float   localr  = 2.0F;
char    *localc = "abc";
void sub ( );
printf ( " \ n %2i %4.1f [%3s] %2i %4.1f [%3s] \ n",
        locali,localr,localc,globali,globalr,globalc );
for ( i=1; i< =2; i++ ) {
    printf ( " \ nCALL #%i to subroutine ... \ n", i );
    sub( );
}
printf ( " \ nMAIN regained control ... \ n" );
printf ( " \ n %2i %4.1f [%3s] %2i %4.1f [%3s] \ n",
        locali,localr,localc,globali,globalr,globalc );
return;
}
```

```
    void sub ( )
{
    static int     locali;
    static float    localr;
    static char  *localc;
    printf ( "\n %2i %4.1f [%3s] %2i %4.1f [%3s]\n",
         locali,localr,localc,globali,globalr,globalc );
    locali  = 3;
    localr  = 4.0;
    localc  = "def";
    printf ( "\n %2i %4.1f [%3s] %2i %4.1f [%3s]\n",
         locali,localr,localc,globali,globalr,globalc );
    return;
}
```

The program generates the same display as the Fortran example program except for the third line (i.e., directly below the line that begins CALL #1), which reads as follows:

0   0.0 [(null)] 10 20.0 [ABC]

Both programs carry three variables—globali, globalr, and globalc—that are available to any subprogram. Fortran does this by mentioning them in a common statement and, in turn, naming that common area in a save statement in the main program. C does this by declaring all three variables before the main statement in the main program. Both programs declare two sets of local variables—locali, localr, and localc. The first set of local variables has a scope restricted to the main program. Being in the main program, the value of these variables are always available and would never need to be explicitly "saved." The second set is created in the single subprogram called sub. When the subprogram is executed for the first time, these variables have no initial value. Fortran would typically set them to either zero or blank appropriately; in fact, values for these "local" variables are

0   .0 [   ] 10 20.0 [ABC]

when the subprogram sub is executed for the first time. C would typically set them to zero or null as appropriate, like this:

0   0.0 [(null)] 10 20.0 [ABC]

Both programs preserve the value of these "local" variables for the next execution of the subprogram sub: Fortran uses the save statement, and C uses the static qualifier on the type definition statement for these variables.

Stop

Execution of a program can be terminated at any point in Fortran by using the `stop` statement. Typically, a single `stop` statement will appear at the end of the main program. Fortran's `stop` statement can take one argument that can be either a 1-to-5 digit number or a character string. ANSI 77 standard Fortran requires that the value of this argument is then "accessible" to the host operating system. Typically, the host operating system will display the value of the argument to the `stop` statement. The following Fortran program can execute any one of the three forms of the `stop` statement:

```
      program main
      integer i
      i = 1
      go to ( 1, 3, 5 ), i
    1 continue
      write ( 6,2 )
    2 format ( 1H , 'Executing STOP N statement ...' )
      stop 12345
    3 continue
      write ( 6,4 )
    4 format ( 1H , 'Executing STOP CHARACTER ',
     -                'statement ...' )
      stop 'ABCDE'
    5 continue
      write ( 6,6 )
    6 format ( 1H , 'Executing STOP statement ...' )
      stop
      end
```

The program generates this display:

```
Executing STOP N statement ...
12345
```

A C program that accomplishes the same function is as follows:

```
#include <stdio.h>
#include <stlib.h>
main ()
{
int i = 1;
switch ( i ) {
        case 1: goto lab_1;
        case 2: goto lab_3;
```

```
                  default: goto lab__5;
            }
   lab__1: printf ( "Executing STOP N statement ... \ n" );
            exit ( 12345 );
   lab__3: printf ( "Executing STOP CHARACTER "
                    "statement ... \ n" );
            exit ( 'A' );
   lab__5: printf ( "Executing STOP statement ... \ n" );
            exit ( EXIT__SUCCESS );
            }
```

C's exit function can signal the host operating system whether it completed successfully or encountered a failure. The values of EXIT__SUCCESS and EXIT__FAILURE are defined in the C standard file stdlib.h and typically are zero and one, respectively. The host operating system accepts these values as indicators of program success or failure. Arguments to the exit function with any other value than EXIT__SUCCESS or EXIT__FAILURE (such as the number 12345 or the character A in the C example program) have no standard interpretation. In other words, the host operating system would handle such values in whatever manner chosen by the implementer.

Subroutine

Fortran	subroutine NAME (VARIABLE, *LABEL)
C Primary	none
C Secondary	static, void

Most Fortran programs are built as a collection of subroutines and functions. These subprograms are used to partition the program's work into manageable units that can be programmed coherently. The following Fortran program exercises two subroutines with single variable, array element, and whole array arguments:

```
      program main
      integer      j
      integer      i,iarray(3)
      real         r,rarray(3)
      character *3 c ,
                   carray(3)
      i         = 1
      iarray(1) = 2
      iarray(2) = 3
      iarray(3) = 4
      r         = 5.0
      rarray(1) = 6.0
      rarray(2) = 7.0
      rarray(3) = 8.0
      c         = 'ix '
      carray(1) = 'x  '
      carray(2) = 'xi '
      carray(3) = 'xii'
      write ( 6,1 ) i, iarray, r, rarray, c, carray
    1 format ( / 1H , 'MAIN: ' 4 ( 1x, i3.3 ),
     -                         4 ( 1x, f4.1 ),
     -                         4 ( 1x, 1H[, a3, 1H] ) )
      write ( 6,2 )
    2 format ( 1H )
      call sub1 ( i,        r,        c        )
      write ( 6,2 )
      call sub1 ( 1,        5.0,      'ix'     )
      write ( 6,2 )
      do 3 j = 1, 3, 1
      call sub1 ( iarray(j), rarray(j), carray(j) )
    3 continue
      write ( 6,2 )
      call sub2 ( iarray, rarray, carray )
      write ( 6,1 ) i, iarray, r, rarray, c, carray
      write ( 6,2 )
      stop
      end
      subroutine sub1 ( i, r, c )
      integer      i
```

```
      real          r
      character*3  c
      write ( 6,1 ) i, r, c
1  format ( 1H , 'SUB1: ', 1x, i3.3, 13x,
   -               f4.1, 16x, 1H[, a3, 1H] )
      return
      end
      subroutine sub2 ( iarray, rarray, carray )
      integer     iarray(3)
      real        rarray(3)
      character*3 carray(3)
      write ( 6,1 ) iarray, rarray, carray
1  format ( 1H , 'SUB2: ',   4x, 3 ( 1x, i3.3 ),
   -                5x, 3 ( 1x, f4.1 ),
   -                6x, 3 ( 1x, 1H[, a3, 1H] ) )
      return
      end
```

The program generates this display (n.b., program and subprogram names have been removed):

001	002	003	004	5.0	6.0	7.0	8.0	[ix]	[x]	[xi]	[xii]
001				5.0				[ix]			
001				5.0				[ix]			
002				6.0				[x]			
003				7.0				[xi]			
004				8.0				[xii]			
002	003	004		6.0	7.0	8.0		[x]	[xi]	[xii]	
001	002	003	004	5.0	6.0	7.0	8.0	[ix]	[x]	[xi]	[xii]

A C program that accomplishes the same function is as follows:

```
     main ( )
     {
     int     j;
     int     i          =    1;
     int     iarray[3]  = {  2,    3,    4     };
     float   r          =    5.0F;
     float   rarray[3]  = {  6.0F, 7.0F, 8.0F };
     char   *c          =    "ix ";
     char    carray[3]  = {  "x ", "xi ", "xii" };
     void sub1 ( int, iarray[ ], float,char * );
     void sub2 ( int iarray[ ], float rarray[ ],
               char *carray[ ] );
     printf ( " \ nMAIN: %3.3i %3.3i %3.3i %3.3i "
               "%4.1f %4.1f %4.1f %4.1f "
               "[%3s] [%3s] [%3s] [%3s] \ n",
               i, iarray[0], iarray[1], iarray[2],
```

```
             r,  rarray[0],  rarray[1],  rarray[2],
             c, carray[0], carray[1], carray[2] );
        printf ( " \ n" );
        sub1 ( i,          r,      c          );
        printf ( " \ n" );
        sub1 ( 1,          5.0,   "ix "       );
        printf ( " \ n" );
        for ( j = 0; j < = 2; j + + ) {
             sub1 ( iarray[j], rarray[j], carray[j] );
        }
        printf ( " \ n" );
        sub2 ( iarray,   rarray,   carray );
        printf ( " \ nMAIN:  %3.3i %3.3i %3.3i %3.3i "
                           "%4.1f %4.1f %4.1f %4.1f "
                           "[%3s] [%3s] [%3s] [%3s] \ n",
                      i, iarray[0],      iarray[1],  iarray[2],
                      r, rarray[0],      rarray[1],  rarray[2],
                      c, carray[0],   carray[1],  carray[2]     );
        printf ( " \ n" );
        return;
    }
    void sub1 ( int i, float r, char *c )
{
    printf ( "SUB1: %3.3i         "
                   "%4.1f          "
                   "[%3s] \ n",
                    i, r, c );
    return;
}
    void sub2 ( int iarray[ ], float rarray[ ],
             char *carray[ ] )
{
    printf ( "SUB2:    %3.3i %3.3i %3.3i"
                 "     %4.1f %4.1f %4.1f"
                 "       [%3s] [%3s] [%3s] \ n",
                  iarray[0],   iarray[1],  iarray[2],
                  rarray[0],  rarray[1],  rarray[2],
                  carray[0],  carray[1],  carray[2]     );
    return;
}
```

Both programs invoke subprogram sub1 in two different ways. First, the single variables i, r, and c are specified as the arguments to sub1. Second, sub1 is invoked three times; and each time, a different element of the arrays iarray, rarray, and carray are specified as arguments. The second subroutine, sub2, is then invoked with all three arrays—iarray, rarray, and carray—passed in their entirety as arguments.

Before the ANSI C standard was developed, the data type of a C function was declared only when it was not an integer, and arguments were declared in separate lines. For example, the first few lines of a pre-ANSI version of the C example program sub1 function would be as follows:

```
void sub1 ( )
    int     i;
    float   r;
    char  *c;
{
    (body of function)
}
```

The function would have been declared in the main program as follows:

```
void sub1 ( );
```

Advantages of the current ANSI specification is that the number and type of a function's arguments are known by the main program, and the first line of the function is virtually a duplicate of the function prototype statement that appeared in the main program.

Fortran requires that each subroutine or function name must be unique across the entire program. C does not have such a requirement. In C, if a function is declared with a static qualifier, then it is local to the source code file in which it appears. Static functions supersede a global function of the same name. Furthermore, static functions cannot be invoked by any function not in the same source code file. For example, the function sub1 is defined globally in this source code file:

```
main ( )
{
    void sub1 ( );
    void static2 ( );
    printf ( "STATIC1 source code file: "
            "top of MAIN program. \ n" );
    sub1( );
    static2( );
    sub1( );
    printf ( "STATIC1 source code file: "
            "bottom of MAIN program. \ n" );
    return;
}
    void sub1 ( )
{
    printf ( "STATIC1 source code file: "
            "SUB1 function. \ n" );
    return;
}
```

In this source code file, sub1 is declared locally:

```
void static2 ( )
{
    static void sub1 ( );
```

```
        printf ( "STATIC2 source code file: "
                "top of STATIC2 function. \ n" );
        sub1( );
        printf( "STATIC2 source code file: "
                "bottom of STATIC2 function. \ n");
        return;
    }
        static void sub1 ( )
    {
        printf ( " \ nSTATIC2 source code file: "
                "SUB1 function. \ n \ n" );
        return;
    }
```

When both source code files are compiled and linked as one program and then run, the following display is generated:

STATIC1 source code file: top of MAIN program.
STATIC1 source code file: SUB1 function.
STATIC2 source code file: top of STATIC2 function.

STATIC2 source code file: SUB1 function.

STATIC2 source code file: bottom of STATIC2 function.
STATIC1 source code file: SUB1 function.
STATIC1 source code file: bottom of MAIN program.

This program demonstrates that different functions with the same name can co-exist in the same program, with only one restriction: at most, one version of the function is global and all others are declared static in the source code file in which they appear.

Write

Fortran	write (NUMBER, LABEL) VARIABLE
	write (UNIT=N,REC=N,ERR=LAB) VARIABLE
	write (ARRAY, LAB, ERR=LAB) VARIABLE
C Primary	fprintf, fwrite, sprintf
C Secondary	! = , fclose, FILE, fopen, fseek, sizeof, struct

Fortran file output is accomplished through the use of the write statement. Four distinct file types can be processed by the write statement: formatted sequential access files, list-directed sequential access files, unformatted direct access files, and internal files. Each of these file types will be described in turn.

Formatted sequential access files represent the modern analogue of yesterday's line printer. Such "flat files" are often the means to export data from one application for subsequent processing by another application program. The following Fortran program writes a sequential access file and displays what is being written:

```
      program main
      integer  i(3), j, iunit
      real      r(3)
      character*3  c(3)
      data i/  1,      2,      3      /
      data r/  2.0,    3.0,    4.0    /
      data c/  'abc',  'def',  'ghi'  /
      iunit = 7
      open ( unit=iunit, file='writesf.dat' )
      do 6 j = 1, 3, 1
         write ( iunit,1,err=2 ) i(j), r(j), c(j)
1     format ( i1, 1x, f3.1, 1x, a3 )
      go to 4
2        continue
         write ( 6,3 ) j
3        format ( 1H , 'WRITE error ... record ',
     -                 i1, ' skipped!' )
         go to 6
4     continue
      write ( 6,5 ) j, i(j), r(j), c(j)
5     format ( 1H , 'Record ', i5.5, ': ',
     -                 i1, 1x, f3.1, 1x, a3 )
6     continue
      write ( 6,8 ) j-1
8     format ( 1H , 'Last data record was ', i5.5, '.' )
      close ( unit=iunit )
      stop
      end
```

175

It uses this data file

    1 2.0 abc
    2 3.0 def
    3 4.0 ghi

and generates this display:

    Record 00001: 1 2.0 abc
    Record 00002: 2 3.0 def
    Record 00003: 3 4.0 ghi
    Last data record was 00003.

A C program that accomplishes the same function is as follows:

```
#include <stdio.h>
main ( )
{
    int     j;
    int     i[3]    = {  1,      2,       3       };
    float   r[3]    = {  2.0F,   3.0F,    4.0F    };
    char    *c[3]   = {  "abc",  "def",   "ghi"   };
    FILE    *iunit;
    int     bytes;
    iunit = fopen ( "writesf.dat", "wa" );
    for ( j=0; j<=2; j++ ) {
        bytes = fprintf ( iunit, "%i %3.1f %3s \ n",
                          i[j], r[j], c[j]        );
        if ( bytes < 0 ) {
            printf ( "WRITE error ... "
                     "record %i skipped! \ n", j );
        }
        else
            printf ( "Record %5.5i: %i %3.1f %3s \ n",
                     j, i[j], r[j], c[j]                     );
    }
    printf ( "Last data record was %5.5i. \ n", j );
    fclose ( iunit );
    return;
}
```

Both programs open the same type of output file. By default, Fortran will open the file with the keyword for the access option set to SEQUEN- TIAL and the keyword for the form option set to FORMATTED. C's fopen function is explicitly told to open the file for output to the file's end in text mode. Then, three records are written into the file. Fortran's write state- ment is programmed here with an error trap that will inform the user, by record number, where the write error occurred. C's fprintf function returns the number of bytes written into the file. The program displays an error

176

message if fprintf signals a problem in updating the file (by returning a negative number as the number of bytes written). Finally, the number of records written is reported to the user, and the single output file is closed.

List-directed sequential access files are convenient because they avoid the requirement to develop a detailed output layout and to code a format statement. The following Fortran program writes three records into a file in a list-directed format:

```
      program main
      integer      i(3), j, iunit
      real         r(3)
      character*3  c(3)
      data i/ 1,      2,      3       /
      data r/ 2.0,    3.0,    4.0     /
      data c/ 'abc', 'def', 'ghi' /
      iunit = 7
      open ( unit=iunit, file='writeslf.dat' )
      do 6 j = 1, 3, 1
         write ( iunit,*,err=2 ) i( j ), r( j ), c( j )
         go to 4
2        continue
         write ( 6,3 ) j
3        format ( 1H , 'WRITE error ... record ',
    -                 i1, ' skipped!' )
         go to 6
4        continue
         write ( 6,5 ) j, i( j ), r( j ), c( j )
5        format ( 1H , 'Record ', i5.5, ': ',
    -                 i1, 1x, f3.1, 1x, a3 )
6  continue
      write ( 6,8 ) j-1
8  format ( 1H , 'Last data record was ', i5.5, '.' )
      close ( unit=iunit )
      stop
      end
```

It creates this output file:

```
1    2.000000abc
2    3.000000def
3    4.000000ghi
```

The program also generates this display:

```
Record 00001: 1 2.0 abc
Record 00002: 2 3.0 def
Record 00003: 3 4.0 ghi
Last data record was 00003.
```

A C program that accomplishes the same function is as follows:

```
#include <stdio.h>
main ()
{
int      j;
int      i[3]  = {  1,      2,      3       };
float    r[3]  = {  2.0F,   3.0F,   4.0F    };
char    *c[3]  = {  "abc",  "def",  "ghi"   };
FILE    *iunit;
int      bytes;
iunit = fopen ( "writeslc.dat", "wa" );
for ( j=0; j< =2; j++ ) {
    bytes = fprintf ( iunit, "%i %f %s \ n",
                      i[j], r[j], c[j] )   ;
    if ( bytes < 0 ) {
        printf ( "WRITE error ... "
                "record %i skipped! \ n", j );
    }
    else
        printf ( "Record %5.5i: %i %3.1f %3s \ n",
                 j, i[j], r[j], c[j] )   ;
}
printf ( "Last data record was %5.5i. \ n", j );
fclose ( iunit );
return;
}
```

It creates this output file:

```
1    2.000000 abc
2    3.000000 def
3    4.000000 ghi
```

The program also generates the identical display as the Fortran example program.

Both programs open the same type of output file. By default, Fortran will open the file with the keyword for the access option set to SEQUEN-TIAL and the keyword for the form option set to FORMATTED. C's fopen function is explicitly told to open the file for output to the file's end in text mode. Then, three records are written into the file. Fortran's write statement is programmed here with an error trap that will inform the user, by record number, where the write error occurred. Fortran writes each numeric value, right-justified, into an implementation-defined fixed-length field (i.e., 12 bytes long for integers and 16 bytes long for reals) and left-justifies character data into a field exactly as long as the character string. C's fprintf function returns the number of bytes written into the file. The program displays an error message if fprintf signals a problem in updating the file (by returning a negative number as the number of bytes written). C writes each field separated by as many spaces as appear

178

between each format specification in the fprintf statement. Finally, the number of records written is reported to the user, and the single output file is closed.

Unformatted direct access files are the only "structured" file directly supported by Fortran. The following Fortran program writes three records:

```fortran
      program main
      integer      i(3), j, iunit
      real         r(3)
      character*3  c(3)
      data i /  1,      2,      3      /
      data r /  2.0,    3.0,    4.0    /
      data c / 'abc',  'def',  'ghi'   /
      iunit = 7
      open ( unit=iunit, file='writedf.dat',
     -       access='direct', recl=11 )
      do 6 j = 1, 3, 1
         write ( iunit,rec=j,err=2 ) i(j), r(j), c(j)
         go to 4
2        continue
         write ( 6,3 ) j
3        format ( 1H , 'WRITE error ... record ',
     -                  i1, ' skipped!' )
         go to 6
4        continue
         write ( 6,5 ) j, i(j), r(j), c(j)
5        format ( 1H , 'Record ', i5.5, ': ',
     -                  i1, 1x, f3.1, 1x, a3 )
6     continue
      write ( 6,8 ) j-1
8     format ( 1H , 'Last data record was ', i5.5, '.' )
      close ( unit=iunit )
      stop
      end
```

The program generates this display:

```
Record 00001: 1 2.0 abc
Record 00002: 2 3.0 def
Record 00003: 3 4.0 ghi
Last data record was 00003.
```

A C program that accomplishes the same function is as follows:

```c
#include <stdio.h>
main ( )
{
int      j;
FILE    *iunit;
int      items;
```

```
int     count = 3;
struct  binary  { long    i;
                  float   r;
                  char    c[4];   }
                  record [3] =
                  { 1L, 2.0F,  'a','b','c','\0',
                    2L, 3.0F,  'd','e','f','\0',
                    3L, 4.0F,  'g','h','i','\0' };
iunit  = fopen  ( "writedc.dat", "wb+" );
items  = fwrite (  record, sizeof ( struct binary ),
                   count, iunit );
for ( j = 0; j < = 2; j++ ) {
    printf ( "Record %5.5i: %ld %f %s \n",
    j, record[j].i, record[j].r, record[j].c );
}
printf ( "Last data record was %5.5i. \n", j );
fclose ( iunit );
return;
}
```

It generates a display identical to the Fortran example program.

Both programs opened similar files. These two files were nearly identical but differ in the length of each logical record. Fortran wrote eleven bytes into the file for each logical record: four for the integer variable, four for the real variable, and three for the character string. C wrote twelve bytes into the file for each logical record: four for the int variable, four for the float variable, and four for the character string (i.e., three characters plus the null character—\0—used to terminate the string). Consequently, direct access files that contain any character data are not interchangeable between Fortran and C unless the null character is handled explicitly. For files written by a Fortran program to be read by a C program, an additional variable needs to be output after each character string. This variable should be defined as

```
character*1 null
```

and initialized as

```
null = char ( 0 )
```

For files written by a C program to be read by a Fortran program, an additional variable defined just as the null variable above needs to be read and disregarded after processing each character string.

Fortran wrote each record individually from integer, real, and character three-element arrays. C's fwrite function performs unformatted output of the entire file at a time where the individual variables are combined into a C struct construct. In the C example program, individual variables i, r, and the c character array are combined into a C struct named binary. Three instances of this struct, record[3], are then defined. C's fwrite function writes all three variables across all three instances at once into the file. The length of the struct is computed by the sizeof function; and all three instances of record is processed in one write because fwrite's third argument, the variable count, is set to three. If the file can be written, fwrite returns the number of instances of record processed correctly (i.e., variables items and count will be equal).

The C example program could have been written to write one record at a time with the following code:

```
count = 1
for ( j=0; j< =2; j++ ) {
    items = fwrite ( &record[j],
                    sizeof ( struct record[j] ),
                    count, iunit                    )
}
```

Under that syntax, any given record could be rewritten by positioning the file to the beginning of that record, as

```
position = ( j − 1 ) * ( sizeof ( record[j] ) );
fseek ( iunit, position, SEEK_SET );
```

changing the value of record[j].i, record[j].r, and/or record[j].c, and then invoking fwrite to update the file. This method of file positioning is the same one used earlier in this chapter in the section on the Fortran read statement.

ANSI 77 standard Fortran permits in-memory buffers to be treated as if they were files. The following Fortran program writes such a buffer:

```
      program main
      integer       i(3),j
      real          r(3)
      character*3   c(3)
      character*9   buffer(3)
      data i/  1,    2,    3     /
      data r/  2.0,  3.0,  4.0   /
      data c/  'abc', 'def', 'ghi'  /
      do 6 j = 1, 3, 1
         write ( buffer(j),1,err=2 ) i(j), r(j), c(j)
1        format ( i1, 1x, f3.1, 1x, a3 )
         go to 4
2        continue
         write ( 6,3 ) j
3        format ( 1H , 'WRITE error ... buffer ',
   -                  i1,' skipped!' )
         go to 6
4        continue
         write ( 6,5 ) j, buffer(j)
5        format ( 1H , 'Record ', i5.5, ': ', a9 )
6 continue
   write ( 6,8 ) j-1
```

```
8 format ( 1H , 'Last data buffer was ', i5.5, '.' )
  stop
  end
```

The program generates this display:

```
Record 00001: 1 2.0 abc
Record 00002: 2 3.0 def
Record 00003: 3 4.0 ghi
Last data buffer was 00003.
```

A C program that accomplishes the same function is as follows:

```c
#include <stdio.h>
main( )
{
    int     j;
    int     i[3]  = {  1,     2,     3     };
    float   r[3]  = {  2.0,   3.0,   4.0   };
    char    *c[3] = {  "abc", "def", "ghi" };
    struct  record  {  char cc[10]; } buffer[3];
    int     bytes;
    for ( j=0; j<=2; j++ ) {
        bytes = sprintf ( buffer[j].cc,"%i %3.1f %3s",
                                i[j], r[j], c[j]          );
        if ( bytes != 9 ) {
            printf ( "Write error ... "
                     "buffer %i skipped! \n", j+1 );
        }
        else
            printf ( "Record %5.5i: %s \n",
                      j+1, buffer[j].cc );
    }
    printf ( "Last data buffer was %5.5i. \n", j );
    return;
}
```

Both programs "write" an in-memory character array named buffer. Fortran declares a three-element array called buffer in which each element is nine characters long. C specifies a struct of a type named record that contains a single ten-character array and declares three instances of such a struct to exist in the buffer array.

Fortran supports processing such character arrays through the use of the write statement. If an error occurs, the err option on the write statement is exercised and control passes to a series of statements that will display an error message. C's sprintf function writes numeric and/or character data into character strings from a list of individual variables. The number of bytes correctly written is returned by the sprintf function into the variable bytes. If nine bytes are not written, an error message is produced. Finally, both programs report the number of buffers processed.

6
Arrays

Arrays are integral to scientific computing. Referred to as vectors, tables, or matrices, arrays allows large amounts of information to be structured in a way meaningful to the numerical problem at hand. Fortran allows arrays of multiple dimensions and user-specified ranges for the index of each dimension, thereby providing a flexible way to create and manipulate arrays. Data is stored in a Fortran array in column-major order. Likewise, C allows arrays of multiple dimensions. By default, however, C does not support user-specified index ranges. Data is stored in a C array in row-major order. Differences between Fortran and C array handling are instructive and manageable.

This chapter will concentrate on six issues regarding C arrays: row-major data storage, ranging array indices, pointers to arrays and arrays of pointers, run-time array dimensioning, character arrays, and structures.

Array data storage

Fortran permits arrays to have up to seven dimensions and stores array data in column-major order. Column-major order requires that array elements in the last declared dimension are stored in adjacent memory locations and in ascending index order followed by elements in the next-to-last declared dimension, etc. For example, if the following 3 by 3 table

```
1  4  7
2  5  8
3  6  9
```

was stored in a Fortran array called m, then values for m(1,1), m(2,1), and m(3,1) would be followed by values for m(1,2), m(2,2), and m(3,2), which would in turn be followed by values for m(1,3), m(2,3), and m(3,3). Examination of these nine adjacent memory locations would show the following:

1 2 3 4 5 6 7 8 9

C permits arrays to have up to twelve dimensions and stores array data in row-major order. Row-major order requires that array elements in the first declared dimension are stored in adjacent memory locations and in ascending index order followed by elements in the next declared dimension, etc. In other words, if the preceding table was stored in a C array called m, then values for m(1,1), m(1,2), and m(1,3) would be followed by values for m(2,1), m(2,2), and m(2,3), which would in turn be followed by values for m(3,1), m(3,2), and m(3,3). Examination of these nine adjacent memory locations would show the following:

1 4 7 2 5 8 3 6 9

Column- and row-major storage techniques are further demonstrated in FIG. 6-1 and FIG. 6-2. In the Fortran program, seven arrays are declared with one, two, three, four, five, six, and seven dimensions, respectively, where each dimension contains two elements. Initialized in a single nested do loop, each array element is assigned a number equal to its storage location by varying the first index most quickly. The Fortran subroutine display takes as arguments the number of elements per dimension, the number of dimensions, the name of the array, and the total number of elements in the array. Dimensioning the dummy name for the array as a one-dimensional vector of length size allows the array to be written in the order in which it is stored.

6-1 Fortran array sample program.

```
      program main
      integer   one, two, three, four, five, six, seven
      integer   n1, n2, n3,   n4,  n5,  n6, n7, n
      integer   i1, i2, i3,   i4,  i5,  i6, i7, k
      dimension one(2),            two(2,2),
     -          three(2,2,2),      four(2,2,2,2),
     -          five(2,2,2,2,2),   six(2,2,2,2,2,2),
     -          seven(2,2,2,2,2,2,2)
      n  = 2
      n1 =       n
      n2 = n1 * n
      n3 = n2 * n
      n4 = n3 * n
      n5 = n4 * n
      n6 = n5 * n
      n7 = n6 * n
      k  = 0
```

```
do 1 i7 = 1, n, 1
do 1 i6 = 1, n, 1
do 1 i5 = 1, n, 1
do 1 i4 = 1, n, 1
do 1 i3 = 1, n, 1
do 1 i2 = 1, n, 1
do 1 i1 = 1, n, 1
k = k + 1
if ( k .le. n1 ) one(i1) = k
if ( k .le. n2 ) two(i1,i2) = k
if ( k .le. n3 ) three(i1,i2,i3) = k
if ( k .le. n4 ) four(i1,i2,i3,i4) = k
if ( k .le. n5 ) five(i1,i2,i3,i4,i5) = k
if ( k .le. n6 ) six(i1,i2,i3,i4,i5,i6) = k
                 seven(i1,i2,i3,i4,i5,i6,i7) = k
1 continue
call display ( n, 1, one, n1 )
call display ( n, 2, two, n2 )
call display ( n, 3, three, n3 )
call display ( n, 4, four, n4 )
call display ( n, 5, five, n5 )
call display ( n, 6, six, n6 )
call display ( n, 7, seven, n7 )
stop
end
subroutine display ( elements, dimensions, array, size )
integer elements, dimensions, array, size
dimension array(size)
write ( 6,1 ) dimensions, elements
1 format ( / 1H, 'Display of ', i1, '-dimensional array ',
-                'with ', i1, ' elements per dimension ...' )
write ( 6,2 ) array
2 format ( 16 ( 1x, i3 ) )
return
end
```

Display of 1-dimensional array with 2 elements per dimension . . .
```
   1    2
```

Display of 2-dimensional array with 2 elements per dimension . . .
```
   1    2    3    4
```

Display of 3-dimensional array with 2 elements per dimension . . .
```
   1    2    3    4    5    6    7    8
```

Display of 4-dimensional array with 2 elements per dimension . . .
```
   1    2    3    4    5    6    7    8    9   10   11   12   13   14   15   16
```

Display of 5-dimensional array with 2 elements per dimension . . .
```
   1    2    3    4    5    6    7    8    9   10   11   12   13   14   15   16
  17   18   19   20   21   22   23   24   25   26   27   28   29   30   31   32
```

6-1 Continued.

Display of 6-dimensional array with 2 elements per dimension . . .

1	2	3	4	5	6	7	8	9	10	11	12	13	14	15	16
17	18	19	20	21	22	23	24	25	26	27	28	29	30	31	32
33	34	35	36	37	38	39	40	41	42	43	44	45	46	47	48
49	50	51	52	53	54	55	56	57	58	59	60	61	62	63	64

Display of 7-dimensional array with 2 elements per dimension . . .

1	2	3	4	5	6	7	8	9	10	11	12	13	14	15	16
17	18	19	20	21	22	23	24	25	26	27	28	29	30	31	32
33	34	35	36	37	38	39	40	41	42	43	44	45	46	47	48
49	50	51	52	53	54	55	56	57	58	59	60	61	62	63	64
65	66	67	68	69	70	71	72	73	74	75	76	77	78	79	80
81	82	83	84	85	86	87	88	89	90	91	92	93	94	95	96
97	98	99	100	101	102	103	104	105	106	107	108	109	110	111	112
113	114	115	116	117	118	119	120	121	122	123	124	125	126	127	128

6-2 C array sample program.

```
#define n 2
main ( )
{
int     one[n];
int     two[n][n];
int     three[n][n][n];
int     four[n][n][n][n];
int     five[n][n][n][n][n];
int     six[n][n][n][n][n][n];
int     seven[n][n][n][n][n][n][n];
int     n1,  n2,  n3,  n4,  n5,  n6,  n7;
int     i1,  i2,  i3,  i4,  i5,  i6,  i7,  k;
void  display ( int elements, int dimensions,
                int *array, int size   );
n1  =        n;
n2  = n1 * n;
n3  = n2 * n;
n4  = n3 * n;
n5  = n4 * n;
n6  = n5 * n;
n7  = n6 * n;
k  = 0;
for (   i7 = 0; i7 < n; i7 + +   ) {
 for (   i6 = 0; i6 < n; i6 + +   ) {
  for (   i5 = 0; i5 < n; i5 + +   ) {
   for (   i4 = 0; i4 < n; i4 + +   ) {
    for (   i3 = 0; i3 < n; i3 + +   ) {
     for (   i2 = 0; i2 < n; i2 + +   ) {
      for (   i1 = 0; i1 < n; i1 + +   ) {
       k = k + 1;
       if (   k < = n1   ) one[i1] = k;
```

```
                if (  k < = n2  )   two[i2][i1] = k;
                if (  k < = n3  )   three[i3][i2][i1] = k;
                if (  k < = n4  )   four[i4][i3][i2][i1] = k;
                if (  k < = n5  )   five[i5][i4][i3][i2][i1] = k;
                if (  k < = n6  )   six[i6][i5][i4][i3][i2][i1] = k;
                                    seven[i7][i6][i5][i4][i3][i2][i1] = k;


              }
            }
          }
        }
      }
    }
  }
    display  (  n,   1,   &one[0], n1  );
    display  (  n,   2,   &two[0][0], n2  );
    display  (  n,   3,   &three[0][0][0], n3  );
    display  (  n,   4,   &four[0][0][0][0], n4  );
    display  (  n,   5,   &five[0][0][0][0][0], n5  );
    display  (  n,   6,   &six[0][0][0][0][0][0], n6  );
    display  (  n,   7,   &seven[0][0][0][0][0][0][0], n7  );
    return;
}

void display  (  int elements, int dimensions,
                 int  *array,     int size  )
{
    int i,   j,  k;
    printf ( "Display of %i-dimensional array "
           "with %i elements per dimension ... \ n",
           dimensions, elements  );
    j =  - 1;
     for  (  i=0;   i < size ;  i + +   )  {
            for    ( k = 1;  k < = 16; k + +   ) {
                 j + = 1;
                 if ( j > = size )
                        break;
                 else
                        printf (   " %3i", *(array + j)  );
        }
        if     ( j < size-1  )
                printf (   " \ n"  );
    }
    printf (   " \ n \ n"  );
    return;
}
```

Display of 1-dimensional array with 2 elements per dimension . . .
   1   2

Display of 2-dimensional array with 2 elements per dimension . . .
   1   2   3   4

Display of 3-dimensional array with 2 elements per dimension . . .

1	2	3	4	5	6	7	8

Display of 4-dimensional array with 2 elements per dimension . . .

1	2	3	4	5	6	7	8	9	10	11	12	13	14	15	16

Display of 5-dimensional array with 2 elements per dimension . . .

1	2	3	4	5	6	7	8	9	10	11	12	13	14	15	16
17	18	19	20	21	22	23	24	25	26	27	28	29	30	31	32

Display of 6-dimensional array with 2 elements per dimension . . .

1	2	3	4	5	6	7	8	9	10	11	12	13	14	15	16
17	18	19	20	21	22	23	24	25	26	27	28	29	30	31	32
33	34	35	36	37	38	39	40	41	42	43	44	45	46	47	48
49	50	51	52	53	54	55	56	57	58	59	60	61	62	63	64

Display of 7-dimensional array with 2 elements per dimension . . .

1	2	3	4	5	6	7	8	9	10	11	12	13	14	15	16
17	18	19	20	21	22	23	24	25	26	27	28	29	30	31	32
33	34	35	36	37	38	39	40	41	42	43	44	45	46	47	48
49	50	51	52	53	54	55	56	57	58	59	60	61	62	63	64
65	66	67	68	69	70	71	72	73	74	75	76	77	78	79	80
81	82	83	84	85	86	87	88	89	90	91	92	93	94	95	96
97	98	99	100	101	102	103	104	105	106	107	108	109	110	111	112
113	114	115	116	117	118	119	120	121	122	123	124	125	126	127	128

In the C program, the same seven arrays are declared with the same number of dimensions and number of elements per dimension. Initialized in a series of nested for loops, each array element is assigned a number equal to its storage location by varying the last index most quickly. The C function display takes as arguments the number of elements per dimension, the number of dimensions, the address of the first element in the array, and the total number of elements in the array. Declaring the name for the array as a pointer to an int data type allows the array to be accessed in storage order when written. If these seven arrays had been initialized in the C program in the same manner as the Fortran program, then they would be displayed as in FIG. 6-3. Such a display clearly shows the difference between Fortran's column-major and C's row-major array storage priority. Given the major difference between Fortran and C array storage techniques, array index manipulation needs to be carefully examined when recasting a Fortran program into the C programming language.

Array index range

By default, each dimension of a Fortran array is indexed by a number ranging from one to the number of elements in that dimension of the array. User-specified index ranges are supported by Fortran so that negative, zero, or positive integer valued indices are valid for any given dimen-

```
.
.
.
for (  i7 = 0; i7 < ; i7 + +   )  {
 for (  i6 = 0; i6 < ; i6 + +   )  {
  for (  i5 = 0; i5 < ; i5 + +   )  {
   for (  i4 = 0; i4 < ; i4 + +   )  {
    for (  i3 = 0; i3 < ; i3 + +   )  {
     for (  i2 = 0; i2 < ; i2 + +   )  {
      for (  i1 = 0; i1 < ; i1 + +   )  {
      k = k + 1;
      if (  k < = n1   ) one[i1] = k;
      if (  k < = n2   ) two[i1][i2] = k;
      if (  k < = n3   ) three[i1][i2][i3] = k;
      if (  k < = n4   ) four[i1][i2][i3][i4] = k;
      if (  k < = n5   ) five[i1][i2][i3][i4][i5] = k;
      if (  k < = n6   )  six[i1][i2][i3][i4][i5][i6] = k;
                         seven[i1][i2][i3][i4][i5][i6][i7] = k;
       }
      }
     }
    }
   }
  }
 }
.
.
.
```

Display of 1-dimensional array with 2 elements per dimension . . .
```
  1   2
```

Display of 2-dimensional array with 2 elements per dimension . . .
```
  1   3   2   4
```

Display of 3-dimensional array with 2 elements per dimension . . .
```
  1   5   3   7   2   6   4   8
```

Display of 4-dimensional array with 2 elements per dimension . . .
```
  1   9   5  13   3  11   7  15   2  10   6  14   4  12   8  16
```

Display of 5-dimensional array with 2 elements per dimension . . .
```
  1  17   9  25   5  21  13  29   3  19  11  27   7  23  15  31
  2  18  10  26   6  22  14  30   4  20  12  28   8  24  16  32
```

Display of 6-dimensional array with 2 elements per dimension . . .
```
  1  33  17  49   9  41  25  57   5  37  21  53  13  45  29  61
  3  35  19  51  11  43  27  59   7  39  23  55  15  47  31  63
  2  34  18  50  10  42  26  58   6  38  22  54  14  46  30  62
  4  36  20  52  12  44  28  60   8  40  24  56  16  48  32  64
```

6-3 Continued.

Display of 7-dimensional array with 2 elements per dimension . . .

1	65	33	97	17	81	49	113	9	73	41	105	25	89	57	121
5	69	37	101	21	85	53	117	13	77	45	109	29	93	61	125
3	67	35	99	19	83	51	115	11	75	43	107	27	91	59	123
7	71	39	103	23	87	55	119	15	79	47	111	31	95	63	127
2	66	34	98	18	82	50	114	10	74	42	106	26	90	58	122
6	70	38	102	22	86	54	118	14	78	46	110	30	94	62	126
4	68	36	100	20	84	52	116	12	76	44	108	28	92	60	124
8	72	40	104	24	88	56	120	16	80	48	112	32	96	64	128

sion of an array. Figure 6-4 declares four arrays: minus with wholly negative indices; split with negative, zero, and positive indices; normal with default indices; and plus with wholly positive indices offset from unity. The single do loop initializes each successive element for all four arrays to the same value by calculating the array index as an offset from the value of i, the loop control variable. After the value of the first and last element and index range of all four arrays is displayed, the contents of the arrays split and normal are written.

6-4 Fortran array index sample program.

```
      program main
      integer    minus,        split,      normal,     plus,       i
      dimension minus(-9:-3), split(-3:3), normal(7), plus(3:9)
      do 1 i=1, 7, 1
      minus(i-10) = i
      split(i-4) = i
      normal(i) = i
      plus(i+2) = i
    1 continue
      write ( 6,2 )
    2 format ( 1H )
      write ( 6,3 )
    3 format ( 1H , '            First Element          Last Element'
     -       / 1H , 'Array      Index    Value          Index     Value'
     -       / 1H , '-------    ----     ----           ----      ----' )
      write ( 6,4 )   minus(-9),  minus(-3),  split(-3), split(3),
     -                normal(1),  normal(7),  plus(3),   plus(9)
    4 format ( 1H , 'minus            -9', i8, '        -3', i7
     -       / 1H , 'split            -3', i8, '         3', i7
     -       / 1H , 'normal            1', i8, '         7', i7
     -       / 1H , 'plus              3', i8, '         9', i7
      write ( 6,5 )   ( split(i), i=-3, 3 )
    5 format ( / 1H , 'split array:', 7i2 )
      write ( 6,6 )   ( normal(i), i=1, 7 )
    6 format ( / 1H , 'normal array:', 7i2 )
      write ( 6,2 )
      stop
      end
```

6-4 Continued.

Array	First Element Index	First Element Value	Last Element Index	Last Element Value
minus	-9	1	-3	7
split	-3	1	3	7
normal	1	1	7	7
plus	3	1	9	7

split array: 1 2 3 4 5 6 7

normal array: 1 2 3 4 5 6 7

Coded in C, FIG. 6-5 shows the same kind of program. All four arrays are declared with seven elements per row, and an array index offset value is initialized for each array (i.e., m for the array minus, s for the array split, etc.). Initializing each array is accomplished in the first for loop where the array index is calculated as an offset from the value of i, the loop control variable. As in the Fortran version, the value of the first and last element and array index of those values for all four arrays is displayed. In each case, the first and last array index values are zero and six, respectively, because each dimension of a C array is indexed from zero to one less than the number of elements in that dimension.

6-5 C array index sample program.

```
main ( )
{
int    minus[7], split[7],  normal[7],  plus[7], i;
int    m=0,     s=0,      n=0,        p=0;
int    *SPLIT;
int    *NORMAL;
m  - =  -9;
s  - =  -3;
n  - =   1;
p  - =   3;
for ( i=1; i< =7; i+ + ) {
      minus[i+m-10] = i;
      split[i+s-4]     = i;
      normal[i+n]      = i;
      plus[i+p+2]      = i;
}
printf ( " \ n" );
printf (   "              First Element     Last Element \ n"
           "Array     Index    Value     Index      Value \ n"
           " -----     ----    ------     ----     -----\ n" );
printf (   "minus      %i      %i       %i        %i \ n"
           "split      %i      %i       %i        %i \ n"
           "normal     %i      %i       %i        %i \ n"
           "plus       %i      %i       %i        %i \ n",
           m-9,  minus[m-9],  m-3,  minus[m-3],
```

```
                  s − 3,    split[s − 3],   s + 3,   split[s + 3],
                  n + 1,    normal[n + 1],  n + 7,   normal[n + 7],
                  p + 3,    plus[p + 3],    p + 9,   plus[p + 9]                    );
     SPLIT = &split[3];
     printf ( " \ nsplit array:" );
     for ( i = − 3; i < = 3; i + + ) {
          printf ( "%2i", SPLIT[i] );
     }
     printf ( " \ n" );
     NORMAL = normal − 1;
     printf ( " \ nnormal array:" );
     for ( i = 1; i < = 7; i + + ) {
          printf ( "%2i", NORMAL[i] );
     }
     printf ( " \ n" );
     return;
     }
```

Array	First Element Index	First Element Value	Last Element Index	Last Element Value
minus	0	1	6	7
split	0	1	6	7
normal	0	1	6	7
plus	0	1	6	7

split array: 1 2 3 4 5 6 7

normal array: 1 2 3 4 5 6 7

As an alternative to an array index syntax with an explicit offset variable, a pointer to what would be the zero element in the range for an array index can be declared and the array referenced through that pointer. For example, *SPLIT is a pointer to the int array called split and is initialized to the address of the fourth element of the split array. Consequently, valid array indices are 0 through 6 for split and −3 through 3 for SPLIT as shown in the for loop in which SPLIT is displayed. Fortran's default initial index of one versus C's default initial index of zero can be consolidated by initializing the pointer *NORMAL so that NORMAL [1] through NORMAL [7] are synonyms for normal[0] through normal[6]. Note two different ways of creating the SPLIT and NORMAL offset arrays: the methods used could have been reversed so that the two lines of code might read

```
SPLIT  =  split + 3
NORMAL  =  &normal[0]  −  1
```

because the name of an array is totally conforming to the address of the first element of that array. It is significant to fully appreciate that SPLIT and NORMAL are not duplicates of the split and normal arrays, respectively. They do add a slight amount of storage (i.e., usually two bytes, an exact measurement can be computed as sizeof(int *)) but that additional storage is independent of the size of the array. In Fortran terms, SPLIT and NORMAL have been "equivalence-d" to the split and normal arrays.

Pointers and arrays

Pointers to arrays are common in C language programs. As described in the previous paragraph, the name of an array is an equivalent syntax for the first element of that array. In FIG. 6-6, several arrays are alternatively referenced directly by or through a pointer. A 3-by-3 matrix named square is declared, initialized, and displayed row by row. Pointing to the address of the first element of square, successive elements of that array can be referenced through the pointer SQUARE as SQUARE + 0, SQUARE + 1, ..., SQUARE + 8 as shown in the second for loop. Alternatively, each row of the square array can be referenced through a pointer to the address of the initial element in each row. Whereas SQUARE was a single pointer to the beginning of the whole square array, Square is a three-element array of pointers where each element of Square points to the beginning of the respective row in the square matrix.

6-6 C arrays treated as pointers.

```
    main ( )
{
    int    i, j, k;
    int    square[3][3] = { 1, 2, 3, 4, 5, 6, 7, 8, 9 };
    int    *SQUARE;
    int    *Square[3];
    int    even[3][3] = { {10}, {40, 50}, {70, 80, 90} };
    int    *uneven[3];
    int    unrow0[1] = { 10 };
    int    unrow1[2] = { 40, 50 };
    int    unrow2[3] = { 70, 80, 90 };
    printf ( " \nsquare array ... \n" );
    for ( i = 0; i < 3; i + + ) {
        for ( j = 0; j < 3; j + + ) {
            printf ( " %i", square[i][j] );
        }
        printf ( " \n" );
    }
    SQUARE = &square[0][0];
    printf ( " \nSQUARE (1 pointer to "
            "square array) ... \n" );
    k = -1;
    for ( i = 0; i < 3; i + + ) {
        for ( j = 0; j < 3; j + + ) {
            k + = 1;
        printf ( " %i", *(SQUARE + k) );
        }
        printf ( " \n" );
```

6-6 Continued.

```
        }
    Square[0] = &square[0][0];
    Square[1] = &square[1][0];
    Square[2] = &square[2][0];
    printf ( "\nSquare (array of 3 pointers: "
            "1 per row of square array) ...\n" );
    for ( i = 0; i < 3; i + + ) {
        for ( j = 0; j < 3; j + + ) {
            printf ( " %i", Square[i][j] );
        }
        printf ( "\n" );
    }
    printf ( "\neven array (%i bytes) ...\n",
            sizeof ( even ) / sizeof ( int ) );
    for ( i = 0; i < 3; i + + ) {
        for ( j = 0; j < 3; j + + ) {
            printf ( " %2i", even[i][j] );
        }
        printf ( "\n" );
    }
    uneven[0] = &unrow0[0];
    uneven[1] = &unrow1[0];
    uneven[2] = &unrow2[0];
    k = sizeof ( unrow0 ) + sizeof ( unrow1 ) + sizeof ( unrow2 );
    k / = sizeof ( int );
    printf ( "\nuneven array (%i bytes) ...\n", k );
    for ( i = 0; i < 3; i + + ) {
        for ( j = 0; j < = i; j + + ) {
            printf ( " %2i", uneven[i][j] );
        }
        printf ( "\n" );
    }
    return;
}
```

```
square array ...
1   2   3
4   5   6
7   8   9


SQUARE (1 pointer to square array) ...
1   2   3
4   5   6
7   8   9


Square (array of 3 pointers: 1 per row of square array) ...
1   2   3
4   5   6
7   8   9


even array (9 bytes) ...
10   0   0
40  50   0
70  80  90
```

6-6 Continued.

```
uneven array (6 bytes) ...
10
40   50
70   80   90
```

A major advantage of pointer arrays is that each additional dimension need not be the same size. For example, the 3-by-3 triangular matrix even has six values on and below the diagonal and zero above and also requires twelve bytes of storage. A perfectly equivalent arrangement is the array of pointers called uneven in which successive rows have one, two, and three elements. As such, the storage required for uneven is six bytes for the three pointers in uneven and six bytes for the values in unrow0, unrow1, and unrow2. In this specific case, the total storage requirement is identical; but the slight storage required to create an array of pointers such as uneven could easily be amortized over longer individual rows to realize a net storage reduction using pointer arrays.

Dynamic array dimensions

C allows run-time array dimensioning. Fortran always requires the dimensions of an array to be totally fixed somewhere in a program, and this cannot be changed without re-compilation. Of course, smaller arrays can be processed by such a program, but storage for the full array is always set aside at each program invocation. Figure 6-7 is a C program in which the dimensions of a table called adjust are specified by the user on the command line that begins program execution.

6-7 C array memory allocation sample program.

```
#include <stdio.h>
#include <stdlib.h>
main ( int argc, char *argv[ ] )
{
    int      i, j, k;
    int      fixed[3][3]  =  { 1, 2, 3, 4, 5, 6, 7, 8, 9 };
    int      rows         =  0;
    int      columns      =  0;
    int      **adjust;
    void     adisplay ( int **array, int I, int J );
    void     fdisplay ( int array[3][3] );
    printf ( "\n%s program invoked with %i arguments ... \n",
             argv[0], argc - 1 );
    if ( argc != 3 ) {
        printf ( "ERROR! Usage is %s rows columns! \n",
                 argv[0] );
        exit ( EXIT__FAILURE );
    }
```

6-7 Continued.

```
        rows      = (int) strtol ( argv[1], NULL, 10 );
        columns   = (int) strtol ( argv[2], NULL, 10 );
        printf ( " \ nallocating space for %i x %i array ... \ n",
                rows, columns );
        adjust = ( int ** ) calloc ( (size__t) rows,
                                    (size__t) sizeof ( int ) );
        if ( adjust = = NULL ) {
            printf ( "ERROR! Can not allocate "
                    "per-row pointers! \ n" );
            exit ( EXIT__FAILURE );
        }
        for ( i = 0; i < rows; i + + ) {
            adjust[i] = ( int * ) calloc ( (size__t) columns,
                                    (size__t) sizeof ( int ) );
            if ( adjust[i] = = NULL ) {
                printf ( "ERROR! Can not allocate column"
                        "pointers for row %i! \ n" );
                exit ( EXIT__FAILURE );
            }
        }
        k = 0;
        for ( i = 0; i < rows; i + + ) {
            for ( j = 0; j < columns; j + + ) {
                k + = 1;
                adjust[i][j] = k;
            }
        }
        printf ( " \ nadjustable dimension %i x %i array is ... \ n",
                rows, columns );
        adisplay ( adjust, rows, columns );
        printf ( " \ nfree allocated memory for adjust array ... \ n" );
        for ( i = 0; i < rows; i + + ) {
            free ( adjust[i] );
        }
        free ( adjust );
        printf ( " \ nfixed dimension 3 x 3 array is ... \ n" );
        fdisplay ( fixed );
        return;
    }
    void adisplay ( int **array, int I, int J )
    {
    int   i, j;
    for   ( i = 0; i < I; i + + ) {
        for ( j = 0; j < J; j + + ) {
            printf ( " %3i", array[i][j] );
        }
        printf ( " \ n" );
    }
    return;
    }
    void fdisplay ( int array[3][3] )
    {
    int   i, j;
```

6-7 Continued.

```
for  ( i = 0; i < 3; i + + ) {
      for ( j = 0; j < 3; j + + ) {
            printf ( " %3i", array[i][j] );
      }
      printf ( " \ n" );
   }
   return;
}
```

FIG67.RUN program invoked with 2 arguments ...

allocating space for 3 x 9 array ...

adjustable dimension 3 x 9 array is ...
```
 1   2   3   4   5   6   7   8   9
10  11  12  13  14  15  16  17  18
19  20  21  22  23  24  25  26  27
```

free allocated memory for adjust array ...

fixed dimension 3 x 3 array is ...
```
1  2  3
4  5  6
7  8  9
```

If the program was invoked with this command line

fig67.run 3 9

then the array adjust would be defined to have 27 elements arranged into three rows and nine columns. These three strings are passed to the program as argv[0], argv[1], and argv[2]. It is common for the program name string, argv[0], to be used in the text of an error message describing program usage. Row and column strings are converted from characters to integers with the C standard strtol function. Memory is allocated for this array in two stages. First, the C standard calloc function is called to allocate space for pointers to each of the three rows. Second, that same function is called on a per row basis in the first for loop to allocate space for nine columns per row.

Memory can be allocated in three ways in C: the calloc function, to reserve space for a particular number of elements of a certain data type; the malloc function, to reserve space for a block of memory a specified number of bytes in length; and the realloc function to reallocate memory reserved by calloc or malloc. The example program works with a two-dimensional adjustable array; but if three dimensions were needed (i.e., cube[x][y][z]), the following code would be used:

```
int * * *cube, b, x, y, z, i, j, k, l;
b = ( size_t ) sizeof ( int );
cube = (int * * *) calloc ((size_t) x,b);
```

```
for ( i = 0; i < x; i++ ) {
    cube[i] = (int **) calloc ((size_t) y,b);
    for ( j = 0; j < y; j++ ) {
    cube[i][j] = (int *) calloc ((size_t) z,b);
    }
}
```

For one dimensions (i.e., vector[x]), this code would be used:

```
int *vector, b, x;
b = ( size_t ) sizeof ( int );
vector = ( int * ) calloc ((size_t) x,b );
```

In either case, arrays of other data types (i.e., float, double, etc.) could be defined by changing int to the desired type in the declaration of the array, the assignment of b, and the cast preceding the invocation of calloc. Also, these code fragments could be changed to use malloc instead of calloc by replacing each invocation of calloc with an invocation of malloc and modifying calloc's two arguments into a product to calculate the single argument to malloc (i.e., (size_t) x,b to (size_t) x*b).

The example program then initializes each element of the adjust array in the second for loop and displays it using the adisplay function. Then memory reserved for adjust is released in the order in which it was claimed: storage for columns in each row, followed by storage for rows. Memory is released by the C standard free function. For comparative purposes, a fully specified three-by-three array called fixed is created, initialized, and displayed in the example program.

Character arrays

Character arrays are the major advantage ANSI 77 standard Fortran enjoys over Fortran 66. C provides several constructions to store and manipulate character data. Figure 6-8 demonstrates a number of methods in C to handle characters.

6-8 C character array sample program.

```
#include <stdio.h>
main( )
{
    int     i, I = 3, j, J = 3, k;
    int     cints0d      =        'a';
    int     cints1d[3]   = {      'b', 'c', 'd'    };
    int     cints2d[3][3] = { {   'e', 'f', 'g'  },
                              {   'h', 'i', 'j'  },
                              {   'k', 'l', 'm'  } };
    char    chars0d      =        'A';
    char    chars1d[3]   = {      'B', 'C', 'D'    };
    char    chars2d[3][3] = { {   'E', 'F', 'G'  },
                              {   'H', 'I', 'J'  },
```

Continued.

```
                                              {   'K', 'L', 'M'   }  };
    char    fixed[2][9]    =  {   {  "nl" }, { "opqrstuv"   }  };
    char    *adjust[ ]     =  {       "NL", "OPQRSTUV"         };
    char    *string0d      =          "An isolated string.";
    char    *string1d[ ]   =  {       "A collection of strings",
                                      "stored",
                                      "in a one-dimensional char *",
                                      " \ n ",
                                      "array with, intially,",
                                      "an unspecified number of rows." };
    char    *string2d[ ][3]  =  {  {  "A table", "of strings"            },
                                   {  "with a variable"                  },
                                   {  "number of rows"                   },
                                   {  " \ n ",
                                      "and a fixed number (3)",
                                      "of columns per row."        }  };
    int     string2d__cols  =  3;
    printf ( " \ n \ Single characters (int) ... \ n" );
    printf ( " %c", cints0d );
    printf ( " %c %c %c", cints1d[0], cints1d[1], cints1d[2] );
    for ( i = 0; i < I; i + + ) {
        for ( j = 0; j < J; j + + ) {
            printf ( " %c", cints2d[ i ][ j ] );
        }
    }
    printf ( " \ n \ nSingle characters (char) ... \ n" );
    printf ( " %c", chars0d );
    printf ( " %c %c %c", chars1d[0], chars1d[1], chars1d[2] );
    for ( i = 0; i < I; i + + ) {
        for ( j = 0; j < J; j + + ) {
            printf ( " %c", chars2d[ i ][ j ] );
        }
    }
    printf ( " \ n \ nFixed and adjustable arrays ... \ n" );
    printf ( " fixed array ( [%s] [%s] ) \ n",
             fixed[0], fixed[1] );
    printf ( " adjust array ( [%s] [%s] ) \ n",
             adjust[0], adjust[1] );
    printf ( " \ nStrings ... \ n" );
    printf ( " %s \ n", string0d );
    k = sizeof ( string1d ) / sizeof ( char * );
    for ( i = 0; i < k; i + + ) {
        printf ( " %s", string1d[ i ] );
    }
    printf ( " \ n" );
    k  = ( sizeof ( string2d ) / sizeof ( char * ) );
    k /= string2d__cols;
        for ( j = 0; j < string2d__cols; j + + ) {
            if ( string2d[ i ][ j ] ! = NULL )
                printf ( " %s", string2d[ i ][ j ] );
        }
    }
```

6-8 Continued.

```
    printf ( " \ n" );
    return;
}
```

Single characters (int) ...
a   b   c   d   e   f   g   h   i   j   k   l   m

Single characters (char) ...
A   B   C   D   E   F   G   H   I   J   K   L   M

Fixed and adjustable arrays ...
fixed array   ([nl]   [opqrstuv]   )
adjust array   ([NL]   [OPQRSTUV]   )

Strings ...
An isolated string.
A collection of strings stored in a one-dimensional char *
    array with, initially, an unspecified number of rows.
A table of strings with a variable number of rows
    and a fixed number (3) of columns per row.

Individual characters can be stored in variables and arrays of either int or char data types. Variables cints0d, cints1d, and cints2d hold single characters as a scalar, a vector, and a table, respectively, of int data type and are exactly matched by the char data type variables chars0d, chars1d, and chars2d. In the statements where cints2d and chars2d are initialized, a set of curly brackets (i.e., {}) delimit each row in the table: this is not required but is included to show how to explicitly denote the initialization of an individual array dimension.

Arrays fixed and adjust each hold the same character strings, but storage requirements for these two representations differ: fixed takes 18 bytes, and adjust takes 16 bytes. Array fixed is stored in a two by nine table with one byte per entry as

Row	Col 0	Col 1	Col 2	Col 3	Col 4	Col 5	Col 6	Col 7	Col 8
0	n	l	\0						
1	o	p	q	r	s	t	u	v	\0

which requires 18 bytes of storage. Array adjust takes two bytes for each string pointer (i.e., *adjust[0] and *adjust[1]) for a subtotal of four bytes, plus three bytes for the string "NL\0", plus nine bytes for the string "OPQRSTUV\0", for a grand total of 16 bytes of storage. Data storage is conserved using an array of pointers to strings rather than a fixed table declaration.

Character strings can be stored individually or in arrays. A single string of words are stored and accessed through the pointer *string0d. An open-ended list of strings are stored and accessed through an array of pointers in *string1d. The number of strings in the list is calculated by dividing the number of bytes set aside for the pointer array string1d by the number of bytes required to define a pointer to the char data type. A table of strings are stored and accessed through a two-dimensional array of pointers named string2d. This table is declared with three columns and initialized with four rows.

Column 0	Column 1	Column 2
A table with a variable number of rows	of strings	
\n	and a fixed number (3)	of columns per row.

The number of rows are computed using the sizeof function and the known number of columns per row. Finally, the seven initialized elements of the string table are displayed.

Structures

C also allows arrays that are comprised of different data types. A struct in C is a data structure defined to hold several components, each of which may be of any data type including another structure. Furthermore, arrays can be created in which each element is a struct data structure.

Figure 6-9 is an example of a telephone list application. An array called person is defined to hold two elements of a struct type called whole. In turn, whole is established as a data structure containing a telephone number, an array of characters to hold the full name of the entry, and a data structure called nameparts of a struct type called part. Furthermore, struct type part is created with five character arrays, each representing a portion of a name. Each part of a name is read from the users keyboard, a punctuation mark and/or space is added to the users entry, and that part of the name is concatenated to produce a combined name in the array fullname.

6-9 C structures.

```
#include <stdio.h>
main( )
{
struct part     { char   title[10];
                  char   first[25];
                  char   middle[25];
                  char   last[30];
                  char   suffix[10];   };
struct whole { struct part nameparts;
                  char   fullname[100];
                  long   telno;               }         person[2];
```

```
struct whole                              *individual;
int   newline;
int   i,   l=2, j;
for  (  i=0; i<l;  i++  )  {
        printf  (   "\nEnter a name and "
                    "telephone number  . . . \n"  );
        printf  (  "title (without punctuation):   "  );
        gets  (   person[i].nameparts.title  );
        printf  (  "first name:   "  );
        gets  (   person[i].nameparts.first  );
        printf  (  "middle initial (with .) or name:   "  );
        gets  (   person[i].nameparts.middle  );
        printf  (  "last name|:   "  );
        gets  (   person[i].nameparts.last  );
        printf  (  "I, Jr., Esq. or other suffix :   "  );
        gets  (   person[i].nameparts.suffix  );
        person[i].fullname[0] = '\0';
        strncat  (   person[i].fullname,
                     person[i].nameparts.title, 10  );
        if  (  strlen  (  person[i].nameparts.title  ) > 0  )
            strncat  (   person[i].fullname, ". ", 2  );
        strncat  (   person[i].fullname,
                     person[i].nameparts.first, 25  );
        if  (  strlen  (  person[i].nameparts.first  ) > 0  )
            strncat  (   person[i].fullname, " ", 1  );
        strncat  (   person[i].fullname,
                     person[i].nameparts.middle, 25  );
        if  (  strlen  (  person[i].nameparts.middle  ) > 0  )
            strncat  (   person[i].fullname, " ", 1  );
        strncat  (   person[i].fullname,
                     person[i].nameparts.last, 30  );
        if  (  strlen  (  person[i].nameparts.last  ) > 0  )
            strncat  (   person[i].fullname, " ", 1  );
        if  (  strlen  (  person[i].nameparts.suffix  )  > 0  )  {
            j = strlen  (  person[i].fullname  ) - 1;
        if  (  person[i].fullname[j] == ' '  )
            person[i].fullname[j] = '\0';
        strncat  (   person[i].fullname, ", ", 2  );
        strncat  (   person[i].fullname,
                     person[i].nameparts.suffix, 10  );
        }
            j = strlen  (  person[i].fullname  ) - 1;
            if  (  person[i].fullname[j] == ' '  )
                person[i].fullname[j] = '\0';
            printf  (  "telephone number   :  "  );
            scanf  (  "%ld", &person[i].telno  );
            newline = getchar( );
        }
        printf  (   "\n"   );
        for  (   i=0; i<l; i++   )  {
            individual = &person[i];
            printf  (  "%s can be reached at %ld. \n",
                      person[i].fullname,   individual->telno  );
```

```
   }
   return
}
```

Enter a name and telephone number . . .
title (without punctuation)	:	Mr
first name	:	John
middle initial (with .) or name:		K.
last name	:	Smith
I, Jr., Esq. or other suffix	:	Jr.
telephone number	:	6671234

Enter a name and telephone number . . .
title (without punctuation)	:	Ms
first name	:	Mary
middle initial (with .) or name:		Elizabeth
last name	:	Jones
I, Jr., Esq. or other suffix	:	
telephone number	:	5568000

Mr. John K. Smith, Jr. can be reached at 6671234.
Ms. Mary Elizabeth Jones can be reached at 5568000.

Note that all five parts of the entered name as well as the combined name are carried in each element of the person array. Then a telephone number is read from the keyboard and placed into the appropriate slot in the data structure contained in the person array. When each element of the person array is displayed, the full name is retrieved directly from the person array, but the telephone number is accessed through a pointer to the current row in the person array. This is not required, but it demonstrates the syntax of referring to a piece of a structure declared as a pointer.

7

Interprogram communication

Finished programs are the end result of many cooperating components. Under immediate control of the programmer are those components of source code and the way that code interacts with host operating system. Hardly any Fortran language feature directly supports source code maintenance and modularity, whereas C has several. Furthermore, Fortran does not define a way to interact with the operating system beyond file access and the exit and pause statements, but C does.

This chapter will concentrate on C support services loosely categorized under a heading of interprogram communication. Five specific areas to be covered are source code markers, included files, command execution, signal handling, and program completion control.

Source code markers

Source code markers are C macros that brand the binary file output by the compiler with information about the source code file. The C macro names and the information they convey to the binary are as follows:

  ___DATE___ date on which source code was compiled.
  ___FILE___ time at which source code was compiled.
  ___LINE___ line number in source code file.
  ___TIME___ name of source code file.

Embedding attributes of the source code file into the binary allows the executable program to post very informative error messages. These macros are used in an example program shown in FIG. 7-1. Of particular interest is the __LINE__ macro, as it is a running count of the number of newlines (plus one) from the beginning of the source code file. In other

7-1 C source code file attributes.

```
main ( )
{
  printf ( " \nAttributes for [%s] source code file ... \n", ____FILE____ );
  printf ( " \n" );
  printf ( "last compiled on: %s \n", ____DATE____ );
  printf ( "last compiled at: %s \n", ____TIME____ );
  printf ( " \n" );
  printf ( "actual line number %d corresponds ", ____LINE____ + 2 );
  #line 1000
  printf ( "to formal line number %d. \n", ____LINE____ );
  printf ( " \n" );
  return;
}
```

Attributes for [fig71.c] source code file ...

last compiled on: Nov 26 1990
last compiled at: 09:52:09

actual line number 10 corresponds to formal line number 1000.

words, it counts blank lines, lines of source code, comments, compiler directives, etc., but does not count lines included into the current source code file (see the next paragraph). Line counts reported by __LINE__ can be set or reset to an arbitrary datum at any point through the use of the #line compiler preprocessing directive. The example program uses that directive to associate a line count of 1000 with the 10th line in the file, 1001 with the 11th, etc. These source code markers give the programmer a rudimentary means to have an executing program refer to characteristics of the underlying source code.

Included files

Included files contain repeated source code, data structure definitions, or function prototypes. They are brought into a source code file at a particular point by the #include compiler preprocessing directive. Figure 7-2 shows a trivial use of an included file. A single printf statement comprises the entire inc.one file, which in turn is inserted twice into the major source code file at the first #include in the main program and the second #include in the func function. Figure 7-2 introduces a convention used in this chapter to show where a new file begins in source code listings: the string '/* inc.one */' is not used as a C comment but as a convention to indicate that a new file begins at that point. Files can be nested using the #include mechanism up to eight levels deep, as shown in FIG. 7-3.

The #include statement uses two different methods to signal the name of the file to be included. Angle brackets (i.e., < and >) are used to references files that the C compiler will retrieve from a specific location in a

7-2 C include file demonstration program.

```
    main ( )
{
  void func ( );
  printf ( "MAIN " );
  #include "inc.one"
  func ( );
  return;
}
  void func ( )
{
  printf ( "FUNC " );
  #include "inc.one"
}

  /* inc.one */

  printf ( ". . . printed from the inc.one file. \ n" );
```

MAIN   . . . printed from the inc.one file.
FUNC   . . . printed from the inc.one file.

7-3 C include file nesting program.

```
  main( )
{
  printf (    " \ nInclude files nested 8 deep. \ n \ n" );
  #include "inc.d01"
  printf (    " \ nReturned to MAIN program. \ n" );
}

/* inc.d01 */

  printf (    "              inc.d01  . . . level 1 \ n" );
  #include "inc.d02"

/* inc.do2 */

  printf (    "              inc.d02   . . . level 2 \ n" );
  #include "inc.d03"

/* inc.d03 */

  printf (    "          inc.d03    . . . level 3 \ n" );
  #include "inc.d04"

/* inc.d04 */

  printf (    "          inc.d04        . . . level 4 \ n" );
  #include "inc.d05"

/* inc.d05 */
```

7-3 Continued.

```
    printf (   "        inc.d05          . . . level 5 \ n" );
    #include "inc.d06"

    /* inc.d06 */

    printf (   "        inc.d06          . . . level 6 \ n" );
    #include "inc.d07"

    /* inc.d07 */

    printf (   "      inc.d07            . . . level 7 \ n" );
    #include "inc.d08"

    /* inc.d08 */

    printf (    " inc.d08               . . . level 8 \ n" );
```

Include files nested 8 deep.

```
              inc.d01 . . . level 1
            inc.d02    . . . level 2
          inc.d03      . . . level 3
        inc.d04        . . . level 4
      inc.d05          . . . level 5
    inc.d06            . . . level 6
  inc.d07              . . . level 7
inc.d08                . . . level 8
```

Returned to MAIN program.

---

host's file system. The exact location changes from host to host. C standard files that define C standard macros, manifest constants, and function prototypes are retrieved automatically from this specific location. Double quotation marks (i.e., " and ") are used to delimit files written by the programmer and, unless otherwise qualified with a path name, usually will be retrieved from the same location in a host's file system as the source code file.

Real uses of included files come in the software development process when a single program is constructed of many functions and data definitions. Reworking even a moderate program to use included files improves its readability and modularity. Figures 7-4 and 7-5 are the same program using the same code but with a different arrangement of source code files.

Both programs manipulate two sets of three variables: an integer, a floating point number, and a character string. One set of three variables is global to the entire program, and the other set is local to each individual function. Both sets of three variables are initialized in the main program, displayed to the user, passed to a function for modification, displayed to the user, returned to the main program, displayed to the user, modified in the main program, and displayed to the user one final time. Included files

7-4 C program structure sample program.

```c
#include <string.h>
int     globali;
float   globalf;
char    *globalc;
main ( )
{
int     locali;
float   localf;
char    *localc;
char    *unit;
void    gdisplay ( );
void    gmodify ( );
void    ldisplay ( int, float, char * );
void    lmodify ( int *, float *, char * );
void    udisplay ( char * );
unit = "MAIN";
globali  = 1;
globalf  = 2.0F;
globalc  = "a";
locali   = 3;
localf   = 4.0F;
localc   = "b";
udisplay ( unit );
printf (   "initial values ..." );
gdisplay ( );
ldisplay ( locali, localf, localc );
udisplay ( unit );
printf (   "modified in subprograms ..." );
gmodify ( );
lmodify ( &locali, &localf, localc );
udisplay ( unit );
printf (   "returned from subprograms ..." );
gdisplay ( );
ldisplay ( locali, localf, localc );
udisplay ( unit );
printf (   "modified in main program ..." );
globali  = 9;
globalf  = 10.0F;
globalc  = "e";
locali   = 11;
localf   = 12.0F;
localc   = "f";
gdisplay ( );
ldisplay ( locali, localf, localc );
printf (   "\n" );
return;
}
    void udisplay ( char *unit )
{
if ( strcmp ( unit, "MAIN " ) == 0 )
    printf ( "\n" );
printf ( "\n[ %-8s ] ", unit );
return;
```

7-4 Continued.

```
    }
        void gdisplay ( )
    {
      char *unit = "GDISPLAY";
      udisplay ( unit );
      printf ( "%2i %4.1f %s", globali, globalf, globalc );
      return;
    }
        void ldisplay ( int locali, float localf, char *localc )
    {
      char *unit = "LDISPLAY";
      udisplay ( unit );
      printf ( "%2i %4.1f %s", locali, localf, localc );
      return;
    }
        void gmodify ( )
    {
      char *unit = "GMODIFY";
      udisplay ( unit );
      globali = 5;
      globalf = 6.0F;
      globalc = "c";
      printf (    "%2i %4.1f %s", globali, globalf, globalc );
      return;
    }
        void lmodify ( int *locali, float *localf, char *localc )
    {
      char *unit = "LMODIFY";
      udisplay ( unit );
     *locali = 7;
     *localf = 8.0F;
      strcpy  ( localc, "d ");
      printf  ( "%2i %4.1f %s", *locali, *localf, localc );
      return;
    }
```

```
[ MAIN       ] initial values . . .
[ GDISPLAY ]   1   2.0   a
[ LDISPLAY ]   3   4.0   b

[ MAIN       ] modified in subprograms . . .
[ GMODIFY ]   5   6.0   c
[ LMODIFY ]   7   8.0   d

[ MAIN       ] returned from subprograms . . .
[ GDISPLAY ]   5   6.0   c
[ LDISPLAY ]   7   8.0   d

[ MAIN       ] modified in main program . . .
[ GDISPLAY ]   9  10.0   e
[ LDISPLAY ]  11  12.0   f
```

7-5 C program structure include file sample program.

```
#include <string.h>
#include "global"
main ( )
{
int    locali;
float  localf;
char *localc;
#include "local"
#include "proto"
unit = "MAIN";
globali = 1;
globalf = 2.0F;
globalc = "a";
locali   = 3;
localf   = 4.0F;
localc   = "b";
udisplay ( unit );
printf (   "initial values . . ." );
gdisplay ( );
ldisplay ( locali, localf, localc );
udisplay ( unit );
printf (   "modified in subprograms . . ." );
gmodify ( );
lmodify ( &locali, &localf, localc );
udisplay ( unit );
printf (   "returned from subprograms . . ." );
gdisplay ( );
ldisplay ( locali, localf, localc );
udisplay ( unit );
printf (   "modified in main program . . ." );
globali = 9;
globalf = 10.0F;
globalc = "e";
locali   = 11;
localf   = 12.0F;
localc   = "f";
gdisplay ( );
ldisplay ( locali, localf, localc );
printf (   "\n" );
return;

/* global */

int    globali;
float  globalf;
char *globalc;

/* local */

char *unit;
```

```
/* proto */

void    gdisplay ( );
void    gmodify ( );
void    ldisplay ( int, float, char * );
void    lmodify ( int *, float *, char * );
void    udisplay ( char * );

/* UDISPLAY */

#include "global"
void udisplay ( char *dummy )
{
#include "local"
#include "proto"
unit = dummy;
if ( strcmp ( unit, "MAIN" ) = = 0 )
    printf ( "\n" );
printf ( "\n[ %-8s ] ", unit );
return;
}

/* GDISPLAY */

#include "global"
void gdisplay ( )
{
#include "local"
#include "proto"
unit = "GDISPLAY";
udisplay ( unit );
printf ( "%2i %4.1f %s", globali, globalf, globalc );
return;
}

/* LDISPLAY */

#include "global"
void ldisplay ( int locali, float localf, char *localc )
{
#include "local"
#include "proto"
unit = "LDISPLAY";
udisplay ( unit );
printf ( "%2i %4.1f %s", locali, localf, localc );
return;
}

/* GMODIFY */

#include "global"
void gmodify ( )
{
```

```
    #include "local"
    #include "proto"
    unit = "GMODIFY";
    udisplay ( unit );
    globali  = 5;
    globalf  = 6.0F;
    globalc = "c";
    printf ( "%2i %4.1f %s", globali, globalf, globalc );
    return;
}

    /* LMODIFY */

    #include "global"
    void lmodify ( int *locali, float *localf, char *localc )
{
    #include "local"
    #include "proto"
    unit = "LMODIFY";
    udisplay ( unit );
  *locali = 7;
  *localf = 8.0F;
    strcpy ( localc, "d" );
    printf ( "%2i %4.1f %s", *locali, *localf, localc );
    return;
}
```

```
[ MAIN      ] initial values . . .
[ GDISPLAY ]   1    2.0   a
[ LDISPLAY ]   3    4.0   b

[ MAIN      ] modified in subprograms . . .
[ GMODIFY ]    5    6.0   c
[ LMODIFY ]    7    8.0   d

[ MAIN      ] returned from subprograms . . .
[ GDISPLAY ]   5    6.0   c
[ LDISPLAY ]   7    8.0   d

[ MAIN      ] modified in main program . . .
[ GDISPLAY ]   9   10.0   e
[ LDISPLAY ]  11   12.0   f
```

in FIG. 7-5 group variable definitions for global and local variables and function prototype statements. Then, source code for each function—gdisplay, gmodify, ldisplay, lmodify, and udisplay—can be stored in individual source code files, compiled separately, and yet refer to a single copy of common code stored in the included files.

Command execution

Command execution allows an executing program to invoke an operating system command, have it run, and return control to the original program. A simple example is shown in FIG. 7-6, which uses C's system function to execute three commands. Initially, C's system function is used with a NULL argument to determine if a command processor exists. If a command processor exists, the example program passes three commands to the host operating system in turn. The syntax of such commands and the value returned by the system function are not defined by C but vary from host to host.

7-6 C system function.

```
#include <stdlib.h>
main ( )
{
    int   error;
    int   i, l=3;
    char *commands[3] = { "DATE", "DIRECTORY *.C", "VERSION" };
    error = system ( NULL );
    if ( error = = 0 ) {
        printf ( "ERROR! Command processor does "
                "not exist! \ n"                          );
        exit ( EXIT__FAILURE );
    }
    for ( i=0; i<l; i+ + ) {
        error = system ( commands[i] );
        printf ( " \ n> > > C system function returned %i "
                "executing '%s' command. \ n",
                error, commands[i] );
    }
    printf ( " \ n" );
    return;
}
```

Mon 26 Nov 1990

> > > C system function returned 0 executing 'DATE' command.

FIG71.C
FIG72.C
FIG73.C
FIG74.C
FIG75.C
FIG76.C

> > > C system function returned 0 executing 'DIRECTORY *.C' command.

Operating System Version 1.23

> > > C system function returned 0 executing 'VERSION' command.

Signal handling

Signal handling enables an executing program to manage external interrupts and certain internal conditions. The C standard signal function can establish a trap for, at a minimum, these six specific conditions:

SIGABRT	abnormal termination (i.e., the C standard abort function).
SIGFPE	erroneous arithmetic operation (i.e., zero divide, overflow, etc).
SIGILL	illegal instruction.
SIGINT	interrupt (i.e., some keyboard entry defined by the host system to get the attention of the executing program: often a ctrl-C).
SIGSEGV	invalid access to storage.
SIGTERM	program termination (i.e., some signal defined by the host system to force program completion).

Other conditions might be defined on any given host, but these six will exist for each standard-conforming C compiler. C's signal function can either register the name of the function that will execute when a signal is received or indicate that a signal should be ignored. Figure 7-7 sets a trap for the interrupt signal, springs the trap, handles the signal, and disables the trap. The first call to signal registers the user-written function bother as a handler for the interrupt signal. C's raise function causes the interrupt signal to be sent. When received by the program, the function bother is invoked and displays a message to the screen. Finally, the user-written interrupt handler is disabled, and the host's default interrupt handler is restored by invoking the signal function with the single argument set to the value of the SIG__DFL macro.

7-7 C signal processing.

```
#include <stdio.h>
#include <stdlib.h>
#include <signal.h>
main ( )
{
    int error;
    void bother( );
    printf (" \ nRegister SIGINT handler . . . \ n" );
    if ( signal ( SIGINT, bother ) = = SIG__ERR ) {
        printf ( "ERROR! Can not register bother as "
            "SIGINT handler! \ n" );
        perror ( " " );
        exit ( EXIT__FAILURE );
    }
    printf ( " \ nRaising SIGINT signal " );
```

7-7 Continued.

```
    if ( raise ( SIGINT ) ! = 0 ) {
        printf ( "ERROR! Can not raise SIGINT signal! \ n" );
        perror ( " " );
        exit ( EXIT__FAILURE );
    }
    printf ( " SIGINT handler returned. \ n" );
    printf ( " \ nUn-register SIGINT handler . . . \ n" );
    if ( signal ( SIGINT, SIG__DFL ) = = SIG__ERR ) {
        printf ( "ERROR! Can not un-register bother as "
                "SIGINT handler! \ n" );
        perror ( " " );
        exit ( EXIT__FAILURE );
    }
    printf ( " \ nSIGINT handler un-registered. \ n" );
    return;
}

void bother ( void )
{
    printf ( ". . . HANDLER . . ." );
    return;
}
```

Register SIGINT handler . . .

Raising SIGINT signal . . . HANDLER . . . SIGINT handler returned.

Un-register SIGINT handler . . .

SIGINT handler un-registered.

Keyboard entry of the interrupt signal can be trapped or ignored. Figure 7-8 demonstrates how a handler for the ctrl-C interrupt signal can be written to manage keyboard entry. When executed the first time, a ctrl-C was entered at the prompt, causing the user-written function controlc to be invoked. When executed the second time, the letter X was entered at the prompt and the interrupt signal was not raised. Figure 7-9 shows the same program, but the second invocation of C's signal function causes the interrupt signal to be ignored. Consequently, the program behaved in the same way the first time the program was run (when a ctrl-C was entered at the prompt) and the second time (when the letter X was entered).

7-8 C signal processing: Ctrl-C entered from keyboard.

```
    #include < stdio.h >
    #include < stdlib.h >
    #include < signal.h >
    main ( )
{
    int   error;
    int   entry;
```

```
    void controlc( );
    printf (" \ nRegister CTRL-C handler . . . \ n" );
    if ( signal ( SIGINT, controlc ) = = SIG__ERR ) {
        printf ( "ERROR! Can not register controlc as "
            "CTRL-C handler! \ n" );
        perror ( " " );
        exit ( EXIT__FAILURE );
    }
    printf ( " \ nEnter a CTRL-C: " );
    entry = getchar ( );
    printf ( " \ nUn-register CTRL-C handler . . . \ n" );
    if ( signal ( SIGINT, SIG__DFL ) = = SIG__ERR ) {
        printf ( "ERROR! Can not un-register controlc as "
            "CTRL-C handler! \ n" );
        perror ( " " );
        exit ( EXIT__FAILURE );
    }
    printf ( " \ nCTRL-C handler un-registered. \ n" );
    return;
}
    void controlc ( void )
{
    printf ( " \ n. . . CTRL-C ENTERED . . ." );
    return;
}
```

Register CTRL-C handler . . .

Enter a CTRL-C: ^C

. . . CTRL-C ENTERED . . .

Un-register CTRL-C handler . . .

CTRL-C handler un-registered.

Register CTRL-C handler . . .

Enter a CTRL-C: X

Un-register CTRL-C handler . . .

CTRL-C handler un-registered.

7-9 C signal processing: Ctrl-C entered and ignored.

```
#include <stdio.h>
#include <stdlib.h>
#include <signal.h>
main ()
{
```

7-9 Continued.

```
        int   error;
        int   entry;
        void controlc( );
        printf ("\nRegister CTRL-C handler . . . \n" );
        if ( signal ( SIGINT, controlc ) = = SIG__ERR ) {
            printf ( "ERROR! Can not register controlc as "
                    "CTRL-C handler! \n" );
            perror ( " " );
            exit ( EXIT__FAILURE );
        }
        printf ( "\nPrepare to ignore CTRL-Cs . . . \n" );
        if ( signal ( SIGINT, SIG__IGN ) = = SIG__ERR ) {
            printf ( "ERROR! Can not ignore CTRL-C "
                    "signal! \n" );
            perror ( " " );
            exit ( EXIT__FAILURE );
        }
        printf ( "\nEnter a CTRL-C: " );
        entry = getchar ( );
        printf ( "\nUn-register CTRL-C handler . . . \n" );
        if ( signal ( SIGINT, SIG__DFL ) = = SIG__ERR ) {
            printf ( "ERROR! Can not un-register controlc as "
                    "CTRL-C handler! \n" );
            perror ( " " );
            exit ( EXIT__FAILURE );
        }
        printf ( "\nCTRL-C handler un-registered. \n" );
        return;
}
        void controlc ( void )
{
        printf ( "\n. . . CTRL-C ENTERED . . ." );
        return;
}
```

Register CTRL-C handler . . .

Prepare to ignore CTRL-Cs . . .

Enter a CTRL-C: ^C

Un-register CTRL-C handler . . .

CTRL-C handler un-registered.

Register CTRL-C handler . . .
Prepare to ignore CTRL-Cs . . .
Enter a CTRL-C: X

Un-register CTRL-C handler . . .

CTRL-C handler un-registered.

Program completion control

Often the completion of a program needs some special handling: file management, transaction log updates, final user instructions, etc. C's standard atexit function is a mechanism to register a series of up to 32 different functions that will be invoked in turn at program completion. Two functions will execute at the end of the program in FIG. 7-10. C's standard atexit function registers the user-written function accounting and then the user-written function finished. When the exit function is invoked, both user-written functions will run. Note that they will run in the reverse order in which they were registered with the atexit function. In essence, if user-written functions FF, EE, DD, . . ., C, B, and A were registered in that order with 32 separate invocations of the atexit function, then they would be executed in the order A, B, C, . . ., DD, EE, and FF.

7-10 C atexit function example program.

```
#include <stdlib.h>
main ( )
{
  void finished ( );
  void accounting ( );
  if ( atexit ( accounting ) != 0 ) {
     printf ( "ERROR! Can not register accounting "
           "routine! \ n" );
     exit ( EXIT_FAILURE );
  }
  if ( atexit ( finished ) != 0 ) {
     printf ( "ERROR! Can not register finished "
           "routine! \ n" );
     exit ( EXIT_FAILURE );
  }
  printf ( " \ nExecution begins. \ n" );
  printf ( " \ nExecution ends. \ n \ n" );
  exit ( EXIT_SUCCESS );
}
  void finished ( )
{
  printf ( "END OF EXECUTION (finished) \ n" );
}
  void accounting ( )
{
  printf ( "JOB ACCOUNTING DATA UPDATED (accounting) \ n" );
}
```

Execution begins.

Execution ends.

END OF EXECUTION (finished)
JOB ACCOUNTING DATA UPDATED (accounting)

8

Input/Output

Input and output to files and CRTs comprise the bulk of work of the vast majority of programs. Aspects of I/O covered in this chapter include Fortran "internal files" (i.e., writing/reading to/from a buffer), keyboard and display processing, sequential and direct access method files, and Fortran `format` statements.

Internal files

Long before the ANSI 77 standard provided a definition for internal files, Fortran programmers used "encode" and "decode" to exchange data between character and numeric representations. Internal file input and output is no different than any other Fortran `read` and `write` operation. Most file operations can be performed on these internal files. However, it is typical to see them employed where a single record in an internal file is written and read over and over again, converting numeric data to character form or reversing that process.

C has two functions—sscanf and sprintf—that perform conversion to and from character buffers. As an example, FIG. 8-1 exercises both functions on a variety of data types. Four variables representing four major data types are read from the terminal using C's scanf function. Packing these four variables—an integer, a floating point number, a character string, and an array of characters—into a single character string is accomplished by the sprintf function. In effect, sprintf "writes" the values of these individual values into a single character string and appends the null character onto the end. Individual variables are reset to arbitrary values before being "read" back from the single character string by C's sscanf function. Throughout the course of the program, values for selected variables are displayed to chart progress of the program's execution.

8-1 C read-and-write internal record example program.

```
#include <stdio.h>
main ( )
{
    int    j;
    int    J = 2;
    int    fields;
    int    i;
    float  f;
    char   c[65];
    char   b[3];
    int    bytes__read;
    int    newline;
    int    bytes__converted;
    char   string[81];
    for ( j = 1; j <= J; j + + ) {
        printf ( " \ nEnter data (%i of %i): ", j, J );
        fields = scanf ( "%i %f %s %c%c%c%c%n",
                         &i, &f, c, &b[0], &b[1], &b[2],
                         &bytes__read );
        newline = getchar( );
        printf ( " \ n%i fields read from CRT . . ."
                 " \ n%i bytes read from CRT . . . ",
                 fields, bytes__read );
        if ( fields ! = 6 ) {
            printf ( "ERROR! Read error after %i-th "
                     "field! \ n", fields );
            break;
        }
        bytes__converted = sprintf ( string,
                         "%i %f %s %.3s",
                         i, f, c, &b[0] );
        printf ( " \ n%i bytes converted into characters . . ."
                 " \ ncharacter string is [%.*s] \ n",
                 bytes__converted, bytes__converted, string );
        i = 7;
        f = 8.9F;
        c[0] = 'w';
        c[1] = ' \ 0';
        b[0] = 'X';
        b[1] = 'Y';
        b[2] = 'Z';
        printf ( " \ nvariables reset to %i %f %s %c%c%c \ n",
                 i, f, c, b[0], b[1], b[2] );
        fields = sscanf ( string,
                         "%i %f %s %c%c%c%n",
                         &i, &f, c, &b[0], &b[1], &b[2],
                         &bytes__converted );
        printf ( " \ n%i fields read from string . . ."
                 " \ n%i bytes converted from string . . . ",
                 fields, bytes__converted );
        if ( fields ! = 6 ) {
            printf ( "ERROR! Conversion error after %i-th "
                     "field! \ n", fields );
```

```
        break;
    }
    printf ( " \ nvariables now equal to %i %f %s %c%c%c \ n",
        i, f, c, b[0], b[1], b[2] );
}
return;
}
```

Enter data (1 of 2): 1 2.3 aaaaaaaaaa BBB

6 fields read from CRT . . .
20 bytes read from CRT . . .
25 bytes converted into characters . . .
character string is [1 2.300000 aaaaaaaaaa BBB]

variables reset to 7 8.900000 w XYZ

6 fields read from string . . .
25 bytes converted from string . . .
variables now equal to 1 2.300000 aaaaaaaaaa BBB

Enter data (2 of 2): 4 5.6 ccc DDD

6 fields read from CRT . . .
13 bytes read from CRT . . .
18 bytes converted into characters . . .
character string is [4 5.600000 ccc DDD]

variables reset to 7 8.900000 w XYZ

6 fields read from string . . .
18 bytes converted from string . . .
variables now equal to 4 5.600000 ccc DDD

Files

Files represent a fundamental means of interprogram communication. Standard operating procedures call for data written by one program to be available, given security clearance, for reading by one or more programs. Fortran supports formatted or unformatted sequential and direct access method files. Virtually every Fortran compiler implementation also allows data to be read from a user's keyboard and written to user's video display. Furthermore, it is common to have a single program access multiple files and the user's terminal to acquire, display, retrieve, and store data. C provides support comparable to Fortran for a variety of devices under several formats.

Fortran does not make a great distinction between access to formatted sequential files and terminal data handling. Usually, two distinct unit numbers are preassigned by the host operating system for keyboard and monitor input and output (i.e., often units 5 and 6, respectively). Most file input/output operations are valid for a CRT (except for Fortran's back- space, endfile, and rewind statements, which are not meaningful for terminal input/output). C restricts certain functions to the CRT, but others are defined independently of the intended device. The biggest difference between terminal handling by Fortran and by C revolves around recogni- tion of the carriage return and line feed combination that signals a new line. On output, ANSI 77 standard Fortran always generates a new line at the end of a print or write statement. Fortran has no standard-compli- ant way to display a prompt and then, without advancing to a new line, wait for the user to respond. C can accomplish this prompt/response cycle with ease because the programmer is totally in control of when and if a new line is generated. C forces the programmer to explicitly recognize and manage the presence of the new line indicator in order to acquire the amount of data expected per line of input.

This section will demonstrate methods of C input/output for terminals and files. CRT input/output is shown in eight examples: per character, strings, whole numbers, floating point numbers, strings (again), individ- ual words in a string, character type recognition (i.e., alphanumeric, upper- or lowercase, punctuation marks, etc.), and character-to-numeric conversion. C sequential file input/output functions are presented followed by an exercise of C's methods to perform direct file access.

Terminal input/output

Individual characters can be accepted and displayed by C's getchar and put- char functions (see FIG. 8-2). Single characters are accepted from the key- board by C's getchar function. Each character is stored in a variable of int data type. A char data type might be a logical choice, but the numeric range of character variables (i.e., at best 0 to 255 for unsigned char—see FIG. 3-2) is too small to allow arbitrary definitions for "special" values such as the end-of-file constant EOF. Once a single character is accepted, it is tested to make sure that it does not signal the end of data. The getchar function returns this indicator of end of "file" if an error occurred or the user entered the implementation defined key sequence that indicated end of data (i.e., often either the two-key sequence Ctrl-D or Ctrl-Z). Until that value is returned by getchar, the putchar function continues to copy every- thing entered on the keyboard to the screen.

Character strings can be read and written to a CRT using terminal- specific C functions or device independent functions. Functions gets and puts perform input and output for strings oriented to the terminal, and fgets and fputs can handle both terminals and files as shown in the example program in FIG. 8-3. A string is read from the keyboard by gets until the user presses the return key or enters the key sequence that signals an end- of-file. In effect, gets will read one line at a time from the keyboard. After a

8-2 C program for single character terminal I/O.

```
#include <stdio.h>
main ( )
{
    int character;
    while ( ( character = getchar( ) ) != EOF )
            putchar ( character );
    return;
}
```

```
a
a
A
A
letter
letter
```

8-3 C program for string terminal I/O.

```
#include <stdio.h>
#include <stdlib.h>
main ( )
{
int     i;
int     trials = 2;
char    buffer[20];
int     error;
for ( i = 1; i < = trials; i + + ) {
    printf ( "\nEnter GETS/PUTS string %d of %d: ",
            i, trials );
    if ( gets ( buffer ) = = NULL ) {
        printf ( "ERROR! gets failed!" );
        exit ( EXIT_FAILURE );
    }
    error = puts ( buffer );
    if ( error < 0 ) {
        printf ( "ERROR! puts failed!" );
        exit ( EXIT_FAILURE );
    }
}
for ( i = 1; i < = trials; i + + ) {
    printf ( "\nEnter FGETS/FPUTS string %d of %d: ",
            i, trials );
    if ( fgets ( buffer, sizeof(buffer), stdin ) = = NULL ) {
        printf ( "ERROR! fgets failed!" );
        exit ( EXIT_FAILURE );
    }
    error = fputs ( buffer, stdout );
    if ( error < 0 ) {
        printf ( "ERROR! fputs failed!" );
        exit ( EXIT_FAILURE );
    }
```

8-3 Continued.

```
    }
    return;
}
```

Enter GETS/PUTS string 1 of 2: its a
its a

Enter GETS/PUTS string 2 of 2: grand old flag
grand old flag

Enter FGETS/FPUTS string 1 of 2: a high
a high

Enter FGETS/FPUTS string 2 of 2: flying flag
flying flag

---

line is read, C's puts function writes the string to the CRT screen. Comparable to gets and puts, fgets and fputs can manage terminal input and output in addition to files.

Whole numbers are processed by scanf, a general purpose formatted CRT input function. As coded in the example program in FIG. 8-4, scanf reads a single integer value into a variable through the address of that variable (i.e., &number). If successful, the number of bytes read will be recorded in the variable bytes through the %n format, and the number of fields processed will be captured by the variable error. Under error conditions, scanf will set error equal to the number of conversions it could accomplish before the error occurred and equal to a value signifying EOF if no conversions were possible. Note that scanf will do as much of the conversion as possible before giving up; in the example program, scanf accepted the 4 in the entry of 4.99 and converted it to an integer before stopping at the decimal point.

8-4 C program for integer numeric terminal I/O.

```
    #include < stdio.h >
    #include < stdlib.h >
    main ( )
{
  int   i;
  int   trials = 2;
  int   number;
  int   bytes;
  int   error;
  int   newline;
  for ( i = 1; i < = trials; i + + ) {
       printf ( " \ nEnter number %d of %d: ",
              i, trials );
       error = scanf ( "%i%n", &number, &bytes );
       if ( ( error = = EOF ) ) {
           printf ( "ERROR! scanf failed!" );
```

```
            exit ( EXIT__FAILURE );
      }
      else
         printf ( "%d items %d bytes "
                  "read . . . [",
                  error, bytes );
      newline = getchar( );
      error = printf ( "%i%n", number, &bytes );
      if ( error < 0 ) {
         printf ( "ERROR! printf failed!" );
         exit ( EXIT__FAILURE );
      }
      else
         printf ( "] . . . %d (that is %d) "
                  "bytes written. \ n",
                  error, bytes );
      printf ( " \ n" );
   }
   return;
}
```

```
Enter number 1 of 2: 123
1 items 3 bytes read . . . [123] . . . 3 (that is 3) bytes written.

Enter number 2 of 2: 4.99
1 items 1 bytes read . . . [4] . . . 1 (that is 1) bytes written.
```

C's scanf function will read up to but not through the carriage return / line feed sequence marking the end of a line. Consequently, this new line mark must be disposed of between each call to scanf: the example program accomplishes this with the following code:

```
newline = getchar( );
```

Formatted output to the terminal is done by C's printf function. As coded in the example program, it counts the number of bytes written and simultaneously updates the error variable and the variable bytes through the %n format. Should a mistake occur, printf sets the error variable to a negative number.

Floating point numbers are also processed by scanf (see FIG. 8-5). The conventions of scanf and printf are the same for this program as the previous example in respect to error control, input character counts, and new line processing. Note here that a whole number—123 in the example—can be read under an %f format and will be correctly converted to 123.0.

Character strings can be processed by scanf (see FIG. 8-6). The conventions of scanf and printf are the same for this program as the previous example program in respect to error control, input character counts, and new line processing.

8-5 C program for floating point numeric terminal I/O.

```
#include <stdio.h>
#include <stdlib.h>
main ( )
{
int      i;
int      trials = 2;
float    number;
int      bytes;
int      error;
int      newline;
for ( i = 1; i < = trials; i + + ) {
    printf ( " \ nEnter number %d of %d: ",
            i, trials );
    error = scanf ( "%f%n", &number, &bytes );
    if ( ( error = = EOF ) ) {
        printf ( "ERROR! scanf failed!" );
        exit ( EXIT__FAILURE );
    }
    else
        printf ( "%d items %d bytes "
                "read . . . [",
                error, bytes );
    newline = getchar( );
    error = printf ( "%f%n", number, &bytes );
    if ( error < 0 ) {
        printf ( "ERROR! printf failed!" );
        exit ( EXIT__FAILURE );
    }
    else
        printf ( "] . . . %d (that is %d) "
                "bytes written. \ n",
                error, bytes );
    printf ( " \ n" );
}
return;
}
```

Enter number 1 of 2: 123
1 items 3 bytes read . . . [123.000000] . . . 10 (that is 10) bytes written.

Enter number 2 of 2: 4.56
1 items 4 bytes read . . . [4.560000] . . . 8 (that is 8) bytes written.

8-6 C program for string terminal I/O.

```
#include <stdio.h>
#include <stdlib.h>
main ( )
{
int      i;
int      trials = 2;
```

```
char    *string;
int     bytes;
int     error;
int     newline;
for ( i = 1; i < = trials; i + + ) {
    printf ( " \ nEnter string %d of %d: ",
            i, trials );
    error = scanf ( "%s%n", string, &bytes );
    if ( ( error = = EOF ) ) {
        printf ( "ERROR! scanf failed!" );
        exit ( EXIT__FAILURE );
    }
    else
        printf ( "%d items %d bytes "
                "read . . . [",
                error, bytes );
    newline = getchar( );
    error = printf ( "%s%n", string, &bytes );
    if ( error < 0 ) {
        printf ( "ERROR! printf failed!" );
        exit ( EXIT__FAILURE );
    }
    else
        printf ( "] . . . %d (that is %d) "
                "bytes written. \ n",
                error, bytes );
    printf ( " \ n" );
}
return;
}
```

Enter string 1 of 2: sometime
1 items 8 bytes read . . . [sometime] . . . 8 (that is 8) bytes written.

Enter string 2 of 2: someplace
1 items 9 bytes read . . . [someplace] . . . 9 (that is 9) bytes written.

Whole sentences can be processed by a combination of C's gets and strtok functions. The example program (FIG. 8-7) uses C's gets function to read line of characters from the keyboard and C's printf function to echo those characters back to the CRT display.

The line

```
piece = strtok ( buffer, " " );
```

updates the variable piece with the address of the first word in the collection of characters called buffer. The second argument to C's strtok function defines a set of characters to use as word separators. In this example, the blank was designated as the marker between tokens in the long character string. Depending on the context of the data a program might process,

8-7 C program for string token terminal I/O.

```
#include <stdio.h>
#include <stdlib.h>
#include <string.h>
main ( )
{
    int      i;
    int      trials = 2;
    char     buffer[60];
    int      error;
    int      bytes;
    int      words;
    char     *piece;
    struct   tokens { char *word; }
             sentence[10];
    int      j;
    for ( i = 1; i < = trials; i + + ) {
        printf ( " \ nEnter string %i of %i: ",
                i, trials );
        if ( ( gets ( buffer ) = = NULL ) ) {
            printf ( "ERROR! gets failed!" );
            exit ( EXIT__FAILURE );
        }
        error = printf ( "%s%n", buffer, &bytes );
        if ( error < 0 ) {
            printf ( "ERROR! printf failed!" );
            exit ( EXIT__FAILURE );
        }
        else
            printf ( " . . . string is"
                    " %i (that is %i) "
                    "bytes long \ n", error, bytes );
        piece = strtok ( buffer, " " );
        words = 0;
        while ( piece != NULL ) {
            words + +;
            sentence[words – 1].word = piece;
            piece = strtok ( NULL, " " );
        }
        printf ( " \ nString %i contains these %i words: \ n",
                i, words );
        for ( j = 0; j < = words – 1; j + + ) {
            printf ( "word number %2.2i: %s \ n",
                    j + 1, sentence[j].word );
        }
    }
    return;
}
```

Enter string 1 of 2: now is the time for
now is the time for . . . string is 19 (that is 19) bytes long

String 1 contains these 5 words:
word number 01: now

8-7 Continued.

word number 02: is
word number 03: the
word number 04: time
word number 05: for

Enter string 2 of 2: all good men to rally
all good men to rally . . . string is 21 (that is 21) bytes long

String 2 contains these 5 words:
word number 01: all
word number 02: good
word number 03: men
word number 04: to
word number 05: rally

---

other choices for token separators suggest themselves: the hyphen for telephone numbers, the comma for monetary figures, and the dash for command line options. The next portion of the program sets up a loop that will continue to execute until the last token has been extracted from the character string. At that point, the address return by C's strtok function will be NULL. The line

        sentence[words-1].word = piece;

stores the address of the most recently extracted token into the next element of a data structure called sentence. Note that the variable words keeps a running count of the number of tokens in the character string. Finally, the example program displays each individual word in the string.

Not only can individual words be processed, but individual characters can be classified by an entire family of C functions. Once a character has been read from the keyboard by C's getchar, it can be classified as alphanumeric, printable, upper- or lowercase, etc., by one of C's is functions. A sample program (FIG. 8-8) reads a single line of characters from the keyboard and classifies each character using a C is function. Note that some characters are correctly classified as belonging to several groups: the letter d is simultaneously a letter, a hexadecimal digit, and an alphanumeric, printable, lowercase character.

8-8 C isX function sample program.

```
#include <stdio.h>
#include <ctype.h>
main( )
{
 int   c;
 int   isa;
 int   i;
 while  (( c = getchar( )) != '\n') {
        printf ( "[%c] is", c );
```

8-8 Continued.

```
            if ( isalnum(c) )
                printf   ( " alphanumeric" );
            if ( isalpha (c) )
                printf   ( " letter" );
            if ( iscntrl  (c) )
                printf   ( " control" );
            if ( isdigit   (c) )
                printf   ( " numeral" );
            if ( isgraph(c) )
                printf   ( " printable" );
            if ( islower (c) )
                printf   ( " lower-case" );
            if ( isprint  (c) )
                printf   ( " printable" );
            if ( ispunct (c) )
                printf   ( " punctuation" );
            if ( isspace(c) )
                printf   ( " white space" );
            if ( isupper(c) )
                printf   ( " upper-case" );
            if ( isxdigit (c) )
                printf   ( " hex__numeral" );
            printf ( " \ n" );
        }
    return;
    }
```

```
[W]  is alphanumeric letter printable printable upper-case
[h ] is alphanumeric letter printable lower-case printable
[e ] is alphanumeric letter printable lower-case printable hex__numeral
[n ] is alphanumeric letter printable lower-case printable
[  ] is printable white space
[i ] is alphanumeric letter printable lower-case printable
[n ] is alphanumeric letter printable lower-case printable
[  ] is printable white space
[d ] is alphanumeric letter printable lower-case printable hex__numeral
[o ] is alphanumeric letter printable lower-case printable
[u ] is alphanumeric letter printable lower-case printable
[b ] is alphanumeric letter printable lower-case printable hex__numeral
[t ] is alphanumeric letter printable lower-case printable
[, ] is printable printable punctuation
[  ] is printable white space
[d ] is alphanumeric letter printable lower-case printable hex__numeral
[o ] is alphanumeric letter printable lower-case printable
[n ] is alphanumeric letter printable lower-case printable
[' ] is printable printable punctuation
[t ] is alphanumeric letter printable lower-case printable
[! ] is printable printable punctuation
```

A final example of terminal input and output is accepting numeric data. A sample program (FIG. 8-9) accepts a string from the keyboard and converts it in stages from a double precision floating point number

8-9 C program to convert character to numeric values.

```
#include <stdio.h>
#include <stdlib.h>
#include <limits.h>
#include <float.h>
#include <errno.h>
main( )
{
char      source[10];
int       itarget;
long      ltarget;
float     ftarget;
double    dtarget;
printf    ( "\nEnter a number: " );
while ( ( gets ( source ) ) ! = NULL ) {
        errno = 0;
        dtarget = strtod ( source, NULL );
        if ( dtarget = = 0.0 ) {
            printf ( "ERROR! strtod failed to "
                    "convert '%s'!\n", source );
            printf ( "errno = %i\n", errno );
            perror ( "CONVERT.C" );
            goto ERR;
        }
        if ( ( fabs(dtarget) > = FLT__MIN ) &&
             ( fabs(dtarget) < = FLT__MAX ) )
            ftarget = (float) dtarget;
        else
            ftarget = 0.0F;
        if ( ( ftarget > = LONG__MIN ) &&
             ( ftarget < = LONG__MAX ) )
            ltarget = (long) ftarget;
        else
            ltarget = 0L;
        if ( ( ltarget > = INT__MIN ) &&
             ( ltarget < = INT__MAX ) )
            itarget = (int) ltarget;
        else
            itarget = 0;
        printf ( "\n[%-10s] = > %d %ld %f %f\n",
                source,
                itarget, ltarget, ftarget, dtarget );
ERR:            ;
        printf ( "\nEnter a number: " );
    }
    return;
}
```

```
Enter a number: number
ERROR! strtod failed to convert 'number'!
errno = 0

Enter a number: -1
[-1        ] = >    -1 -1 -1.000000 -1.000000
```

8-9 Continued.

```
Enter a number: 2
[2        ] = >    2 2 2.000000 2.000000

Enter a number: 3.0
[3.0      ] = >    3 3 3.000000 3.000000

Enter a number: 4.0e4
[4.0e4    ] = >    0 40000 40000.000000 40000.000000

Enter a number: 5.0e9
[5.0e9    ] = >    0 0 5000000000.000000 5000000000.000000

Enter a number: 6.0e37
[6.0e37   ] = >    0
                   0
                   600000021381960800000000000000000000000.000000
                   600000000000000000000000000000000000000.000000
```

through a single precision floating point number through an extended range integer to a standard whole number. Initially, a character string of up to ten bytes is acquired from the keyboard by the C's gets function. It is converted to a double precision number by C's strtod function. Should this conversion fail, strtod returns zero. This double precision value is then checked to see if it falls within the range that can be represented as a single precision floating point number; the reference used is the smallest and largest values accepted as a single precision floating point number (i.e., the macros FLT_MIN and FLT_MAX, respectively, as defined in the float.h file). The single precision floating point value is converted to an extended precision integer if it falls within the numerical limits of a long data type (i.e., the macros LONG_MIN and LONG_MAX as defined in the limits.h file). Next, the extended precision integer is reduced to a normal integer if it fits by comparison to the limits of an int data type (i.e., the macros INT_MIN and INT_MAX as defined in the limits.h file). Finally, all four numeric representations of the number are displayed on the terminal screen by C's printf function. Six test values are processed by the sample program to demonstrate handling of negative numbers, positive whole numbers, floating point numbers, and numbers that successively exceed the limits of the int and long data types.

C offers a rich collection of functions to support terminal input and output. Without question, the greatest benefit C offers over Fortran is its ability to allow the programmer to control if and when a carriage return / new line sequence is processed. Initially, however, C's disadvantage comes by providing several CRT accept and display functions of varying capabilities that must be selected with care, rather than Fortran's binary choice of read and write.

Sequential access method files

Sequential access files have a simple implementation in most computer languages, and C is one of them. In the example program shown in FIG. 8-10, a "card image" data file is read to the end of file.

8-10 C sequential file access program.

```
#include <stdio.h>
#include <limits.h>
#include <stdlib.h>
main ( )
{
FILE    *input;
int     line;
int     MAX__LINES = INT__MAX;
char    record[81];
int     error;
if ( ( input = fopen ( "sam.dat", "r" ) ) = = NULL ) {
    printf ( "ERROR! Can not open [sams.dat] file! \ n" );
    exit ( EXIT__FAILURE );
}
for ( line = 1; line< = MAX__LINES; line + + ) {
    if ( fgets ( record, sizeof(record), input ) = = NULL ) {
        if ( feof ( input ) )
            break;
        else
            printf ( "ERROR! Read error line %i! \ n", line );
            exit ( EXIT__FAILURE );
    }
    printf ( "Line %5.5i: ", line );
    error = fputs ( record, stdout );
    if ( error < 0 ) {
        printf ( "ERROR! Display error line %i! \ n", line );
        exit ( EXIT__FAILURE );
    }
}
if ( !feof ( input ) ) {
    printf ( "ERROR! Premature EOF at line %i! \ n", line – 1 );
    exit ( EXIT__FAILURE );
}
printf ( " \ nA total of %i records were read. \ n", line – 1 );
fclose ( input );
exit ( EXIT__SUCCESS );
}
```

```
Line 00001:        #include <stdio.h>
Line 00002:        #include <limits.h>
Line 00003:        #include <stdlib.h>
Line 00004:        main ( )
Line 00005:        {
Line 00006:        FILE    *input;
```

```
Line 00007:        int       line;
Line 00008:        int       MAX__LINES = INT__MAX;
Line 00009:        char      record[81];
Line 00010:        int       error;
    .
    .
    .
Line 00035:        fclose ( input );
Line 00036:        exit ( EXIT__SUCCESS );
Line 00037:        }
A total of 37 records were read.
```

Initially, the program opens the data file in a mode—"r"—that signifies that the file is a text (i.e., formatted) file that must exist prior to program execution. Then up to MAX_LINES are read from that file using C's fgets function. Note that this function will return NULL under two conditions: the end of file has been reached or a read error has occurred. C's feof function is used to distinguish between those two conditions. If the file has been read to the end, the break statement stops further processing of the for loop. If the file has not been read to the end, a read error message is displayed and execution of the entire program is terminated. Each line as read with fgets from the file is then displayed on the terminal screen with C's fputs function. When the for loop has stopped, C's feof function is used again to check for the end of file condition. If there is more data in the file, the user is warned that the file was not read to conclusion with this message:

ERROR! Premature EOF at line 10!

Otherwise, the count of records read is displayed like the following:

A total of 37 records were read.

Finally, the file is closed with C's fclose function. Sections on Fortran's read and write statements in Chapter 5 give other examples of sequential file input and output.

Direct access method files

Direct access files are Fortran's only native file structure. Access to data is controlled exclusively by the record number in such files with only three significant rules: a record must be written before being read, record N cannot be written until records one through N-1 have been written, and each record has a fixed logical record length. C's binary file type managed by C's fwrite and fread functions operating on fixed-length data structures provide an exact duplicate of Fortran's direct access files. By example, FIG. 8-11 shows a program that gathers information from the CRT, populates a

8-11 C direct access file program.

```
#include <stdio.h>
#include <stdlib.h>
main ( )
{
FILE      *unit;
size_t    lrecl;
char      buffer[64];
int       error;
int       line;
int       MAX_LINES = 3;
struct binary { long number;
                char message[60]; } record;
size_t    length;
int       i;
int       newline;
long      position;
printf ( "\nOpening [dam.dat] file . . . \n" );
if ( ( unit = fopen ( "dam.dat", "wb+" ) ) = = NULL ) {
    printf ( "ERROR! Can not open [dam.dat] file! \n" );
    exit ( EXIT_FAILURE );
}
lrecl = sizeof ( buffer );
printf ( "\nSetting logical record length "
         "to %i bytes . . . \n \n", lrecl );
error = setvbuf ( unit, buffer, _IOFBF, lrecl );
if ( error != 0 ) {
    printf ( "ERROR! Can not set logical "
             "record length!\n" );
    exit ( EXIT_FAILURE );
}
for ( line = 1; line < = MAX_LINES; line + + ) {
    printf ( "Enter message #%i: ", line );
    fgets ( record.message, lrecl, stdin );
    length = strlen ( record.message );
    record.message[length – 1] = '\0';
    record.number = (long) line;
    error = fwrite ( &record, lrecl, 1, unit );
    if ( error != 1 ) {
        printf ( "ERROR! Write error record "
                 "%i!\n", line );
        exit ( EXIT_FAILURE );
    }
}
rewind ( unit );
printf ( "\nFile contains these records . . . \n \n" );
for ( line = 1; line < = MAX_LINES; line + + ) {
    error = fread ( &record, lrecl, 1, unit );
    if ( error != 1 ) {
        printf ( "ERROR! Read error "
                 "record %i!\n", line );
        exit ( EXIT_FAILURE );
    }
```

8-11 Continued.

```
                printf ( printf ( "%4.4ld%s \ n",
                        record.number, record.message );
        }
        printf ( " \ nRetrieve records randomly . . . \ n \ n" );
        for ( i = 1; i < = 3; i + + ) {
AGAIN:          ;
                printf ( "Display what record? " );
                scanf ( "%i", &line );
                newline = getchar( );
                if ( ( line < 1 ) ||
                    ( line > 3 ) ) {
                    printf ( "Record number out of range! " );
                    goto AGAIN;
                }
                position = ( line − 1 ) * lrecl;
                error = fseek ( unit, position, SEEK__SET );
                if ( error ! = 0 ) {
                    printf ( "ERROR! fseek can not "
                            "position file! \ n" );
                    exit ( EXIT__FAILURE );
                }
                error = fread ( &record, lrecl, 1, unit );
                if ( error ! = 1 ) {
                    printf ( "ERROR! Read error record "
                            "%i! \ n", line );
                    exit ( EXIT__FAILURE );
                }
                printf ( "%4.4ld%s \ n",
                        record.number, record.message );
        }
        fclose ( unit );
        exit ( EXIT__SUCCESS );
    }
```

Opening [dam.dat] file . . .

Setting logical record length to 64 bytes . . .

Enter message #1:   "Gone Fishin" said the
Enter message #2:   sign in
Enter message #3:   the drug store window.

File contains these records . . .

0001"Gone Fishin" said the
0002sign in
0003the drug store window.

Retrieve records randomly . . .

Display what record? 3
0003the drug store window.

Display what record? 1
0001"Gone Fishin" said the
Display what record? 2
0002sign in

---

three record direct access file, displays that file sequentially, and then displays any given record from the file.

At the beginning of the example program, the file is opened in a mode—"wb"—signifying that the file is a new binary file that can be written to and read from at any record, as opposed to only at the end of the file. C's sizeof function computes the length, in bytes, of the data structure that will be used to set up data for input and output. The setvbuf function then establishes that record length as operative for that file. Then, three lines are read from the terminal with C's fgets function. Because this function reads the carriage return / line feed generated by the user when the enter (or return) key is struck, it is explicitly over-written with the null character. The other element of the record data structure is initialized to be the record number in the file. This is not required: any numeric data could have been placed in this field, or any other field definition could have been substituted in its place. Data being ready for output, C's fwrite function writes lrecl bytes to the file from the area pointed to by the address &record. Once rewound, the file is then read sequentially by C's fread function and displayed to the user.

Concluding this program is a section where the user specifies the order in which to read records. When prompted, the user enters a record number that, after checking for validity, is used to compute the file position. The line of code that reads

```
position = ( line − 1 ) * lrecl;
```

calculates the position in the file of the beginning of record number line as measured in bytes from file's beginning. In other words, with a 64 byte logical record length, the first record begins at byte 0 and extends through byte 63, the second record stretches from byte 64 to byte 127, and the third record occupies bytes 128 to 191. C's fseek function places the file pointer at that byte offset from the file's beginning in preparation for the next read. Once acquired randomly from the file, the record is displayed on the user's screen. Finally, the file is closed. Sections on Fortran's read and write statements in Chapter 5 give other examples of direct access file input and output.

One difference between Fortran and C direct access files needs to be highlighted. C terminates each character string with the null character (i.e., the "\0" character). So, a "ten-character" string actually contains nine characters and the null character. In Fortran, a ten character string contains ten characters. This causes a mismatch in binary direct access files. As mentioned in the read and write sections in Chapter 5, Fortran needs to read and discard a character*1 variable at the end of each C character string and write a character*1 variable initialized to char(0) at the end of each character string. Note that this "extra" character on input and output will affect the logical record length of such files.

Both Fortran and C provide comparable means of terminal and file input and output. C certainly offers a wider variety of functions from which to choose than Fortran's read, print, and write; and this translates into more control being placed in the hands of the programmer. For compatibility purposes, both languages support the same range of file types and that neither language has a file type that cannot be processed by the other. Lastly, you should not overlook the fact that C provides superior error control information on a per-read and write basis than available under Fortran; counts of fields and bytes correctly processed up to the point of an error can be used to develop quite specific error messages.

Formats

A significant percentage of source code for most programs deal solely with acquiring data and preparing such data for output. Interactive front ends for programs that began life in a batch mode and generic "report writers" are excellent examples of programs where nearly all processing is directed towards packaging data for input or output. Both Fortran and C provide means to edit incoming data and convert internal data representations into printable or displayable form. Fortran uses nearly thirty different edit descriptors in a format statement to massage data (see TABLE 8-1). C uses a dozen conversion specifiers with eight flags and modifiers qualifying those specifiers to accept and display formatted data (see TABLE 8-2).

Combinations of each valid flag with C's conversion specifiers is shown in FIG. 8-12. In the absence of a flag, C displays any given datum in as compact a field as possible. Once qualified by a flag, C can display information left-justified, with or without sign, with or without leading zeros, and with some field-sensitive editing for numeric data.

Some flag / conversion specifiers are not legal (i.e., leading zeros for character data). Most of the conversion specifiers include a field definition in the form of "width.precision," where the width number measures the span of the field on the output device and the precision number generally defines the number of digits to appear to the right of a decimal point. On output, width and/or precision can be replaced by an asterisk that will be evaluated when the program executes:

```
width     =   10;
precision =    5;
value     = 123.0;
printf ( "%*.*f\n", width, precision, value );
```

Table 8-1　Fortran Format Edit Descriptors.

Descriptor *	Repeatable	Brief Description
' ' apostrophe	no	encloses string (output only)
: colon	no	terminates format control
/ slash	no	advance to next record
A	yes	full character string
Aw	yes	all or part of character string
BN	no	ignore blanks (input only)
BZ	no	treat blanks as zero (input only)
Dw.d	yes	double precision
Ew.d	yes	exponents
Ew.dEe	yes	exponents
Fw.d	yes	without exponents
Gw.d	yes	varied magnitude
Gw.dEe	yes	varied magnitude
nH	no	character constant (output only)
1H	no	single space
1H+	no	no advance (overprint)
1H0	no	double space
1H1	no	form feed (top of form)
Iw	yes	integer
Iw.m	yes	integer with leading zeros
Lw	yes	logical (T or F)
kP	no	scale factor
S	no	processor controlled sign control
SP	no	force sign control (print + or −)
SS	no	suppress sign control
Tc	no	absolute positional editing
TLc	no	backward positional editing
TRc	no	forward positional editing
nX	no	skip n spaces

* Lowercase letters in the first column are defined as:
  c: character position (nonzero positive integer)
  d: digits after decimal point (positive integer)
  e: digits in exponent (nonzero positive integer)
  k: scale factor (any integer)
  m: mandatory digits printed (positive integer)
  n: character count (nonzero positive integer)
  w: field width (nonzero positive integer)

This would produce the following display (n.b., the "_" denotes a blank):

_123.00000

Deferring a full field specification until program execution is "run-time formatting," an example of which appeared in the format statement section in Chapter 5. On input, an asterisk indicates that a field should be skipped. For example, the following line of code

```
scanf ( "%i %*i %i", &first, &last );
```

Table 8-2. C Format Conversion Specifiers.

Conversion Specifier	Flags				Width	Precision	Modifier Input			Modifier Output		
	–	+	#	0			h	l	L	h	l	L
c character	y	n	n	n	n	y	y	n	n	n	n	n	n
d integer	y	y	y	n	y	y	y	y	y	n	y	y	n
e, E floating point	y	y	y	y	y	y	y	n	y	y	n	n	y
f floating point	y	y	y	y	y	y	y	n	y	y	n	n	y
g, G floating point	y	y	y	y	y	y	y	n	y	y	n	n	y
i integer	y	y	y	n	y	y	y	y	y	n	y	y	n
n I/O count	n	n	n	n	n	n	n	y	y	n	y	y	n
o octal	y	n	n	n	y	y	y	y	y	n	y	y	n
p pointer	y	n	n	n	n	y	n	n	n	n	n	n	n
s string	y	n	n	n	n	y	y	n	n	n	n	n	n
u unsigned integer	y	n	n	n	y	y	y	y	y	n	y	y	n
x, X hexadecimal	y	n	n	y	y	y	y	y	y	n	y	y	n

Column headings under the word "Flags" produce the following formats: (–), data is left-justified in field; (+), sign always printed; ( ), if first character is NOT a sign, then print a space; (0), print with leading zeroes; and (#), use an alternate form of output for certain conversion specifiers in which a decimal point is *always* printed for e and f specifiers, a decimal point is *always* printed as well as trailing zeros for g specifier, and prefix with zero or 0x for non-zero values printed with the o and x specifiers.

The precision of a conversion specifier affects printing as follows: (dioux), the minimum number of digits; (ef), the number of digits after the decimal point; (g), the number of significant digits; and (s), the maximum number of characters. Default precision for integer numbers (i.e., dioux) is one, and default precision for floating point numbers (i.e., efg) is six.

Column headings under the input and output modifier columns refer to short or long integers (i.e., the h and l modifiers) or long double (i.e., the L modifier).

Note that the three floating point conversion specifiers, (i.e., efg) convert their corresponding argument to a double on output. However, the default conversion on input is to the float data type. To convert on input to the double data type, use the l modifier.

8-12 C format conversion specifier sample program.

```
    main ( )
{
    int        ix  = 123;
    long       lx  = 456;
    unsigned   ux = 789;
    float      ex  = 0.12F;
    float      fx  = 0.12F;
    float      gx = 0.12F;
```

8-12 Continued.

```
double      dx = 4.5;
int         cx = 'A';
char        *sx = "abcde";
int         bytes[10];
printf ( "\nEach format displayed without flags . . .\n\n" );
printf ( " %c%n %d%n %e%n %f%n %g%n %i%n %o%n %s%n %u%n %x%n\n",
         cx,&bytes[0],  ix,&bytes[1],ex,&bytes[2],
         fx,&bytes [3],  gx,&bytes[4],ix,&bytes [5],
         ix,&bytes [6],  sx,&bytes [7],ux,&bytes[8],
         ix,&bytes [9]                             );
printf ( "\nTen fields ended at character positions . . . \n\n" );
printf ( "%i %i %i %i %i %i %i %i %i %i\n",
             bytes[0],  bytes[1],  bytes[2],
             bytes[3],  bytes[4],  bytes[5],
             bytes[6],  bytes[7],  bytes[8],
             bytes[9]                       );
printf ( "\nEach format displayed with flags . . .\n\n" );
printf ( "c: [%-15c]\n", cx );
printf ( "d: [%-15d] sign %+d space [% d] zeros %0.5d\n",
         ix, ix, ix,   ix );
printf ( "e: [%-15e] sign %+.2e space [% .2e] alt %#.2e\n"
         "                          zeros %0.2e\n",
         ex, ex, ex, ex, ex );
printf ( "f:  [%-15f] sign %+.2f space [% .2f] alt %#.2f "
         "zeros %0.2f\n",
         fx, fx, fx, fx, fx );
printf ( "g: [%-15g] sign %+.2g space [% .2g] alt %#.2g "
         "zeros %0.2g\n",
         gx, gx, gx, gx, gx );
printf ( "i:  [%-15i] sign %+i space [% i] zeros %0.5i\n",
         ix, ix, ix, ix, ix );
printf ( "o: [%-15o] zeros %0.5o\n",
         ix, ix );
printf ( "s: [%-15s]\n",
         sx );
printf ( "u: [%-15u] zeros %0.5u\n",
         ux, ux );
printf ( "x: [%-15o] alt %#x zeros %0.5x\n",
         ix, ix, ix );
    printf ( "\n" );
    return;
}
```

Each format displayed without flags . . .

A 123 1.200000e−001 0.120000 0.12 123 173 abcde 789 7b

Ten fields ended at character positions . . .

1 5 19 28 33 37 41 47 51 54

Each format displayed with flags . . .

c: [A   ]

8-12 Continued.

d:	[123	] sign +123 space [123] zeros 00123
e:	[1.200000e – 001	] sign +1.20e – 001 space [1.20e – 001] alt 1.20e – 001
		zeros 1.20e – 001
f:	[0.120000	] sign +0.12 space [0.12] alt 0.12 zeros 0.12
g:	[0.12	] sign +0.12 space [0.12] alt 0.12 zeros 0.12
i:	[123	] sign +123 space [123] zeros 00123
o:	[173	] zeros 00173
s:	[abcde	]
u:	[789	] zeros 00789
x:	[173	] alt 0x7b zeros 0007b

when reading the following record

123 456 789

would assign 123 to first and 789 to last because the %*i specifier causes the 456 field to be discarded.

For the most part, C is capable of creating an output string similar in appearance to its Fortran counterpart. However, the G floating point format is an exception. ANSI 77 standard Fortran defines the appearance of a number printed in a G format as a function of its value and the precision under which it is printed (see FIG. 8-13). C's G specifier has a similar rule: generally use the f specifier unless the exponent is less than – 4 or exceeds the precision, in which case use the e specifier. Figure 8-14 shows how C's G specifier handles the same range of values processed by a Fortran program.

8-13 Fortran G format example.

```
       program main
       real          x(6)
       integer       d
       character     char_zero
       integer       ichar_zero
       integer       i
       integer       j
       characterp•34 format200
       data          char_zero / 1H0 /
       data          format200 / '(1H ,1H[,g20.d,3H] [,g20.de4,1h])' /
       ichar_zero = ichar ( char_zero )
       do 400 i = 1, 3, 1
       write ( 6,100 )
100    format ( \ 1H , 'Enter fractional part: ' )
       read ( 5,• ) d
       x(1) = 0.01
       x(2) = 0.5
       x(3) = 5.0
       x(4) = 1.0 • ( 10.0 •• ( d–2 ) )
       x(5) = 1.0 • ( 10.0 •• ( d–1 ) )
       x(6) = 1.0 • ( 10.0 •• ( d ) )
       format200(14:14) = char ( ichar_zero + d )
```

8-13 Continued.

```
format200(26:26) = format200(14:14)
do 300 j = 1, 6, 1
write ( 6,format200 ) x(j), x(j)
300 continue
400 continue
stop
end
```

Enter fractional part: 1

```
[          .1E-04] [                .1E-0004]
[          .5     ] [                .5      ]
[          5.     ] [                5.      ]
[          .1     ] [                .1      ]
[          1.     ] [                1.      ]
[          .1E+02] [                .1E+0002]
```

Enter fractional part: 5

```
[        .10000E-04] [              .10000E-0004]
[        .50000     ] [              .50000      ]
[        5.0000     ] [              5.0000      ]
[        1000.0     ] [              1000.0      ]
[        10000.     ] [              10000.      ]
[        .10000E+06] [              .10000E+0006]
```

Enter fractional part: 9

```
[     .100000000E-04] [           .100000000E-0004]
[     .500000000     ] [           .500000000      ]
[     5.00000000     ] [           5.00000000      ]
[     10000000.0     ] [           10000000.0      ]
[     100000000.     ] [           100000000.      ]
[     .100000000E+10] [           .100000000E+0010]
```

8-14 C G format example.

```
#include <stdio.h>
#include <math.h>
main( )
{
double  x[6];
int     d;
int     i;
int     newline;
int     j;
for ( i = 0; i < 3; i + + ) {
    printf ( "\nEnter fractional part: \n" );
    scanf ( "%i", &d );
    newline = getchar( );
    x[0] = 0.01;
    x[1] = 0.5;
    x[2] = 5.0;
    x[3] = 1.0 * pow ( 10.0, (double) (d − 2) );
```

8-14 Continued.

```
        x[4] = 1.0 * pow ( 10.0, (double) (d – 1) );
        x[5] = 1.0 * pow ( 10.0, (double) (d   ) );
        for ( j = 0; j < 6; j + + ) {
            printf ( "[%#20.*g] [%#20.*g] \n",
                    d, x[j], d, x[j] );
        }
    }
    return;
}
```

```
Enter fractional part:    1
[               0.01]  [                   0.01]
[                0.5]  [                    0.5]
[                 5.]  [                     5.]
[                0.1]  [                    0.1]
[                 1.]  [                     1.]
[          1.e+001]  [              1.e+001]

Enter fractional part:    5
[          0.010000]  [              0.010000]
[          0.50000]  [              0.50000]
[          5.0000]  [              5.0000]
[          1000.0]  [              1000.0]
[          10000.]  [              10000.]
[       1.0000e+005]  [           1.0000e+005]

Enter fractional part:    9
[       0.0100000000]  [           0.0100000000]
[       0.500000000]  [           0.500000000]
[       5.00000000]  [           5.00000000]
[       10000000.0]  [           10000000.0]
[       100000000.]  [           100000000.]
[    1.00000000e+009]  [        1.00000000e+009]
```

Form control is provided under Fortran and C through special strings. Fortran's form control consists primarily of managing a line feed at the beginning of an output record (see FIG. 8-15). C can produce the identical display with special format characters such as \f for form feed, \r for a carriage return without a line feed, and \n for a new line (see FIG. 8-16).

8-15 Fortran line control program.

```
    program main
    write ( 6,1 )
  1 format ( // 1H , 'Program shows various slew ',
  -              'control Holleriths' )
    write ( 6,2 )
  2 format ( 1H , 'This is the first line on ',
  -              'the initial page.'
  -        / 1H , 'The next FORMAT will advance ',
  -              'to a new page.' )
```

8-15 Continued.

```
     write ( 6,3 )
   3 format ( 1H1, 'This is the first line on ',
   -               'the second page.' )
     write ( 6,4 )
   4 format ( 1H , '_____s overwritten.' )
     write ( 6,5 )
   5 format ( 1H+, 'This line i' )
     write ( 6,6 )
   6 format ( 1H , 'The next line should appear ',
   -               'after a blank line.' )
     write ( 6,7 )
   7 format ( 1H0, 'The line above should be blank.' )
     write ( 6,8 )
   8 format ( 1H , 'Program shows various slew ',
   -               'control Holleriths' // )
     stop
     end
```

Program shows various slew control Holleriths
This is the first line on the initial page.
The next FORMAT will advance to a new page.
This is the first line on the second page.
This line is overwritten.
The next line should appear after a blank line.

The line above should be blank.
Program shows various slew control Holleriths

8-16 C line control program.

```
     main ( void )
   {
     printf ( " \ n \ nProgram shows various "
              "slew control characters \ n" );
     printf ( "This is the first line "
              "on the initial page. \ n"
              "The next PRINTF will "
              "advance to a new page. \ n" );
     printf ( " \ fThis is the first line "
              "on the second page. \ n" );
     printf ( "_____s overwritten. \ r" );
     printf ( "This line i \ n" );
     printf ( "The next line should appear "
              "after a blank line. \ n" );
     printf ( " \ nThe line above should be blank. \ n" );
     printf ( "Program shows various slew "
              "control characters \ n \ n" );
     return;
   }
```

Program shows various slew control Holleriths
This is the first line on the initial page.

The next PRINTF will advance to a new page.
This is the first line on the second page.
This line is overwritten.
The next line should appear after a blank line.

The line above should be blank.
Program shows various slew control Holleriths

Fortran `format` statements can be emulated in C. When a `format` statement is needed to display the same information without variation, then C's #define statement is the best mechanism. When the information varies from time to time, then a complete formal function subprogram can be written or C's #define can be used to establish a statement function. Figure 8-17 shows how both kinds of `format` statements can be programmed in C. In the example program, the first #define statement instructs the compiler to replace the string format1 with that printf statement throughout the file. The second #define statement creates a statement function called format2 that accepts five arguments and feeds those arguments to a printf output statement. Note that the fourth argument, narg, is the number of characters to print from the character array b and is used to complete the specifier %.*s by "filling" in the asterisk. Also, the first two lines in this function end with the backslash character. This character tells the compiler that the logical line is "continued" on the next physical line of source code. The third #define statement establishes a statement function called format3 that takes four arguments and sends those arguments to a scanf input statement. The fourth and final #define statement creates another statement function that accepts text strings and the value of an int variable as arguments.

8-17 C emulation of Fortran format statement.

```
#include <stdio.h>
#define format1 printf ( "format1: \ n" )
#define format2( iarg, farg, carg, narg, barg ) \
        printf ( "format2: %i %f %s %.*s \ n", \
                iarg, farg, carg, narg, barg )
#define format3( iarg, farg, carg, barg ) \
        scanf ( "%i %f %s %3c", \
                iarg, farg, carg, barg )
#define format4( sarg1, sarg2, iarg ) \
        printf ( "%s %s %i \ n", sarg1, sarg2, iarg )
main ( )
{
int    i   = 123;
float  f   = 4.5F;
char *c   = "abc";
char  b[3] = { 'D', 'E', 'F' };
```

```
int    newline;
format1;
format2 ( i, f, c, sizeof(b)/sizeof(char), &b[0] );
format1;
printf ( "  Enter new values: " );
format3 ( &i, &f, c, &b[0] );
newline = getchar( );
format1;
format2 ( i, f, c, sizeof(b)/sizeof(char), &b[0] );
format1;
format4 ( "format4:", "i = ", i );
return;
}
```

```
format1:
format2: 123 4.500000 abc DEF
format1:
        Enter new values: 678 9.0 xyz UVW
format1:
format2: 678 9.000000 xyz UVW
format1:
format4: i = 678
```

Managing input and output is a major portion of the effort of any programmer working on a large suite of programs. Above and beyond file design, data storage methodology, and terminal interface schemes, basic data I/O consumes a large proportion of programming time. Differences exist between Fortran and C input/output mechanisms; but both can perform nearly all of the other's operations, and files created under one language can be processed by programs written in the other.

9

*C functions
new to Fortran*

C has a number of functions that are foreign to the Fortran programmer. Some of these new functions have been introduced in previous chapters, but six areas have yet to be discussed. This chapter will present C functions covering compiler preprocessing, enumerated constants, sorting and searching, random numbers, time and date handling, and recursive functions.

Compiler preprocessing

C source code lines beginning with the # symbol are interpreted at compile time as compiler directives. Many of the example programs in this book have used the #define directive; the #include directive was covered in Chapter 7; and FIG. 9-1 introduces eight new compiler directives.

After three constants are defined, the program tests the value of a decision variable—COMPUTER—in a very Fortran-like "#if . . . #elif . . . #else . . . #endif" sequence to initialize a data structure called host with an identification of the host computer, C compiler, and C compiler version number. Then, a long version of the #ifdef directive is used to determine if KNOWN is defined and to print a message stating whether or not it is. The #undef directive is then used to "un-define" KNOWN, and its state is tested with the #ifndef directive to confirm whether or not it is indeed undefined.

The last directive, #error, will display a message at compile time if the conditions under test cause it to be executed. The appropriate lines of the program are commented out because MISSING is not defined. If those lines were left intact, #error would be executed and the user-specified message would be displayed by the compiler. This directive is particularly useful to force a compiler error if some special situation arises where the programmer is sure that the compile should not continue.

```
        #define ABC          1
        #define DEF          2
        #define COMPUTER  1
        #define KNOWN
        void main ( )
    {
        struct world {   char    *computer;
                         char    *compiler;
                         float   version; } host;
        #if     COMPUTER == ABC
        host.computer   = "ABC Model D";
        host.compiler   = "ANSI";
        host.version    = 1.23;
        #elif   COMPUTER == DEF
        host.computer   = "EFG Model H";
        host.compiler   = "K&R";
        host.version    = 4.56;
        #else
        host.computer   = "Unknown";
        host.compiler   = "Unknown";
        host.version    = 0.0;
        #endif
        printf  ( " \ nHost is: %s computer"
                  " \ n   %s compiler"
                  " (Version %.2f) \ n",
                  host.computer, host.compiler,
                  host.version );
        #if     defined KNOWN
        printf ( " \ nKNOWN is defined. \ n" );
        #else
        printf ( " \ nKNOWN is NOT defined. \ n" );
        #endif
        #undef  KNOWN
        #ifndef KNOWN
        printf ( " \ nKNOWN is no longer defined. \ n" );
        #else
        printf ( " \ nKNOWN is still defined. \ n" );
        #endif
/*      #ifndef MISSING
        #error MISSING is NOT defined!
        #endif  */
        return;
    }
```

Host is: ABC Model D computer
        ANSI compiler (Version 1.23)

KNOWN is defined.

KNOWN is no longer defined.

Also, an implementation-defined compiler directive named #pragma has arguments and an interpretation that varies from host to host and from compiler to compiler. In effect, #pragma is a "place holder" defined in the ANSI C standard for each compiler developer to insert compiler and/or host specific preprocessing directives.

Enumerated constants

Enumerated constants are a special form of the C int data type. They are used to assign integer values to a set of variables, as shown in FIG. 9-2.

9-2 C enum data type sample program.

```
main( )
{
    enum cardinal__directions    { north,    south,    east,    west,    d };
    enum compass__rose           { ne = 10,  se = 20,  sw = 30, nw = 40, c };
    printf ( " \ n" );
    printf ( "directions: %2i %2i %2i %2i d = %2i \ n",
                north, south, east, west, d            );
    printf ( "compass : %2i %2i %2i %2i c = %2i \ n",
                ne,    se,    sw,    nw,   c            );
    return;
}

directions:    0    1    2    3   d= 4
compass :     10   20   30   40   c=41
```

In the example program, two sets of enumerated constants are defined. Each individual constant in the set cardinal_directions is, by default, assigned a successively higher integer starting at zero. Each individual constant in the set compass_rose is explicitly assigned an integer value with the last constant, c, receiving a value one higher than the previous constant, nw. Although the example uses positive integers in a monotonic series of values, the following assignment for compass_rose

$$\{ \text{ne} = 10, \text{se} = -7, \text{sw} = 66, \text{nw} = 9, c \};$$

is legal and would create a series of values for the five constants of $\{10, -7, 66, 9, 10\}$, where both the ne and c constants were assigned an identical value. It is important to realize that the enum statement establishes values for constants such that no element of cardinal_directions or compass_rose can be changed later in the program.

Sorting and searching

Sorting is directly supported in ANSI standard C through the qsort function. In the example program in FIG. 9-3, a list of six words is defined, ini-

9-3 C qsort (quick sort) sample program.

```
#include <stdio.h>
#include <stdlib.h>
#include <string.h>
int comparisons;
main ( )
{
    char *names[6] = {  "Baker",  "Foxtrot",  "Able",
                        "Echo",  "Charlie",  "ABLE"  };
    int   count = 6;
    int   i;
    int   compare ( char *one[ ], char *two[ ] );
    printf ( "UNSORTED" );
    for ( i = 0; i < count; i + + ) {
        printf ( " %s", names[i] );
    }
    printf ( "\n\nQSORT activity . . .\n\n" );
    comparisons = 0;
    qsort ( (void *) names,             (size__t) count,
            (size__t) sizeof ( *names ), compare      );
    printf ( "\nSORTED" );
    for ( i = 0; i < count; i + + ) {
        printf ( " %s", names[i] );
    }
    printf ( "\n\n" );
    return;
}
    int compare ( char *one[ ], char *two[ ] )
{
    int result;
    result = strcmp ( *one, *two );
    comparisons + = 1;
    printf ( "%2d %2d %-7s %-7s\n",
            comparisons, result, *one, *two );
    return result;
}
```

UNSORTED Baker Foxtrot Able Echo Charlie ABLE

QSORT activity . . .

```
 1    1  Foxtrot   Baker
 2  - 1  Able      Foxtrot
 3    1  Foxtrot   Baker
 4    1  Baker     ABLE
 5  - 1  Able      Baker
 6    1  Echo      Baker
 7  - 1  Baker     Charlie
 8  - 1  Baker     Echo
 9    1  Baker     Able
10  - 1  ABLE      Able
11  - 1  Able      Baker
12    1  Able      ABLE
13  - 1  ABLE      Able
```

9-3 Continued.

14	0	ABLE	ABLE
15	–1	Charlie	Echo
16	–1	Echo	Foxtrot
17	1	Echo	Charlie
18	–1	Charlie	Echo
19	0	Charlie	Charlie

SORTED ABLE Able Baker Charlie Echo Foxtrot

tialized, and displayed in the original initialization order. C's standard qsort function is invoked with reference to the array to be sorted, the number of elements in the array, the size of each element in the array, and the name of a user-written function that will "order" any arbitrary pair of array elements. The user-written function must return a negative, zero-valued, or positive number if the first element in the pair is considered less than, equal to, or greater than the second element, respectively. This is a user-written function, so any special ordering rules (i.e., partial key sorts) and data type handling can be explicitly managed by the programmer.

In the example, the compare function keeps a count of the number of times it is invoked, uses C's standard strcmp function to evaluate the lexical relationship of the two words, and also displays the components and result of each comparison. Finally, the list is displayed in sorted order. Usually the qsort function is an implementation of the Hoare's famous "quicksort" algorithm defined in 1961. It has two significant characteristics: it is not a stable sort (i.e., any equal valued elements may or may not be in the same relationship to one another after sorting) and has its worst performance when all N elements of the array to be sorted are already in order (i.e., the worst case execution time is proportional to $N*N$).

Searching is directly supported in ANSI standard C through the bsearch function, of which FIG. 9-4 is an example. In this example program, a table of seven state/region pairs is defined, initialized, and displayed in the original initialization order. The table of state/region pairs is then sorted, by state, using C's standard qsort function. The program then goes down a list of state names entered on the command line, matches each state name entered by the user to the state/region table, and displays the region of the country in which the state is located. C's standard bsearch function is used to match the user entry, argv[i], to the table of state/region pairs, states. The bsearch function is invoked with reference to the target name, the sorted table, the number of elements in the table, the size of each element in the table, and the name of a user-written function that will evaluate the match of the target to any arbitrary table entry. The user-written function must return a negative, zero-valued, or positive number if the target is considered numerically less than, equal to, or greater than the table element, respectively. This is a user-written function, so any special matching rules (i.e., full or partial key match) and data type handling can be explicitly managed by the programmer.

```
#include <stdio.h>
#include <stdlib.h>
#include <string.h>
struct place { char *state, *region; }
main ( int argc, char *argv[ ] )
{
    struct place states[ ] = {
                "Maine",        "northeastern",
                "Washington",   "northwestern",
                "Arizona",      "southwestern",
                "Kansas",       "central",
                "Alabama",      "southern",
                "Florida",      "southeastern",
                "Pennsylvania", "mid-atlantic"   };
    int     count;
    int     i;
    struct  place *result;
    int     scompare ( struct place *one,
                        struct place *two );
    int     bcompare ( char  *one,
                        struct place *two );
    if ( argc <= 1 ) {
        printf ( "\nUSAGE: %s state_1 state_2 "
                "state_i state_n\n", argv[0] );
        exit ( EXIT_FAILURE );
    }
    count = sizeof ( states ) / sizeof ( struct place );
    printf ( "\nSorting table of %i state-and-region "
            "pairs by state ...\n", count );
    qsort ( (void *) states,            (size_t) count,
            (size_t) sizeof ( struct place ), scompare );
    printf ( "\nSearching for regional location of %i "
            "states ...\n\n", argc-1 );
    for ( i=1; i<argc; i++ ) {
        if ( ( result = bsearch (
                        (void *) argv[i],
                        (void *) states,
                        (size_t) count,
                        (size_t) sizeof ( struct place ),
                        bcompare )
                    ) == NULL )
            printf ( "%s is NOT in the state-and-"
                    "region table.\n", argv[i] );
        else
            printf ( "%s is in the %s region.\n",
                    result->state, result->region );
    }
    exit ( EXIT_SUCCESS );
}
    int scompare ( struct place *one,
                    struct place *two )
{
    int result;
```

```
    result = strcmp ( one – > state, two – > state );
    return result;
}
    int bcompare ( char *one, struct place *two )
{
    int result;
    result = strcmp ( one, two – > state );
    return result;
}
```

Sorting table of 7 state-and-region pairs by state . . .

Searching for regional location of 6 states . . .

Maine is in the northeastern region.
Washington is in the northwestern region.
Arizona is in the southwestern region.
Florida is in the southeastern region.
Wherever is NOT in the state-and-region table.
Kansas is in the central region.

In the example, the bcompare function uses C's standard strcmp function to evaluate the match. C's bsearch function will return NULL if no match is found; otherwise, it will return a pointer to the matched element. Having been invoked with six "state" names, the example program then displays the region of the country in which each state is located, including one unmatched "state" (i.e., "Wherever").

Random numbers

A simple random number generator is part of C's standard library. Figure 9-5 demonstrates how to initialize a stream of random numbers with the srand function and produces random numbers until one of those numbers exceeds half the numerical range of the rand function. The random number generator is stable in that it will draw the same series every time if initialized with the same seed.

9-5 C random number functions.

```
    #include <stdlib.h>
    #include <limits.h>
    main ( )
{
    unsigned int seed;
            int i;
            int stop;
            int random;
    printf ( " \ nEnter seed: " );
    scanf ( "%u", &seed );
```

```
srand ( seed );
printf ( " \ nSequence initialized with seed "
        "of %u. \ n", seed );
printf ( " \ nDraw up to %i random integers in range "
        "(0,%ld) \ n", INT__MAX, (long)RAND__MAX );
stop = RAND__MAX / 2;
printf ( "and stop the first time an integer exceeds "
        "%i . . . \ n \ n", stop );
for ( i = 1; i < INT__MAX; i + + ) {
    random = rand( );
    printf ( "%i ", random );
    if ( random > stop )
        break;
}
printf ( " \ n \ n%Draw number %i exceeded %i. \ n",
        i, stop );
return;
}
```

Enter seed: 3

Sequence initialized with seed of 3.

Draw up to 32767 random integers in range (0,32767)
and stop the first time an integer exceeds 16383 . . .

48   7196   9294   9091   7031   23577

Draw number 6 exceeded 16383.

Time and date

C supports several time and date functions, demonstrated here in FIG. 9-6. Initially, time is retrieved from the system using the time function and is recorded as the number of seconds since the beginning of January 1, 1970. The amount of processor time used by the program is returned by the clock function in "ticks per second," which can be converted to seconds by dividing by the value of the macro CLK__TCK.

The ctime function converts the data returned by the time into a string. Time spans can be measured by using the time function at both the beginning and end of a code sequence and allowing the difftime function to calculate that difference in seconds. Functions gmtime and localtime convert the data returned by time into "Greenwich Mean Time" (i.e., UCT or Universal Coordinated Time) and local time, respectively. Both are displayed through the asctime function, which converts the data returned by time into a string. Note that the only difference between the ctime and asctime functions is the type of data on which they operate: ctime works with a pointer established by time and asctime works with a structure initialized on invocation of gmtime and localtime.

```
#include <stdio.h>
#include <stdlib.h>
#include <time.h>
main ( )
{
time__t      time__pointer;
long         seconds;
float        ticks;
float        tocks;
time__t      time__begin;
time__t      time__end;
struct tm *tm__pointer;
int          time__length;
char         time__string[40];
void         tmdisplay ( struct tm *tm__pointer );
printf ( " \ nDate and time functions . . . \ n" );
seconds = time ( &time__pointer );
ticks = ( float ) CLK__TCK;
printf ( " \ nCLK__TCK: %f clock ticks per second \ n", ticks );
tocks = ( float ) clock ( );
printf ( " \ nCLOCK: processor time so far "
         "%f units = %f seconds \ n", tocks, tocks/ ticks );
printf ( " \ nCTIME: " );
printf ( "%s",ctime ( &time__pointer ) );
time ( &time__begin );
printf ( " \ nDIFFTIME: enter anything " );
getchar( );
time ( &time__end );
printf ( ". . . that took %f seconds \ n",
         difftime ( time__end, time__begin ) );
time ( &time__pointer );
tm__pointer = gmtime ( &time__pointer );
printf ( " \ nGMTIME: " );
printf ( "%s", asctime ( tm__pointer ) );
tm__pointer = localtime ( &time__pointer );
printf ( " \ nLOCALTIME: " );
printf ( "%s", asctime ( tm__pointer ) );
printf ( " \ nTIME: %ld seconds since beginning "
         "of 1970 \ n", seconds );
time__length = strftime ( time__string, 40,
                "%A %d %B %Y %I:%M:%S %p",
                tm__pointer );
printf ( " \ nSTRFTIME: (%i bytes) [%s] \ n",
         time__length, time__string );
printf ( " \ nTM components . . . \ n" );
tmdisplay ( tm__pointer );
tm__pointer - >tm__mon - = 4;
printf ( " \ nTM components 4 months prior . . . \ n" );
mktime ( tm__pointer );
tmdisplay ( tm__pointer );
tocks = ( float ) clock ( );
printf ( " \ nCLOCK: processor time so far "
         "%f units = %f seconds \ n", tocks, tocks/ ticks );
```

```
      return;
   }
      void tmdisplay ( struct tm *tm_pointer )
   {
   char    *months[12] = {   "January",    "February",    "March",
                             "April",      "May",         "June",
                             "July",       "August",      "September",
                             "October",    "November",    "December"   };
   char    *days[7] = {   "Sunday",     "Monday",     "Tuesday",
                          "Wednesday",  "Thursday",   "Friday",
                          "Saturday"                                 };
   char    *dst[2] = { "Standard", "Daylight Savings" };
   printf ( "%3.2d tm_sec . . . seconds 0 – 59 \ n",
         tm_pointer – >tm_sec );
   printf ( "%3.2d tm_min . . . minutes 0 – 59 \ n",
         tm_pointer – >tm_min );
   printf ( "%3.2d tm_hour . . . hours 0 – 23 \ n",
         tm_pointer – >tm_hour );
   printf ( "%3.2d tm_mday . . . day of month 1 – 31 \ n",
         tm_pointer – >tm_mday );
   printf ( "%3.2d tm_mon . . . month 0 – 11 (0 = January) %s \ n",
         tm_pointer – >tm_mon, months[tm_pointer – >tm_mon] );
   printf ( "%3d tm_year . . . years since 1900 A.D. \ n",
         tm_pointer – >tm_year );
   printf ( "%3d tm_wday . . . day of week 0 – 6 (0 = Sunday) %s \ n",
         tm_pointer – >tm_wday, days[tm_pointer – >tm_wday] );
   printf ( "%3.3d tm_yday . . . day of year 0 – 366 \ n",
         tm_pointer – >tm_yday );
   printf ( "%3d tm_isdst . . . daylight savings time flag: ",
         tm_pointer – >tm_isdst );
   if ( tm_pointer – >tm_isdst < 0 )
      printf ( "[UNKOWN] " );
   if ( tm_pointer – >tm_isdst = = 0 )
      printf ( "%s", dst[0] );
   if ( tm_pointer – >tm_isdst > 0 )
      printf ( "%s", dst[1] );
   printf ( " Time \ n" );
   printf ( "      %s", asctime ( tm_pointer ) );
   return;
   }
```

Date and time functions . . .

CLK_TCK: 1000.000000 clock ticks per second

CLOCK: processor time so far 60.000000 units = 0.060000 seconds

CTIME: Thu Nov 29 20:44:58 1990

DIFFTIME: enter anything . . . that took 2.000000 seconds

GMTIME: Fri Nov 30 04:45:00 1990

LOCALTIME: Thu Nov 29 20:45:00 1990

9-6 Continued.

TIME: 659940298 seconds since beginning of 1970

STRFTIME: (37 bytes) [Thursday 29 November 1990 08:45:00 PM]

TM components . . .
```
 00 tm__sec    . . . seconds 0 – 59
 45 tm__min    . . . minutes 0 – 59
 20 tm__hour   . . . hours 0 – 23
 29 tm__mday   . . . day of month 1 – 31
 10 tm__mon    . . . month 0 – 11 (0 = January) November
 90 tm__year   . . . years since 1900 A.D.
  4 tm__wday   . . . day of weeek 0 – 6 (0 = Sunday) Thursday
332 tm__yday   . . . day of year 0 – 366
  0 tm__isdst  . . . daylight savings time flag: Standard Time
    Thu Nov 29 20:45:00 1990
```

TM components 4 months prior . . .
```
 00 tm__sec    . . . seconds 0 – 59
 45 tm__min    . . . minutes 0 – 59
 20 tm__hour   . . . hours 0 – 23
 29 tm__mday   . . . day of month 1 – 31
 06 tm__mon    . . . month 0 – 11 (0 = January) July
 90 tm__year   . . . years since 1900 A.D.
  0 tm__wday   . . . day of weeek 0 – 6 (0 = Sunday) Sunday
209 tm__yday   . . . day of year 0 – 366
  1 tm__isdst  . . . daylight savings time flag: Daylight Savings Time
    Sun Jul 29 20:45:00 1990
```

CLOCK: processor time so far 2530.000000 units = 2.530000 seconds

---

Both ctime and asctime create a string with an identical layout. If the date and time string created by asctime or ctime are not suitable, other varieties of date and time formats can be established by the strftime function. Date and time data are also available on a "broken down basis" and held in a nine element data structure. Individual elements of this data structure can be accessed as shown in the tmdisplay function in the example program.

Of special interest is that this full data structure can be projected forward and backward in time to determine the date and time of a past or future moment by manipulating one or more of the elements of this data structure. In the example program, C's standard mktime is used to determine the date and time of a moment four months prior to the execution of the program. Finally, the example program displays the total amount of processing time used by the program.

Recursive functions

Recursive functions are fully supported by C. In essence, a function can call itself in the course of completing its task. Figure 9-7 relies on this fea-

9-7 C recursive program.

```
#include <stdio.h>
#include <stdlib.h>
int count     =    0;
int MAXIMUM = 100;
int MINIMUM =     0;
int number;
main ( int argc, char *argv[ ] )
{
    int result;
    int guess ( int * );
    printf ( " \ n%s program invoked with %i arguments . . . \ n",
          argv[0], argc-1 );
    if ( argc != 2 ) {
        printf ( "ERROR! Usage is %s positive__number! \ n",
              argv[0] );
        exit ( EXIT__FAILURE );
    }
    number = ( int ) strtol ( argv[1], NULL, 10 );
    if ( ( number <        0 ) ||
       ( number > MAXIMUM ) ) {
        printf ( "ERROR! Number > %i . . . too large! \ n",
              MAXIMUM );
        exit ( EXIT__FAILURE );
    }
    printf ( " \ nStarting to guess the number between "
          "%i and %i . . . \ n \ n", MINIMUM, MAXIMUM );
    result = MAXIMUM;
    result = guess ( &result );
    printf ( " \ nGuessed the number %i in %i trys. \ n",
          result, count );
    return;
}

int guess ( int *current )
{
    int local;
    count += 1;
    printf ( "Guess #%i is %i \ n", count, *current );
    if ( *current == number )
        return *current;
    if ( *current > number )
        MAXIMUM = *current;
    else
        MINIMUM = *current;
    local = MINIMUM + ( ( MAXIMUM - MINIMUM ) / 2 );
    local = guess ( &local );
    *current = local;
    return *current;
}
```

FIG97.RUN program invoked with 1 arguments . . .

Starting to guess the number between 0 and 100 . . .

Guess #1 is 100
Guess #2 is 50
Guess #3 is 75
Guess #4 is 87
Guess #5 is 93
Guess #6 is 90
Guess #7 is 91

Guessed the number 91 in 7 trys.

---

ture to guess a number between zero and 100. Starting with an initial guess, the program converges on the target value entered on the command line by halving the difference between the last guess over the target value and the last guess under the target value. Unless a host operating system provides special services, however, Fortran cannot support recursive programs.

10
Summary

This book assumes that circumstances exist in which programmers intimately familiar with Fortran will have opportunities or be required to program in C. However, there is little merit in entertaining any argument as to which language is "better"; the decision to program in one language versus another is a complex function of knowledge of the underlying problem to be solved, mastery of the language being considered, and time and/or business constraints. Even within the "Fortran family," decisions are still made between Fortran 66 versus Fortran 77 and ANSI standard Fortran versus proprietary extensions. Weighing the costs and benefits of the choice of a programming language is a difficult task.

In the near future, Fortran programmers may also change their programming paradigm to accommodate "Fortran Extended." This specification grew out of work to develop a new ANSI standard Fortran as an evolutionary next step beyond Fortran 77 and as Fortran 77's replacement. This work began in 1978 and produced a draft standard—ANSI X3J3/S8.104—in May, 1987. ANSI committees took under advisement public comments on this draft standard and elected to change its status from a replacement for Fortran 77 to a companion specification to Fortran 77. Correspondingly, the 1987 draft was revised—ANSI X3J3/S8.112—and published in June, 1989, as a companion rather than a replacement to Fortran 77. The revised draft received an initial period of public review in the fall of 1989 with a follow-up review in the fall of 1990. A final version could be expected in 1991.

Fortran Extended specifies features that are very useful to the design and development of maintainable code and the programmatic solution of scientific and technical problems. Ten broad classes of these features are source code form, program structure, variable declarations, subprogram arguments, intrinsic functions, variable initialization, arrays, control structures, file handling, and a miscellany. Each of these areas will be described in turn. Several Fortran Extended program fragments are presented in this chapter; but without a commercially available compiler, they could not be fully checked. They were written with careful reference to the ANSI standard but, again, without a compiler's rigid enforcement, errors may persist as evidence of a misunderstanding or misreading of the ANSI standard.

Source code can take two forms under Fortran Extended: free and fixed. Free form source code specifies lines of up to 132 characters, with comments beginning anywhere on the line as long as they are preceded by an exclamation point. Separate Fortran statements can also be "packed" into one line of source code where each statement is separated by a semicolon, such as the following:

```
i=1;r=2.34;c='letter' ! Three statements on one line
```

Lastly, a line in a free form source code file is marked as being continued on another line by ending the line with an ampersand:

```
if ( i .eq. 123 .and. &
     j .eq. 456        ) k = 789
```

Up to 39 continuation lines are accepted. Fixed form source code is the familiar Fortran 77 style with two changes: the exclamation point is accepted along with the letter C and the asterisk as an indication that a line is a comment; and, as with free form, several statements separated by a semi-colon can share one line of code. Fortran Extended also requires that any given program unit must be coded in either free or fixed (but not both) forms.

Program structure is revised in Fortran Extended to accommodate a new means of declaring global data. A simple Fortran 77 program, such as the following,

```
program seven
integer one, two
common / area / one, two
call sub7
stop
end
subroutine sub7
integer one, two
common / area / one, two
one = 123
return
end
```

might be rewritten as

```
program nine
      use area
```

```
       call sub9
   end program nine
   subroutine sub9
         use area
         one = 123
   end subroutine sub9
   module area
           integer one, two
   end module area
```

in which the main program and the subroutine are encapsulated in a
"start/end" syntax not much different from Fortran 77's "if/end if"
pair, global data is defined in a separate program unit called a module that
is referenced in the main program and subprogram by the use statement.
Also, code can be incorporated into a source code file using the INCLUDE
statement (i.e., like C's #include statement).

Fortran Extended specifies new methods for declaring variables. Public or private variables, adjustable sized arrays, and user-selected numerical precision are shown in this example:

```
integer, private :: local
real, dimension (3,3) :: three_by_three
double precision, allocatable, dimension (:) :: adjust
integer, parameter :: percent = selected_int_kind ( 2 )
integer ( percent ) score
integer, parameter :: dp = kind ( 0.0d0 )
real ( dp ) bigone
character ( len = 16 ) first_name
integer, function :: userfunction
score = 98_percent
bigone = 7654321.0_dp
allocate ( adjust(2,5), stat = iaerror )
deallocate ( adjust, stat = iderror )
```

Variable local will be "private" to the programming unit in which it
is declared, so its definition and the scope of its value is restricted. Array
three_by_three is a standard single-precision array. Array adjust is
of data type double precision, but the size of the array is not specified
until later when the allocate statement is executed. Parameter percent is initialized to signal integers with two significant digits (i.e.,
between −99 and 99) and is used to declare a variable score and qualify
the constant assigned to that variable. Similarly, parameter dp is initialized to signal double precision variables and is used to declare a variable bigone and qualify the constant assigned to that variable. Finally, a
character variable and integer-valued function are declared.

Variables used in subprogram arguments also have a new means of
specification in Fortran Extended including keyword calls, generic subroutine names, and "intent" and optional arguments. For example, if
the arguments to a subroutine are declared in an interface section in a

module subprogram unit, then the names of the dummy arguments can be used as keywords in the call:

```
module overall
      interface
            subroutine individual ( age, sex, ssn )
                  integer            age
                  character ( len = 1 ) sex
                  integer            ssn
            end subroutine individual
      end interface
end module overall
call individual ( age=29, sex='F', ssn=123456789 )
```

This functionality is similar to the keyword concept of Fortran open, inquire, and close statements, among others. Generic subroutines can also be defined as

```
interface exchange
      subroutine i_exchange ( i, j )
            integer, intent ( inout ) :: i, j
      end subroutine i_exchange
      subroutine r_exchange ( x, y )
            real,      intent ( inout ) :: x, y
      end subroutine r_exchange
end interface
call exchange ( k, l )
call exchange ( a, b )
```

in which a general purpose subroutine called exchange is defined. It accepts two variables and allows a type specific user-written subroutine i_exchange to be called if exchange's arguments are integer and r_exchange to be called if exchange's arguments are real. This functionality is similar to Fortran 77's generic versus specific names for certain intrinsic functions (i.e., log versus alog, dlog, and clog). The interface definition could also be enclosed within a module subprogram unit, recognized in other subprogram units through the use statement, and thereby made globally accessible across the entire program. In addition, subroutine arguments can be explicitly declared as input to, output from, input-and/or-output, and optional:

```
call subargs ( w, x, y )
call subargs ( w, x, y, z )
subroutine subargs ( a, b, c, d )
      real,            intent ( in    ) :: a
      real,            intent ( inout ) :: b
      real,            intent ( out   ) :: c
      real, optional, intent ( in    ) :: d
      c = a / 2.0
      if ( present ( d ) ) b = b * 2.0
```

Regarding subroutine subargs, the value of the first argument cannot be changed, the value of the second argument might be changed, the value of the third argument will be changed, and the presence of a fourth argument, when present, causes a particular expression to be evaluated.

Fortran Extended defines a number of new intrinsic functions to facilitate some of its novel features. Some of these intrinsic functions are listed in TABLE 10-1.

Table 10-1   Fortran Extended Selected Intrinsic Functions.

Function name	Definition
Numeric functions	
ceiling	least integer greater than or equal to number
floor	greatest integer less than or equal to number
Character functions	
achar	character in position in ASCII collation
adjustl	adjust string left (remove leading blanks)
adjustr	adjust string right (remove trailing blanks)
iachar	position of character in ASCII collation
len_trim	length of string without trailing blanks
repeat	repeated string concatenation
scan	scan for first or last character(s) in string
trim	remove trailing blanks from string
verify	confirm presence of character(s) in string
Numeric inquiry functions	
digits	number of significant digits in numeric model
epsilon	number almost negligible compared to one
huge	largest number in numeric model
maxexponent	maximum exponent in numeric model
minexponent	minimum exponent in numeric model
precision	decimal precision
radix	base in numeric model
range	decimal exponent range
tiny	smallest number in numeric model
Bit inquiry function	
bit_size	number of bits in numeric model
Bit manipulation	
btest	bit testing
iand	logical and
ibclr	clear bit
ibits	bit extraction
ibset	set bit
ieor	exclusive OR
ior	inclusive OR
ishft	logical shift
ishftc	circular shift
not	logical complement

Table 10-1   Continued.

Array manipulation functions

all	.TRUE. if all array values are true
any	.TRUE. if any array value is true
count	number of .TRUE. elements in array
dotproduct	dot product of two vectors
matmul	vector or 2-dimensional matrix multiplication
maxloc	location of maximum value in array
maxval	maximum value in array
minloc	location of minimum value in array
minval	minimum value in array
product	product of all array elements
sum	sum of all array elements
transpose	transpose two-dimensional array

Array inquiry functions

allocated	.TRUE. if array is allocated
lbound	returns vector of lower bounds set for array
size	total number of elements in array
ubound	returns vector of upper bounds set for array

Array construction functions

merge	merge two arrays under mask
pack	pack N-dimensional array into vector
spread	replicate array by adding a dimension
unpack	unpack vector into N-dimensional array

Intrinsic subroutines

date_and_time	retrieve date and time from host system
mvbits	copy bits from one integer to another
random	return pseudo random number
randomseed	initialize pseudo random number generator
system_clock	obtain ticks, ticks/second, maximum ticks

Initializing variables in Fortran Extended is very similar to Fortran 77 with two major additions: number bases other than 10, and data structures. Variables can be declared to have values in any of four bases (i.e., decimal, binary, octal, and hexadecimal) in a data statement:

```
integer decimal, binary, octal, hexadecimal
data decimal        /       127  /
data binary         / B'1111111' /
data octal          / O'   125' /
data hexadecimal / Z    7f'  /
```

All four variables are initialized to the same value as represented in a different base.

Data structures are a major feature of Fortran Extended and are analogous to structures in C. For example, in the following code,

```
type lumber
      character ( len =  4 ) nominal
      integer               length
      character ( len = 10 ) wood
end type lumber
type ( lumber ) :: studs
type ( lumber ) :: planks
data studs / lumber ( '2×4', 8, 'White Pine' ) /
data planks % nominal  /  '1×10'    /
data planks % length   /  6         /
data planks % wood     /  'Red Oak' /
```

a derived data type named lumber is defined with three elements, and two data structures—studs and planks—are declared of type lumber and initialized in two different styles. The flexibility that the combined derived data types and data structures offer might prove useful in coding complex technical and commercial models in Fortran Extended.

Many features are introduced in Fortran Extended to deal with arrays, including dynamic allocation, sections, augmentation, and whole-array operations.

During program execution, storage space for an array can be acquired and released:

```
real, allocatable, dimension (:) :: x
allocate ( x(-5:5,10), stat = iaerror )
if ( allocated ( x ) ) &
      deallocate ( x, stat = iderror )
```

Here, storage is acquired for an 11-by-10 two-dimension array named x using the allocate statement, checked for existence with the allocated intrinsic function, and then released by the deallocate statement.

Array sections are particular slices of an array. For example, look at the following Fortran Extended code:

```
integer, dimension ( 6 ) :: whole
integer, dimension ( 3 ) :: even
character ( len = 32 ), dimension ( 100 ) :: word
character ( len =  1 ), dimension ( 100 ) :: begin
real, dimension ( 5 ) :: all
real, dimension ( 3 ) :: extract, some
even = whole ( 2 : 6 : 2 )
begin = words ( : ) ( 1:1 )
extract = ( / 5, 3, 1 / )
some = all ( extract )
```

Even is comprised of whole(2), whole(4), and whole(6), begin is comprised of the first letters of words, and the three elements of some are equivalent to all(5), all(3), and all(1), in that order.

An array also can be augmented with an additional dimension, like the following,

```
real, dimension ( 2, 2 ) :: column
column = ( / 2, 4 / )
square = reshape (  shape = ( / 2, 2 / ),       &
                    source = ( / 1, 3 / ),      &
                    column              )
```

so that the array square has the values one and three in the first column and values two and four in the second column.

Operations can be performed on entire arrays in a single statement, such as this code,

```
real, dimension ( 10, 20 ) :: x
real average
average = sum ( x ) / size ( x )
```

where the intrinsic function sum totals all 200 values in the array x, and the intrinsic function size reports the number of elements—200—in the array x.

Finally, a whole array can be examined, like the following:

```
real, dimension ( 100 ) :: fever
character ( len = 32 ), dimension ( 100 ) :: action
where ( fever > 100 )
        action = 'Give aspirin and juice.'
        fever = fever - 1.0
elsewhere
        fever = 98.6
        action = 'No action required.'
end where
```

Attributes of arrays also can be queried with some of the new Fortran Extended intrinsic functions (see TABLE 10-1).

Fortran 77 and Fortran Extended share similar if and do control structures but Fortran Extended adds some new features. The if control structure can be named, as in

```
maybe : if ( x .gt. 1.23 ) then
            y = 4.56
        else
            y = 7.89
end if maybe
```

which clearly associates an end if statement with its controlling if statement.

Fortran Extended also supports names and introduces certain branching statements for do loops, such as

```
i = 1
right : do while ( i .le. 10 )
            if ( i .eq. 5 ) cycle right
            left : do j = 1, 10, 1
                        call center
                        if ( j .ge. i ) exit right
            end do left
        i = i + 1
end do right
```

where, in the loop named left, subroutine center is called i times where i is the control variable in the loop named right. When i is equal to five, the loop named left is not executed at all.

Lastly, Fortran Extended establishes a new control structure named select, such as

```
whichever : select  case ( i )
                    case ( 2, 4, 6, 8 )
                            call even
                    case ( 1, 3, 5, 7 )
                            call odd
                    case default
                            call zero_ten
end select whichever
```

in which an action can be taken depending on a set of values specified for the control variable. In each case, named control structures might contribute to the clarity and maintainability of Fortran source code.

File handling is changed in Fortran Extended in regard to three areas: new open statement options, inquire statement syntax, and file input/output (especially read/write statement options and edit descriptors).

When a file is opened in Fortran Extended, four new options can be specified in the open statement:

action   a file can be opened for READ, WRITE, or READWRITE (default) access.

delim   on list-directed output, character constants can be delimited by an APOSTROPHE, QUOTE marks, or without any delimiters (i.e., NONE, which is the default).

pad   on formatted input, the record will or will not (i.e., YES—the default—or NO) be logically padded with blanks if the input list and format requires more data than the record contains in order to be satisfied.

position   sequential access files can be opened with the file positioned ASIS (default), at the beginning (REWIND), or at the end of the file (APPEND).

Also, the `status` keyword in the `open` statement has a new legal value, REPLACE; REPLACE will create a file if a file by the user-supplied name does not exist, or it will delete the file by the user-supplied name if it does exist and then create a new file with the user-supplied name. These Fortran Extended `open` statement changes provide additional file control for the programmer.

The `inquire` statement is extended to cover the new open keywords and is also given a new facility. This new facility is demonstrated by the following line of code:

```
inquire ( iolength = i ) array, b, j, string1, x
```

In this line, i will be set to the "length" of output record if those five variables were written to an unformatted direct access file. This "length" variable, i, will be measured in the same processor-dependent units as are used for the `recl` keyword option in the open statement.

File input and output is extended by five new `read` and/or `write` statement options and three new edit descriptors. The read/write statement options are

advance   formatted sequential access files under an explicit format specification can be processed with partial record input/output (i.e., advance = NO, default is YES).

eor   under no advancing input, if the end-of-record is encountered, control branches to the label given after this keyword.

nml   specifies a name list group name.

nulls   under list-direct input, the variable given after this keyword is set to the number of variables in the input list for which no value appears in the input stream.

size   under no advancing input, the variable given after this keyword is set to the number of characters transferred under the current format.

An example of partial record input is

```
        character ( len = 2 ), dimension ( 5 ) :: vowels
        read ( 5,1,advance='NO',size=n ) ( vowels(i),i=1,3)
     1  format ( 3a2 )
!       backspace 5
        read ( 5,2                      ) ( vowels(i),i=4,5)
     2  format ( 2a2 )
```

in which, if the record read "a e i o u ," then the first `read` would initialize the first three elements of vowels (n.b., n would be equal to six) and the second `read` would provide values for vowels(4) and vowels(5). Note that if the `backspace` command had not been commented out, the file position would have returned to the beginning of the record. Consequently, after the second read, the last two elements of vowels would be "a " and "e " instead of "o " and "u." No advancing and "namelist" input/output under various names and with different syntax have been common extensions to Fortran 77: Fortran Extended recognizes the need for such constructs.

Lastly, four new format edit descriptors are defined (B, O, Z, and EN) that allow binary, octal, hexadecimal, and engineering formats. The last new format descriptor, EN, sets the mantissa between one and 999 (inclusive), a user-specified count of digits after the decimal point, and an exponent that is divisible by three (i.e., 1234.5 would appear as 1.234E+03 with an EN12.3 edit descriptor).

Additional capabilities of Fortran Extended include recursive programming, pointers, and the concept of language evolution. Neither ANSI, the Fortran 66, or Fortran 77 standards required a standard compliant compiler to support recursive programming: Fortran Extended has such a requirement for functions and subroutines. Pointers also have full support in Fortran Extended as a new data type and can be associated, nullified, and disassociated with a target object. Finally, Fortran Extended declares as obsolete several features of the ANSI standard Fortran 77 programming language, including the arithmetic if statement, real and double precision do loop control variables, shared do loop termination statements, do loop termination on other than a continue statement, alternate subroutine routines, the pause statement, the assign statement, the assigned go to construct, and formal labels specified in read/write statements by an assigned variable. The net effect of these features can be implemented by better methods than available in Fortran 77 and may not be recognized in whatever Fortran standard eventually supersedes Fortran Extended.

Any review of Fortran Extended leads towards a conclusion that the standard serves to codify some existing practice and introduce new features. Ten major aspects of Fortran Extended reflect features of C: free form source code, interface statement (i.e., C's function prototypes), dynamic array allocation, data structures, do/while and select control structures, file open action (i.e., READ, WRITE, and READWRITE), other than decimal base format edit descriptors, no advancing partial record input/output, recursive programming, and pointers. Given the different syntax in which these features are implemented in Fortran Extended versus C, it is clear that Fortran Extended is not modeled after C but rather incorporates modern programming language requirements as they have evolved since the late 1970s.

This book is addressed to the experienced Fortran programmer: a programmer who is forever likely to choose Fortran for each and every one-shot programming task. Often this programmer has a thorough applications knowledge of the problem to be solved and is familiar with the scientific, technical, or commercial discipline from which the problem arises. In this book, I attempt to preserve this knowledge and encourage the programmer to apply it effectively when coding in C. If the Fortran programmer receives a solid, reliable understanding of C by reading this book, then that objective has been achieved.

A
C compilers

In practice, you cannot learn C simply by reading and studying. To ensure development of expertise, you must actually use the language in a series of programming projects. You could conveniently experiment with C by gaining access to a C compiler on a microcomputer. Accordingly, this appendix lists nearly four dozen C compilers currently available in the market. The list gives the product name, the microcomputer(s) on which it will run, and the vendor's name, address, and telephone number.

This list of C compilers is provided only as a convenience to readers of this book; the presence of a particular product or vendor does not constitute an endorsement. Similarly, the absence of a particular product or vendor does not imply that any evaluation kept it off the list.

Aztec C
(Amiga, Apple, Atari, PC, Macintosh)
    Manx Software Systems
    P.O. Box 55
    Shrewsbury, NJ 07701
    (201) 542-2121
    (800) 221-0400

C68 (Motorola MC680X0)
    Alcyon Corp.
    6888 Nancy Ridge Dr.
    San Diego, CA 92121
    (619) 587-1155

C86PLUS (PC)
    Computer Innovations
    980 Shrewsbury Av.
    Tinton Falls, NJ 07724
    (201) 542-5920
    (800) 922-0169

C 86 (PC)
    Real-Time Computer Science
    Corp.
    1390 Flynn Rd., Unit E
    Camarillo, CA 93010
    (805) 987-9781

C and C++ Optimizing Compilers
(PC and UNIX)
    Green Hills Software
    510 Castillo St.
    Santa Barbara, CA 93101
    (805) 965-6044

C Compiler
    Supersoft, Inc.
    510 W. Park Av.
    P.O. Box 1628
    Champaign, IL 61820
    (217) 359-2112
    (800) 678-3600

C Compiler
    Wintek Corp.
    1801 S. St.
    Lafayette, IN 47904
    (317) 742-0428
    (800) 742-6809

C Compiler (PC)
    IBM Corp.
    Old Orchard Rd.
    Armonk, NY 10504
    (914) 765-1900

C Cross Compiler
(for PC on Apollo, VAX, Sun)
    Oasys
    230 Second Av.
    P.O. Box 8990
    Waltham, MA 02254-8990
    (617) 890-7889

C Native Compilers
(Atari, DEC PDP-11 & VAX,
IBM 370 & PC)
    Whitesmiths, Ltd.
    59 Power Rd.
    Westford, MA 01886
    (617) 692-7800
    (800) 225-1030

C Network Compiler (Intel 80X86)
    Novell Development Products
    Novell, Inc.
    P.O. Box 9802
    Austin, TX 78766

C Optimizing Compiler (PC)
    Microsoft Corp.
    16011 NE. 36th Way
    P.O. Box 97017
    Redmond, WA 98073
    (206) 882-8080

C++ Compiler
(PC, Intel 386, SUN-3, VAX)
    Oregon Software, Inc.
    6915 SW. Macadam, S-200
    Portland, OR 97219-2397
    (503) 245-2202

C-51 (PC-to-8051 cross compiler)
    Franklin Software, Inc.
    888 Saratoga Av., S-2
    San Jose, CA 95129
    (408) 296-8051

C-terp (PC)
    Gimpel Software
    3207 Hogarth Ln.
    Collegeville, PA 19426
    (215) 584-4261

CrossCode C
(PC or UNIX for HD64180,
68000, Z80)
    Software Development
    Systems, Inc.
    3110 Woodcreek Dr.
    Downers Grove, IL 60515
    (312) 971-8170
    (800) 448-7733

C_talk (PC)
    CNS, Inc.
    Software Products Dept.
    7090 Shady Oak Rd.
    Eden Prairie, MN 55344
    (612) 944-0170

Eco-C88 (PC) and Eco-C
(Macintosh and Z80 CP/M)
Ecosoft, Inc.
6413 N. College Av.
Indianapolis, IN 46220
(317) 255-6476

EPC C
(Intel, SPARC, Motorola 88000)
Migration Software Systems,
Ltd.
2107 N. First St., S-600
San Jose, CA 95131
(408) 452-0527

Guidelines C++ (PC)
Guidelines Software, Inc.
18 Evergreen Dr.
P.O. Box 749
Orinda, CA 94563
(415) 254-9183

High C (PC) and High C386
(Intel 80386)
Metaware, Inc.
903 Pacific Av., Suite 201
Santa Cruz, CA 95060-4429
(408) 429-6382

Hyper-C (Macintosh)
Spectra Micro Development
P.O. Box 41795
Tucson, AZ 85717
(602) 884-7402

Instant C (PC)
Rational Systems
P.O. Box 480
Natick, MA 01760
(508) 653-6194

Lattice C
(Amiga, Atari, PC, NEC 78310/2,
68000, Z80)
Lattice, Inc.
2500 S. Highland Av.
Lombard, IL 60148
(312) 916-1600

Let's C (PC)
Mark Williams Company
1430 W. Wrightwood
Chicago, IL 60614
(312) 472-6659
(800) 692-1700

LPI-C (Intel 80386 and Motorola
680X0)
Liant Software
959 Concord St.
Framingham, MA 01701-4613
(508) 626-0006

MacC (Macintosh)
Consulair
P.O. Box 2192
Ketchum, ID 83340
(208) 726-5846

Microcontroller C
(Hitachi, Intel, Motorola, Zilog)
Archimedes Software, Inc.
2159 Union St.
San Francisco, CA 94123
(415) 567-4010

MPW C (Macintosh)
Apple Programmers and
Developers Ass.
290 SW. 43rd St.
Renton, WA 98055
(206) 251-6548

NDP C-386
(PC and Intel 80386: DOS and UNIX)
MicroWay, Inc.
P.O. Box 79
Kingston, MA 02364
(508) 746-7341

NEW C (UNIX, XENIX, MS-DOS)
Liant Software
959 Concord St.
Framingham, MA 01701-4613
(508) 626-0006

Objective-C (PC)
Stepstone Corp.
75 Glen Rd.
Sandy Hook, CT 06482
(203) 426-1875
(800) 289-6253

Optimizing C (Macintosh-A/UX)
UniSoft Corp.
6121 Hollis St., S-100
Emeryville, CA 94608
(415) 420-6400

Par.C (Inmos Transputer)
Parsec Developments
Witte Singel 66
P.O. Box 782
2300 AT Leiden
The Netherlands
(31) 71 142142

Power C (PC)
Mix Software, Inc.
1132 Commerce Dr.
Richardson, TX 75081
(214) 783-6001

QC88 (PC)
Quality Computer Systems
The Austin Code Works
11100 Leafwood Ln.
Austin, TX 78750-3409
(512) 258-0785

QuickC (PC)
Microsoft Corp.
16011 NE. 36th Way
P.O. Box 97017
Redmond, WA 98073
(206) 882-8080

Run/C and Advantage C++ (PC)
Lifeboat Associates
55 South Broadway
Tarrytown, NY 10591
(914) 332-1875
(800) 847-7078

SC-C (PC)
Silicon Composers, Inc.
210 California Av., Suite K
Palo Alto, CA 94036
(415) 322-8763

Sierra C (68000)
Sierra Systems
6728 Evergreen Av.
Oakland, CA 94611
(415) 339-8200

SVS C (UNIX)
Silicon Valley Software
1710 S. Amphlett Blvd., S-100
San Mateo, CA 94402
(415) 572-8800

THEOS C
(THEOS on various microcomputers)
THEOS Software Corp.
1777 Botelho Dr., S-360
Walnut Creek, CA 94596-5022
(415) 935-1118

THINKS's LightspeedC (Macintosh)
Symantec Corp.
10201 Torre Av.
Cupertino, CA 95014
(408) 253-9600

Turbo C (PC)
Borland International, Inc.
P.O. Box 660001
1800 Green Hills Rd.
Scotts Valley, CA 95066-0001
(408) 438-8400
(800) 543-7543

WATCOM C6.5 and WATCOM
Express C (PC)
  WATCOM Products, Inc.
  415 Phillip St.
  Waterloo, Ontario
  Canada, N2L 3X2
  (519) 886-3700
  (800) 265-4555

Zortech C++ (PC)
  Zortech Inc.
  361 Massachusetts Av., S-303
  Arlington, MA 02174
  (617) 646-6703
  (800) 848-8408

B
Fortran compilers

Recent advances in microcomputer technology have resulted in systems with sufficient power to handle fairly sophisticated science and engineering problems. To take advantage of such hardware platforms, this appendix lists over a dozen Fortran compilers currently available in the market. The list gives the product name, the microcomputer(s) on which it will run, and the vendor's name, address, and telephone number.

This list of Fortran compilers is provided only as a convenience to the readers of this book; the presence of a particular product or vendor does not constitute an endorsement. Similarly, the absence of a particular product or vendor does not imply that any evaluation kept it off the list.

EPC Fortran 77
(Intel, SPARC, Motorola)
> Migration Software Systems, Ltd.
> 2107 N. First St., S-600
> San Jose, CA 95131
> (408) 452-0527

F77L, F77L-EM, Personal
FORTRAN 77 (PC)
> Lahey Computer Systems
> 917 Tahoe Blvd., S-203
> P.O. Box 6091
> Incline Village, NV 89450
> (702) 831-2500

FORTRAN
(Apollo, PC, Intel 386, Sun, VAX)
> OASYS
> 230 Second Av.
> P.O. Box 8990
> Waltham, MA 02254-8990

FORTRAN (Macintosh)
> Language Systems Corp.
> 441 Carlisle Dr.
> Herndon, VA 22070
> (703) 478-0181

Fortran 77
(Amiga, Apple II, Atari, DEC PDP +
VAX, Mac, PC)
    Pecan Software Systems, Inc.
    1410 39th St.
    Brooklyn, NY 11218
    (718) 851-3100
    (800) 637-3226

FORTRAN 86 (PC)
    Real-Time Computer
    Science Corp.
    1390 Flynn Rd.
    Camarillo, CA 93010
    (805) 987-9781

FORTRAN Optimizing Compiler
    Microsoft Corp.
    16011 NE. 36th Way
    P.O. Box 97017
    Redmond, WA 98073-9717
    (206) 882-8080

Fortran Optimizing Compiler
(PC and UNIX)
    Green Hills Software
    510 Castillo St.
    Santa Barbara, CA 93101
    (805) 965-6044

FTN77+ (QNXos)
    Southdale Integrated
    Systems, Inc.
    2838 Highway #7
    Norval, Ontario
    Canada LOP 1KO
    (416) 455-9533

LPI-FORTRAN (PC)
    Liant Software
    959 Concord St.
    Framingham, MA 01701
    (508) 626-0006

NDP Fortran-386
(MS-DOS or UNIX on Intel 80386)
    Microway
    P.O. Box 79
    Kingston, MA 02364
    (508) 746-7341

NKR FORTRAN
(UNIX on Motorola 680X0)
    NKR Research, Inc.
    4040 Moorpack Av., S-209
    San Jose, CA 95117
    (408) 249-2612

Optimizing FORTRAN
(Macintosh under A/UX)
    UniSoft Corp.
    6121 Hollis St., S-100
    Emeryville, CA 94608
    (415) 420-6400

Prospero FORTRAN
(Atari, CP/M, PC and UNIX)
    Prospero Software, Inc.
    100 Commercial St., S-306
    Portland, ME 04101
    (207) 874-0382

RM/FORTRAN
(PC and UNIX on Intel 80386)
    Liant Software
    959 Concord St.
    Framingham, MA 01701
    (508) 626-0006

Salford FTN77 (PC)
    OTG Systems, Inc.
    P.O. Box 239
    Rts. 106 & 374
    Clifford, PA 18413
    (717) 222-9100

SVS FORTRAN 386
(MS-DOS or UNIX on Intel 80386)
    Science Applications International
    Corp.
    5150 El Camino Real, Suite C-31
    Los Altos, CA 94022
    (415) 960-3322

SVS Fortran 77 (UNIX)
    Silicon Valley Software
    1710 South Amphlett
    Blvd., S-100
    San Mateo, CA 94402
    (415) 572-8800

C
Fortran to C
translation tools

One decision made in the course of developing a new application is the selection of the programming language. Modern programming languages each have their own strengths and weaknesses. Often, the nature of the problem itself allows the analyst to pick a suitable language. However, in many cases, company policy regarding a "standard" programming language and/or an individual programmer's skill in a particular language greatly contribute to the final decision.

When existing applications are evaluated for modification and maintenance, the programming language decision can be revisited. An extremely large body of FORTRAN code exists, distributed across a wide variety of hardware platforms and running under diverse operating systems. Some of these existing applications would benefit from being recast into the C programming language. Maintenance could be improved because an accomplished C programmer might be located easier than an accomplished FORTRAN programmer. An application could take advantage of hardware platforms and/or operating systems that have embedded support for C but perhaps less effective support for FORTRAN. In addition, an application could interact more efficiently with other applications written in C or with software utilities—data management, screen handling, etc.—that have a rich C interface and perhaps a less flexible FORTRAN interface.

If an existing FORTRAN application is a candidate for conversion to C, it might make some sense to have the bulk of the "translation" done automatically. Such tools exist, and this appendix is a list of several FORTRAN-to-C converters currently available in the market. The list gives the product name, and the vendor's name, address, and telephone number.

This list of eight FORTRAN-to-C converters is provided only as a convenience to the readers of this book; the presence of a particular product or vendor does not constitute an endorsement. Similarly, the absence of a particular product or vendor does not imply that any evaluation kept it off the list.

ASSISTANT II
MicroTools
1082 E. El Camino Real, S-5
Sunnyvale, CA 94087
(408) 243-7688

f2c
Free Software Foundation, Inc.
675 Massachusetts Av.
Cambridge, MA 02139
(617) 876-3296

F2C
System Simulation Ltd.
250M Bedford Chambers
The Piazza
Covent Gardens, London
England WC2E 8HA
44-1-836-7406

FOR_C and FOR_C++
Cobalt Blue
2940 Union Av., Suite C
San Jose, CA 95124
(408) 723-0474

Fortran-C
Green Hills Software, Inc.
510 Castillo St.
Santa Barbara, CA 93101
(805) 965-6044

FORTRIX-C
Rapitech Systems, Inc.
Montebello Corporate Park
Suffern, NY 10901
(914) 368-3000
(800) 367-8749

FTC
CAS Project Management Ltd.
Marlow Lodge
Station Rd.
Marlowe, Buckinghamshire
England SL7 1NW
44-06284-71141

PROMULA.FORTRAN
PROMULA Development Corp.
3620 N. High St., S-301
Columbus, OH 43214
(614) 263-5512